The [illegible] Promises,
The Harm It Does

The Good It Promises, The Harm It Does

Critical Essays on Effective Altruism

Edited by
CAROL J. ADAMS, ALICE CRARY,
AND LORI GRUEN

OXFORD
UNIVERSITY PRESS

Oxford University Press is a department of the University of Oxford. It furthers the University's objective of excellence in research, scholarship, and education by publishing worldwide. Oxford is a registered trade mark of Oxford University Press in the UK and certain other countries.

Published in the United States of America by Oxford University Press
198 Madison Avenue, New York, NY 10016, United States of America.

Library of Congress Cataloging-in-Publication Data
Names: Adams, Carol J., editor.
Title: The good it promises, the harm it does : critical essays on
effective altruism / Carol J. Adams, Alice Crary, and Lori Gruen, eds.
Description: New York, NY, United States of America : Oxford University Press, [2023] |
Includes bibliographical references and index.
Identifiers: LCCN 2022040672 (print) | LCCN 2022040673 (ebook) |
ISBN 9780197655702 (paperback) | ISBN 9780197655696 (hardback) |
ISBN 9780197655726 (epub) | ISBN 9780197655733 (ebook) | ISBN 9780197655719
Subjects: LCSH: Animal rights—United States. | Anti-racism—United States. |
Altruism—United States.
Classification: LCC HV4764 .G68 2023 (print) | LCC HV4764 (ebook) |
DDC 179/.3—dc23/eng/20221123
LC record available at https://lccn.loc.gov/2022040672
LC ebook record available at https://lccn.loc.gov/2022040673

DOI: 10.1093/oso/9780197655696.001.0001

1 3 5 7 9 8 6 4 2

Paperback printed by Marquis, Canada
Hardback printed by Bridgeport National Bindery, Inc., United States of America

Contents

Foreword

Amia Srinivasan

The movement known as "Effective Altruism" is true to its name in at least one way: it has proven enormously effective at promoting itself and winning powerful adherents. The story of the consequences of Effective Altruism's success has so far been told by those adherents. For them, the success of Effective Altruism is near-definitionally a moral good. Effective Altruism, after all, is a movement committed to doing good in a maximally efficient way, so it might appear to follow that the more sincerely committed adherents it has, the better the world must become. But this reasoning assumes that Effective Altruism—understood not as an ideal type but as an actually existing social formation—in fact achieves its stated commitments. What if Effective Altruism, whatever the intentions of its leaders and followers, systematically harmed those it promised to help, eroding democratic decision-making, creating perverse incentives, and reinforcing the very structures that produce the suffering it purports to target? What if Effective Altruism presupposed an impoverished conception of the good, and of the "reason" it seeks to harness for its promotion? What if Effective Altruism had the ideological function of buttressing systems of oppression, all the while reassuring its adherents—themselves very often beneficiaries of those systems—that they were morally unimpeachable?

These are some of the questions raised when the story of Effective Altruism's success is told not by its proponents, but by those engaged in liberation struggles and justice movements that operate outside Effective Altruism's terms. These struggles, it must be said, long predate Effective Altruism, and it is striking that Effective Altruism has not found anything very worthwhile in them: in the historically deep and ongoing movements for the rights of working-class people, nonhuman animals, people of color, Indigenous people, women, incarcerated people, disabled people, and people living under colonial and authoritarian rule. For most Effective Altruists, these movements are, at best, examples of ineffective attempts to do good; negative examples from which to prescind or correct, not political formations from which to learn, with which to create coalition, or to join.

This fact reveals, on the part of Effective Altruism, not only a certain moral and intellectual presumptuousness. More disturbingly, it reveals Effective Altruism's fundamental conservatism. The historically most significant social movements—none of which, unlike Effective Altruism, were born out of the activism of Oxford philosophers—have offered complex analyses of the interrelations between different structures of oppression: between, say, racial domination and capitalist exploitation; the plight of poor women of the Global South and the climate crisis; or neoliberalism, mass incarceration, and the assault on the dignity of people with disabilities. These social movements have also, at their best, shown us that another, radically different world might be possible—a world not just with less harm and suffering, but with substantially more freedom, democracy, and equality in all its guises—even as they articulate concrete programs for reform. These movements have pushed us to think about a world beyond, for example, capitalism, the gender binary, the nuclear family, prisons, and the nation-state. Effective Altruism, with its monomaniacal insistence on the tractable and the measurable, calls us back from these exercises of radical political imagination. In so doing, Effective Altruism promises us a better world while implicitly encouraging us to accept the world more or less as it is.

Whenever criticisms such as these are put forward, Effective Altruists rush to reply that they only target Effective Altruism as it is currently implemented or practiced, not Effective Altruism "as such" or "in principle." Indeed, Effective Altruists typically go on, since Effective Altruism is simply the idea that we should undertake to do good in the most effective ways possible, it might well turn out that Effective Altruism recommends that we should, say, engage in union organizing or join the Movement for Black Lives—so long as the evidence supports the efficacy of such actions. This reply doesn't always hit its mark, for some of Effective Altruism's critics have offered powerful arguments that target the core principles and background moral epistemology of Effective Altruism—have offered, that is, "in principle" critiques of Effective Altruism. But, more significantly to my mind, this reply fails to understand the force of those criticisms that admittedly don't target Effective Altruism's core principles.

Political critique does not, and should not, merely address what social and political movements say about themselves. Political critique does, and should, also think about what social and political movements *do*: what effects they systematically bring about in the world, which structures they tend to reinforce, and which people they empower and which they silence. When movements fail to "do" what they "say," it is not always just a matter of failed "implementation," easily correctable through a doubling-down on the movement's core principles. Sometimes, contradictions between what a movement "says" and "does" reveal something deep about how the movement practically works—and why it is successful. In turn, such revelations can tell us something about the limits of what such a movement can plausibly achieve.

It is perhaps unsurprising that Effective Altruists do not recognize the force, or indeed form, of such arguments: do not recognize, that is, what it might even mean to think of Effective Altruism not just as a moral philosophy, but as a piece of ideology. Analytic philosophers as a whole, of whatever moral or political persuasion, tend to evaluate social and political movements according to what they say about themselves, as opposed to what they do in the world.

(Thus, for most analytic philosophers, liberalism's seemingly contradictory entanglement with colonialism or the patriarchal family is no more than a historical accident, one that sheds no light on what we should think, normatively speaking, of the prospects of liberalism.) As most students of political history, or practitioners of politics, will tell you, this is a politically disastrous way of thinking about political movements. Ideas have a life beyond what they say, which is partly why ideas matter so very much.

This volume contains many voices to which Effective Altruism as a whole is not in the practice of listening, even when those voices call for things—like the end of farmed animal suffering—that Effective Altruism also supports. Most of the volume's contributors are not philosophers or academics, and do not write in the chosen vernacular of Effective Altruism. They raise worries about the overwhelming whiteness, middle-classness, and maleness of the Effective Altruist community that many of its members are likely to think irrelevant to the assessment of Effective Altruism's value. They often speak from experience, and do not purport to offer alternative general principles that can guide all moral decision-making. There is every possibility, then, that Effective Altruists will ignore what these voices have to say—or fail to take the time to understand what their significance might be. That would be a deep shame, and what's more, a betrayal of what I believe is a real commitment, on the part of many Effective Altruists, to bring about a better world.

All Souls College, Oxford
February 2022

Acknowledgments

We wish to thank all the contributors to this volume for staying with this project through years of a pandemic that imposed severe burdens on many and relentlessly demanded energies elsewhere. We are honored to be able to bring out their wonderful essays. We are grateful for support from The New School, Wesleyan University, and All Souls, College, Oxford, and also from the Brooks Institute for Animal Rights Law and Policy, which hosted the February 2020 event at which the idea for this book was born.

It meant a great deal to us to have Amia Srinivasan's participation, and we are indebted to her for contributing the book's foreword.

We want to express our gratitude to Peter Ohlin of Oxford University Press, who recognized the importance of this collection, and to his colleagues at the press, including Chelsea Hogue, Title Manager for our book. We thank Kavitha Yuvaraj, Project Manager of Newgen Knowledge Works for her oversight of the manuscript and proof preparation and our copy editor, Peter Jaskwaik.

We also acknowledge the gracious and insightful contributions of Tara Mastrelli, who provided an additional editorial eye on the essays and helped us with the manuscript preparation.

Finally, we acknowledge each other, for the individual strengths we each brought to the book, and for the support and insights fostered by our working together.

Acknowledgments

About the Contributors

Elan Abrell is a cultural anthropologist and lawyer whose research focuses on human–animal interactions, environmental justice, and food-related technological innovation. He is an assistant professor in the Environmental Studies Program and the Science in Society Program at Wesleyan University. His award-winning 2021 ethnography *Saving Animals: Multispecies Ecologies of Rescue and Care* explores the material and ethical challenges of caring for rescued animals in US animal sanctuaries. He was formerly a visiting assistant professor of environmental studies at New York University, a visiting assistant professor in urban studies at Queens College, CUNY, and a 2017–2018 Farmed Animal Law and Policy Fellow at the Animal Law and Policy Program at Harvard University.

Carol J. Adams is a feminist scholar and activist whose written work explores the cultural construction of overlapping and interconnected oppressions, as well as the ethics of care. She is the author of *The Sexual Politics of Meat: A Feminist-Vegetarian Critical Theory*; *Burger*; *Living among Meat Eaters*; *Protest Kitchen; Fight Injustice, Save the Planet, and Fuel Your Resistance One Meal at a Time* (coauthored with Virginia Messina), and many other books. With Josephine Donovan, she is the editor of *Women and Animals* (1996) and *The Feminist Care Tradition in Animal Ethics: A Reader* (2007). She has written for the *New York Times*, the *Washington Post*, *Ms. Magazine*, and other publications.

Jennifer Channin has served as the executive director of the Better Food Foundation since 2021. She previously served as director of development at the Better Food Foundation, Farm Forward, and Found in Translation, and has worked in philanthropy for nearly twenty years, raising tens of millions of dollars for farmed animal protection and social justice organizations worldwide. She holds a Masters of Divinity degree from Harvard, is an ordained minister, and is a dual citizen of the US and Brazil. She lives in San Diego with her partner, Aaron, and their dog, Buddy.

David L. Clough is chair of Theology and Applied Sciences at the University of Aberdeen. He has recently completed the landmark two-volume monograph *On Animals* (2012, 2019) on the place of animals in Christian theology and ethics. He is the cofounder of CreatureKind, an organization engaging Christians with farmed animal welfare, founder of DefaultVeg, and principal investigator for a three-year AHRC-funded project on the Christian Ethics of Farmed Animal Welfare in partnership with major UK churches. He is a Methodist lay preacher and has represented the Methodist Church on national ecumenical working groups on the ethics of warfare and climate change.

Alice Crary is University Distinguished Professor of Philosophy at the New School for Social Research and the author of *Beyond Moral Judgment* and *Inside Ethics*. She is the coauthor, with Lori Gruen, of *Animal Crisis*. She has edited and coedited many books and journal issues, including *Social Visibility* (an issue of *Philosophical Topics*), coedited with Matt Congdon. She was a counselor in a battered women's shelter, and she was a one of the founders of the New School's graduate program in Gender and Sexuality Studies. She is completing a book called *Radical Animal*, which argues that revaluing animal lives is decisive for resisting oppressive structures that hurt human beings.

Andrew deCoriolis is the executive director of Farm Forward, where he advocates for safe, healthy, and humane animal farming. Andrew is an expert in animal welfare standards and certifications. He works closely with food companies, universities, and cities to help them improve the welfare of animals and increase the proportion of plant-based food in their supply chains. Andrew's work at Farm Forward has been covered in leading periodicals, including the *New York Times*, *Fast Company*, and *Civil Eats*. Andrew is currently an advisor to the Well/Beings charity, the Game Changers Institute, the Good Food Purchasing Program, and the State Innovation Exchange. Andrew lives in San Francisco with his partner, son, and rescue mutt Tater Tot.

Simone de Lima is a biologist and a retired professor of Developmental Psychology at the Universidade de Brasília, Brazil, where her work focused on innovative education and disability. She's been involved in different forms of activism since her teens, from student organizing against the Brazilian dictatorship to doing feminist, environmental, children's, and animal rights work. She cofounded Brasilia's first animal advocacy organization, as well as its first vegan cafe, Café Corbucci, and directed the Outreach and Education Department of a US animal rights nonprofit. She lives with her husband and dog in Takoma Park, Maryland, volunteers at Poplar Spring Animal Sanctuary, and collaborates with vegan and radical education collectives.

Aaron S. Gross, PhD, is professor of religious studies and cochair of the Food Studies Initiative at the University of San Diego, and founder of the food and farming advocacy group Farm Forward. Gross's work on food has been featured in numerous venues, including the *New York Times*, the *Washington Post*, and the *Guardian*. Gross was cowriter with Jonathan Safran Foer of the 2018 film adaptation of Foer's international bestseller *Eating Animals*. Gross is the author of *The Question of the Animal and Religion: Theoretical Stakes, Practical Implications* (Columbia University Press) and *Feasting and Fasting: The History and Ethics of Jewish Food* (New York University Press). He lives in San Diego with his partner, Jennifer, and their dog, Buddy.

Steve J. Gross, PhD, is a former Fortune 1000 business consultant who helped pioneer the corporate outreach strategies that have transformed both animal advocacy and corporate support for animal welfare improvements since the late 1990s. Gross has led successful negotiations on behalf of animal advocacy groups in their dealings with some of the nation's largest food retailers, including Burger King, McDonald's, Wendy's, Safeway, and Whole Foods. Prior to this work, Gross cofounded and ran the Illinois Humane PAC, passing ten animal protection laws in a decade with an average annual budget of less than fifty thousand dollars. He was a founding board member of Global Animal Partnership and served as board chair of Farm Forward for more than a decade.

Lori Gruen is the William Griffin Professor of Philosophy at Wesleyan University, where she also is a professor in the Feminist, Gender, and Sexuality Studies Program and the Science in Society Program. She is the founder and coordinator of Wesleyan Animal Studies and one of the founding faculty for the Center for Prison Education. She is the author of *Ethics and Animals: An Introduction*, *Entangled Empathy*, and *Animal Crisis*, coauthored with Alice Crary. She has also edited many books, including *Ecofeminism: Feminist Intersections with Other Animals and the Earth*, *Critical Terms for Animal Studies*, and *Animaladies: Gender,*

Animals, and Madness. She has written for the *New York Times*, *Time Magazine*, the *Washington Post*, and other venues.

Matthew C. Halteman is a professor of philosophy at Calvin University in Grand Rapids, Michigan, USA, and Fellow of the Oxford Centre for Animal Ethics, UK. He writes and teaches on philosophy as a way of life, philosophical hermeneutics, and animal ethics, and is the author of *Compassionate Eating as Care of Creation* and the co-editor of *Philosophy Comes to Dinner.* He eats vegan desserts like they are going out of style, even though they are just now coming into style.

Krista Hiddema, PhD, is an animal rights activist whose research highlights the need for ecofeminist principles in matters of board governance within the animal advocacy movement, with an emphasis on the economic, ecological, and social health of employees. Krista has served as a vice president for a global technology company and founded a boutique employment law firm in Toronto. She led Mercy For Animals Canada, overseeing twelve undercover investigations into factory farms and slaughterhouses. Today Krista is the executive director of For the Greater Good, consulting with animal protection organizations on board governance, strategy, and organizational development. She is a reviewer for the *Journal of Critical Animal Studies* and former president of Happily Ever Esther Farm Sanctuary.

pattrice jones is a cofounder of VINE Sanctuary, an LGBTQ-led farmed animal refuge, as well as the author of *The Oxen at the Intersection* and *Aftershock: Confronting Trauma in a Violent World.*

Rachel McCrystal is the executive director of Woodstock Farm Sanctuary, a nonprofit consultant, and an animal rescuer. She speaks and writes about issues of animal rights, farmed animal justice issues, sustainable nonprofit practices, and animal agriculture's impact on the climate crisis.

John Sanbonmatsu is an associate professor of philosophy at Worcester Polytechnic Institute in Massachusetts, where he teaches ethics, critical social theory, and the philosophy of technology. Sanbonmatsu is the author of the books *The Omnivore's Deception: What We Get Wrong about Meat, Animals, and the Nature of Moral Life* (forthcoming, NYU Press) and *The Postmodern Prince: Critical Theory, Left Strategy, and the Making of a New Political Subject* (Monthly Review Press), as well as editor of the anthology *Critical Theory and Animal Liberation* (Rowman & Littlefield). His opinion writing has appeared, among other places, in the *Christian Science Monitor* and *Huffington Post*. A critic of cellular or synthesized meat technology, Sanbonmatsu curates the Clean Meat Hoax website (https://www.cleanmeat-hoax.com/).

Brenda Sanders is a food justice activist who works to make plant-based foods more accessible to everyone. She is the cofounder and executive director of the Afro-Vegan Society, a nonprofit organization that provides online support and resources to inspire people to transition to vegan living; cofounder of Thrive Baltimore, a community resource center that offers classes, workshops, and other programming to assist people in making healthier, kinder, more sustainable choices; and co-owner of The Greener Kitchen, a vegan deli and carry-out that produces plant-based foods that are both affordable and accessible.

Christopher Sebastian is a journalist, researcher, and technical writer. He uses media theory, political science, and cultural analysis in a multidisciplinary approach to helping people understand animal liberation.

Michele Simon is a public health attorney, food policy expert, author, and thought leader in the plant-based foods industry. Simon has written extensively on the politics of food and alcohol. Her first book, *Appetite for Profit: How the Food Industry Undermines Our Health and How to Fight Back*, was published by Nation Books in 2006. NYU Professor Marion Nestle (who calls the book "brilliant") made it required reading for her nutrition students. In 2016, Simon founded the Plant Based Foods Association, the nation's only membership association promoting the interests of plant-based food companies. She has a master's degree in public health from Yale University and received her law degree from the University of California, Hastings College of the Law.

Amia Srinivasan is the Chichele Professor of Social and Political Theory at All Souls College, Oxford.

Kathy Stevens cofounded Catskill Animal Sanctuary (CAS) in New York's Hudson Valley in 2001. Today, CAS is not only one of the world's leading sanctuaries for farmed animals; it is also a leading voice in the call for humanity to adopt veganism as the most impactful way to save animals and reverse climate change. Kathy is the author of two books about the work of CAS: *Where the Blind Horse Sings* and *Animal Camp: Reflections on a Decade of Love, Hope, and Veganism at Catskill Animal Sanctuary.*

Her writing is featured in numerous anthologies, including *The Missing Peace* and *Voices of Animal Liberation.* Kathy speaks on the emotional lives of farm animals, the imperative of a global switch to veganism, and the power of animal sanctuaries as change-makers. Her weekly podcast, *Herd Around the Barn*, was launched in 2021.

Joseph Tuminello is an assistant professor of philosophy at McNeese State University, a program coordinator for Farm Forward, and a Fellow of the Oxford Centre for Animal Ethics. Joey's teaching and research focuses on the intersection of food, animal, and environmental issues. Since 2011, Joey has assisted Farm Forward with numerous research projects and education initiatives that have engaged more than 20,000 students around the world.

Michael D. Wise is an environmental historian and cultural geographer at the University of North Texas. He is the author of the book *Producing Predators: Wolves, Work, and Conquest in the Northern Rockies* (2016), and of many articles and essays on the historical dimensions of food and animal–human relationships in modern North America.

Introduction

Carol J. Adams, Alice Crary, and Lori Gruen

The world contains widespread and acute misery and injustice. As we are finalizing this volume, in the early spring of 2022, close to four million people have been violently displaced by Russia's illegal war against Ukraine. The Conger ice shelf, a chunk of ice the size of Rome, collapsed into the ocean in March 2022, soon after temperatures in Antarctica, the coldest region on the planet, soared seventy degrees (Fahrenheit) above average, further destabilizing the planet's climate. The global COVID-19 pandemic is ongoing, and hunger, poverty, and related health crises are long-standing and systemic issues in many places. The earth is hurtling toward what is being called the sixth mass extinction, with species dying off at dramatically elevated rates. Billions of land animals suffer and die annually in concentrated feeding operations and slaughterhouses across the world. Historically deeply rooted structures of racism, ableism, classism, misogyny, ageism, and transphobia continue to hurt great numbers of people, exposing them to intolerance, economic exclusion, and physical harm. In the face of such grievous problems, people who want to find positive ways to respond often grapple with difficult questions about how to make a difference.

Seizing on people's desire to help and the difficulties associated with figuring out how to do so, members of an entrepreneurial and self-described "utilitarianesque" community, including several Oxford-affiliated philosophers, created various organizations to encourage people to give as much money as they could in the

Carol J. Adams, Alice Crary, and Lori Gruen, *Introduction* In: The Good It Promises, The Harm It Does. Edited by: Carol J. Adams, Alice Crary, and Lori Gruen, Oxford University Press.
DOI: 10.1093/oso/9780197655696.001.0001

most effective ways to address suffering around the globe. Among the most prominent organizations are "Giving What We Can," launched by Toby Ord and William MacAskill in 2009, and "80,000 Hours," founded by Benjamin Todd and MacAskill in 2011.[1] In late 2011, people involved in these organizations came together under a new umbrella organization, which they dubbed the Center for Effective Altruism.

Effective Altruism (EA) subsequently took off as a philosophy of charitable giving that claims to guide adherents in doing the "most good" per dollar donated or time spent. EA has become a popular way of framing decisions about how to have a positive effect on the world. It has grown rapidly and not merely as an academic pursuit. It is represented not only by university-based institutes and research centers, but also by organizations that recommend grants and by foundations that make them. Several hundreds of millions of dollars are now donated annually in accordance with EA's principles, and tens of billions more are committed.

This giving has, from the time of EA's founding, been directed toward minimizing the suffering of nonhuman animals as well as toward working to minimize serious, but preventable, problems that human beings face. EA-related organizations are strikingly influential in the realm of animal advocacy, where affiliated funders are so dominant that it is difficult for any pro-animal group to spurn them, and groups that are deemed "ineffective" stand to suffer significant losses of funds.

• • •

At a 2020 in-person event in Miami, Florida, devoted to discussing practical and policy issues pertinent to the animal protection movement, a group of scholars, activists, scholar-activists, and activist-scholars met over many vegan meals and shared accounts

[1] https://forum.effectivealtruism.org/posts/9a7xMXoSiQs3EYPA2/the-history-of-the-term-effective-altruism.

of how EA was harming their work and the work of others.[2] As our conversations continued over days, some common themes emerged. One was that EA's insistence on its favored quantitative metrics pressures activists to work within the market-structured institutions that in many cases are responsible for the very wrongs they seek to address, pushing them to pursue reformist strategies that contribute to the persistence of harmful institutions. Another theme was that EA tends to overlook or even disparage more radical or transformative social efforts dedicated to building relationships and communities, including multispecies ones, that aren't governed by instrumental, economic values. Yet another was that EA favors calculative, paradigm-driven strategies and treats as irrelevant the kind of responsiveness to particular expressions of human and animal suffering that is a core methodological commitment of many activists and advocates.

These general themes emerged from very specific discussions regarding how organizations and interventions were being harmed by EA. Sanctuary directors talked about how their newly EA-admiring funders had come to favor metrics suggesting that caring for animals and feeding them in sanctuaries were "ineffective" approaches to animal advocacy, and accordingly withdrew funding. Lawyers working to extend rights to nonhumans talked about how the defunding of sanctuaries meant that, even if they prevailed in freeing individual animals from harmful captivity, they could not guarantee there was a safe place for the animals to go. Community activists working in marginalized communities on race- and class-related issues of food access and nutrition, alongside issues of animal advocacy, recounted that EA-funders had told them they would not fund their work because it wasn't effective. Food justice advocates based outside the United States told

[2] The event at which these discussions took place was a congress hosted by the Brooks Institute for Animal Rights Law and Policy. The discussions that led to this book were informal conversations among participants, not part of the Brooks Institute's official program.

stories about how international EA-funded organizations directly interfered with local vegan enterprises dedicated to supporting the plant-based traditions of local communities, among other things, by insisting that funding for vegan initiatives go toward the development of monocrop-based, industrially produced "alternative proteins"—or toward efforts to reform industrial animal agriculture with cage-free campaigns and the like. Vegans of color talked about encountering explicit racism in EA-affiliated groups and implicit racism in EA-based recommendations that favor social methods effective in elite and predominantly white social spaces (e.g., corporate campaigns and efforts to change consumer habits with new products) over forms of engagement with roots in non-white communities (e.g., outreach through local churches and community organizing).[3] #MeToo advocates described how the funding metrics of EA ignored hostile work environments, and how many have been hurt by known serial sexual exploiters who lead groups assessed as "effective" by EA-tied groups.

It became clear to us that a book detailing the dangers of EA would be an important contribution to both activism and scholarship.[4] The fact that EA is part of a tradition that adopts a top-down approach to complex social problems, and that does not treat listening to people's voices, such as those of participants in social movements, as a fundamental methodological precept, is another reason that this book is necessary. This project centers the voices of activists speaking from where they stand in interconnected social justice movements. We believe in the importance of listening

[3] One EA-affiliated group that recommends grants for pro-animal organizations, Animal Charity Evaluators, seems to now believe that all forms of grass-roots outreach (with the possible exception of online ads) have close to zero effect. See https://animalcharityevaluators.org/research/reports/leafleting/.

[4] All three of the current volume's editors were at the conference at which the idea for the book first arose (see note 2), as were some of the other contributors. Although conversations at this conference were the immediate catalyst for the book, these conversations built on years of related interactions and collaborations among members of a larger, loosely organized community of activists and advocates.

to people who are on the ground and engaged in struggle, and in learning from the harms they have experienced. The structure of this volume reflects this commitment.

The Good It Promises, The Harm It Does is the first book-length critique of Effective Altruism. It is distinctive in bringing together writers from diverse activist and disciplinary backgrounds to explore EA's failure to meaningfully address various forms of human and animal suffering. Taken together, the book's chapters show that in numerous interrelated areas of social justice work—including animal protection, antiracism, public health advocacy, poverty alleviation, community organizing, the running of animal sanctuaries, education, feminist and LGBTQ politics, and international advocacy—EA's principles are actualized in ways that support some of the very social structures that cause suffering, thereby undermining its efforts to "do the most good." In addition to describing how EA can harm animals and humans, the book contains critical studies of EA's philosophical assumptions and critical studies of organizations that set out to realize them. It invites readers to recognize EA as an alluring and extremely pernicious ideology, and it traces out a number of mutually reinforcing strategies for submitting this ideology to criticism.

Although all of the authors in the book agree in wanting to talk about substantial harms of EA, they present a range of—sometimes overlapping, sometimes divergent—views about what the problem with EA is and how to address the damage it continues to do. Our aim as editors was not to try to deny or cover up this diversity, but rather to create space for differences to be discussed. The most substantial differences aired here include those that separate the authors who maintain that EA could be a force for good if it were radically reconceived and implemented in socially responsible ways and the authors who believe that EA is irredeemably confused and corrupt, and thus call for jettisoning it altogether.

EA has been a conspicuous force in philanthropy since the early 2010s, and its growth should be understood as part of larger social currents. It is neither wholly new nor wholly distinctive. After World War II, humanitarian nongovernmental organizations proliferated to address natural and human-caused emergencies as well as the increasingly visible problem of hunger. Images of starving people led to donations from those who were relatively well-off to aid those in need. These earlier humanitarian efforts undoubtedly influenced the Peter Singer, a prominent proponent of EA, who published an essay entitled "Famine, Affluence, and Morality" (1972), wherein which he argued that if people can help others without sacrificing anything "of comparable moral importance" they ought to do it. Inspired by Singer, philosopher Peter Unger developed a book-length argument in his *Living High and Letting Die* (1996) that made a vivid case for why relatively well-off people should be giving away much more of their money. Both thinkers were using ideas from the philosophical tradition of utilitarianism, which enjoins us to act in ways that decrease suffering and increase well-being, and in this spirit they emphasized doing the "most good." Their arguments resonated beyond the academy partly due to their fit with notable contemporaneous trends, including the advent of new development economics, characterized partly by its welfarist bent, and the emergence of the idea of impact investing. EA traces its origins to the more philosophical and utilitarian-inspired portion of this bigger social moment, and it stands out for its emphasis on the notion of "effectiveness."

Effective Altruists often demur at the suggestion that utilitarianism undergirds their view. Some defenders of EA even suggest that they aren't committed to any particular moral theory. But advocates of EA overwhelmingly share a number of utilitarian core commitments. These include commitments to impartiality (each person's good is as important as everyone else's), welfarism (promoting well-being is the good to be achieved), and maximization (it's not just doing good, but doing the most good, all things considered). Protest as they may, Effective Altruists get their characteristic orientation from much older utilitarian ideas, reworking them and attracting new attention to them.

Importantly, other non-utilitarian moral theories and traditions reject these combined commitments and represent them as saddling us with a flawed image of morality. EA's commitments are also directly at odds with the aims and practices of numerous liberation movements, many of which are distinguished by their insistence on starting with the voices of the oppressed and taking simultaneously empathetic and critical engagement with these voices to guide the development of strategies for responding to suffering. These immanent and critical methods directly oppose the kind of advance formulation of a one-size-fits-all program for doing good that is EA's hallmark.

The misfit between EA's image of positive social interventions and the images within other ethical and liberating traditions sheds light on how it abandons more familiar understandings of its central notions of "effectiveness" and "altruism" and assigns them new meanings within its familiar but far from sacrosanct moral worldview. The notion of effectiveness gets put through a very specific philosophical filter and is reified, so that it appears to be the exclusive entitlement of a metrics of probable effects or expected utility that itself supposedly has a unique claim to reliance on "reason and evidence." Decisions about what is and isn't effective are then relegated to elite and purportedly expert individuals whose judgments are treated as value-free. This decision process creates a host of well-documented problems, above all those stemming from a failure to interrogate the process's alignment with mechanisms that reproduce severe social injustices. Essays in this volume describe, for instance, how ideas that sustain white supremacy have consistently informed EA's beliefs and practices. That EA animal activists regard the effects of corporate campaigns that aim to mitigate the harms of meat companies as "measurable," while representing community organizing as largely incalculable and unreliable, reflects their privileged social positioning, not the facts on the ground.

Alongside the important critiques of the "effectiveness" of EA in the chapters that follow, there are also concerns raised about its claim to promote "altruism." Talk of altruism suggests that care, compassion, and empathy are important values for EA, but on inspection this turns out not to be the case. One notable strand of thought traced out in the essays included here—familiar from work on the ethics of care—has to do with how global capitalism in its current form either treats care work, animals, and other parts of the natural world as "free resources," or else internalizes them into an economic value system that strips them of their ethical importance. EA doesn't have resources for fundamentally criticizing the pertinent capitalistic structures, and instead tends to speak for preserving them and working within them, in effect reproducing their harms. This collection's contributors challenge this stance, pushing back against structures that contribute to the exploitation of women and Indigenous and racialized people who are made to do care work as well as to the devastation of more-than-human nature.

When concerns about the absence of care and empathy are raised with Effective Altruists, they typically respond that they *do* embrace such engagements, but only when they lead to a greater good. This is a position that a pivotal EA-associated charity-assessor within animal protectionism, Animal Charity Evaluators (ACE), has adopted over the last few years. ACE offers a highly qualified positive assessment of the care work that occurs at animal sanctuaries. ACE is prepared to support such work only on the condition that it can be shown to shift people's attitudes toward animals in ways that increase funding for organizations that, according to ACE's EA-derived calculations, are immediately in the business of doing the "most good." This is not a way of registering the value of care, empathy, and the pursuit of genuine altruism, however, but rather a way of denying these values and reducing them to mere means to other ends. This instrumentalization of deep values makes crucial aspects of the lives of those who bear them invisible—another grave harm of EA.

In the face of a host of criticisms, advocates of EA adopt strategies of response that are both slippery and sticky. To date EA hasn't answered the most telling criticisms of it, but rather assimilated the criticisms by reinterpreting their meanings and significance within its own instrumental and economic scheme of values. This style of response disguises the way in which key modes of social and political engagement have been suppressed, a sleight of hand that makes it seem as though EA's critics are lamenting the loss of mere childish will-o'-the-wisps with no weight or substance in the grown-up world of late capitalism. In this way, we can see EA as an ideology in the insidious sense, a system of belief and practice that covers up systemic injustices embedded in the fabric of existing capitalist societies in a manner that clears the way for the perpetuation of significant wrongs and harms.

All of the chapters in this volume include among their concerns impacts that EA has had in the animal movement. From the major role of EA-related funders to the emergence of ACE as a gatekeeper of animal-focused nonprofit funding, EA has inveigled itself deeply into animal activism. Many activists and organization are susceptible to EA approval and so need to seek assurance that their actions can be deemed effective. For all its distinctness, the case of EA's role in animal advocacy, and of its impact on the lives of animals, is illustrative, making clear the good EA promises and the harm it does.

EA offers a deceptively simple formula and seems to make the task of doing good a straightforward matter of its application. The task of collecting data necessary to use the formula in particular settings may be difficult, but it can be entrusted to experts. This seems to relieve the rest of us of the need to think hard about particular cases, to ask ourselves whether a better appreciation of the social and political terrain might speak for a different understanding and a different intervention. Part of the value of this book lies in revealing that rather than being morally helpful, EA evades morally and politically decisive work. By drawing attention to a wealth of heterogeneous, grass-roots, and community organizing groups that don't fit one pattern, the chapters in this collection plainly show that there is no room for the kind of blanket advance "solution" to these problems that Effective Altruists claim to offer. On the contrary, it is impossible responsibly to judge how best to respond apart from the sort of sensibility fostered by, among other things, experience, thoughtful engagement with local values, and collaborative action. Through its individual essays, which are lively and filled with examples, this book invites the kind of engaged attention to particular cases that it represents as theoretically and practically necessary.

The Good It Promises, The Harm It Does is, in real part, a project of recovery: there are voices and projects much older than EA, keenly needed activist traditions that EA lacks the resources to assess and so threatens to squelch. We seek to recover, positively, what we are in danger of losing.

References

Singer, Peter. (1972). "Famine, Affluence, and Morality." *Philosophy & Public Affairs* 1 (3): 229–243.

Unger, Peter. (1996). *Living High and Letting Die: Our Illusion of Innocence.* Oxford: Oxford University Press.

1

How Effective Altruism Fails Community-Based Activism

Brenda Sanders

I was once told that a prominent animal rights movement donor would never fund my work because "there's no way to prove how effective it is." Over the last decade, my work has focused on hosting workshops, classes, festivals, food tastings, film screenings, and other events that introduce people in low-income communities of color to the benefits of making healthier, kinder, more sustainable choices. Founding a national organization like Afro-Vegan Society and hosting large-scale events like Vegan SoulFest and the Plant-Based Jumpstart, my team and I have been able to reach tens of thousands of people with information and inspiration to transition to plant-based eating.

So this donor's opinion of my work was upsetting to me, but I wasn't sure why at the time. I assumed I was having an ego reaction to the thought of some rich white guy judging my work to be unworthy of his support. But when I finally took the time to contemplate what was at the root of my resentment, I realized that judging the effectiveness of my work based on a "return on investment" model was, at its core, based on a white-centric view of activism. Gauging the impact of community-based activism needs to be done through an entirely different lens, which can only be done by someone who understands how activism works in Black communities.

Brenda Sanders, *How Effective Altruism Fails Community-Based Activism* In: *The Good It Promises, The Harm It Does.* Edited by: Carol J. Adams, Alice Crary, and Lori Gruen, Oxford University Press.
 DOI: 10.1093/oso/9780197655696.003.0001

There are nearly nine million low-income Black people in the United States, yet the animal rights movement has shown very little interest in engaging with this particular segment of the population. In truth, that's been a good thing, since most of the tactics currently being used in mainstream animal rights activism wouldn't have been terribly effective in these spaces anyway. But the glaring disregard for low-income communities of color needs to be addressed. In the time I've been doing on-the-ground vegan activism in low-income Black communities, I've found that the level of trust people have for the messenger as well as the relatability and cultural relevance of the outreach are major factors in people's receptivity to the message.

Trust

For decades now, low-income Black areas have been ground zero for all manner of foundation-funded social programs and "mission-driven" nonprofit initiatives, designed to "fix" the people who live there. Unfortunately, those who have ventured into the 'hood on behalf of those foundations and nonprofits have historically never been from these communities, and so they've had absolutely no frame of reference to truly understand the people they're trying to "save." This ignorance has led, time and time again, to failed initiatives and empty promises.

An unfortunate consequence of this saviorism has been that the people in these communities have been saddled with the emotional debris left behind by decades of social programs being initiated and then deserted, community services being offered and then abandoned, and resources being made available to families and then withdrawn. Since the do-gooders going into these neighborhoods to fix them never actually consulted with those who could best articulate the root causes of their problems and offer viable solutions—the community members themselves—the so-called saviors failed miserably in their goals. This behavior has led people in marginalized communities to have a deep-seated distrust of outsiders coming in with ideas and initiatives to solve their problems.

This is why the kind of outreach I call "drive-by activism" doesn't have the desired effect in low-income Black communities. Swooping in to do a few hours of vegan outreach is going to have very little lasting effect—especially if these outsiders are sharing new information that contradicts what people already believe. Going into churches, community centers, afterschool programs, libraries, and other places where people congregate and offering cooking demos, workshops, film screenings, classes, and plant-based food tastings is a way to reach people in environments where they're already comfortable and open to receiving information.

Another vital component of this work is that this information be conveyed by those of us who understand the specific needs of our communities. Having grown up in the spaces where we're advocating means we can build trust from a place of shared experience. We don't have to constantly worry about saying the wrong thing or being offensive in some way. We know how to talk to people in our community, and we can therefore convey this information in a way that has the potential to gain real momentum and create a cultural shift that will make a tangible difference in the lives of marginalized Black folks.

Relatability

Disregarding Black and brown folks when engaging in vegan advocacy is dismissive, devaluing, and downright racist, but knowing the best way to engage in community-based activism is a must when doing this work. The same would go for targeting animal lovers with information about animal cruelty or educating health-conscious people about the nutritional benefits of plant-based eating. Having this kind of understanding of why certain forms of activism work in certain spaces is essential to doing outreach to people living at the margins of society.

When my team sets out to do outreach in a community, one of the first things we do is reach out to the neighborhood churches and community centers to offer to do free plant-based cooking demos for their members. When these community centers and churches host events like health fairs and holiday marketplaces, we make sure to table at as many of these events as possible, and while tabling we not only offer resources to help people start to make healthier, more sustainable food choices (like recipes, samples, and vegan starter guides); we also pass out flyers for upcoming classes, workshops, and other events we're hosting.

Soon people begin to recognize us from our regular engagements with them, so that when we invite them out to participate in our four-week vegan education classes, cooking workshops, or food tastings, many of them come out and participate. Would folks who had never seen or interacted with us before and don't know anything about us or our organization have been even remotely interested in attending any event we're hosting? Probably not. And if we hadn't offered much-needed services, resources, and support and made personal connections, would folks from these congregations have not only come to our events, but also brought family, friends, and coworkers with them, in many cases filling our space to capacity? Doubtful.

This on-the-ground activism is an integral part of influencing the culture in communities that are closed off to outsiders, and it is important and worthwhile work.

Cultural Relevance

When doing vegan activism at the community level, you figure out fairly early on that food is the most sensible point of entry. In general, people spend a large portion of each day planning meals, purchasing ingredients, and then preparing the food, and with people in marginalized communities, there are often cultural traditions tied into this process as well. For many low-income folks, food choices also tend to be the result of the struggle to find foods that are abundant enough to feed a family but affordable enough to fit within a meager budget. This has created a generational pattern of eating unhealthy, packaged animal products that tend to be abundant in these communities.

Plant-based food manufacturers can produce all the delicious plant-based veggie burgers, sausages, and cheeses in the world, but if no one is going into marginalized communities and introducing information about making different food choices, there will be zero demand for them, and so these plant-based foods won't be making their way into these communities anytime soon. "If we build it, they will come" just doesn't apply to folks who have no idea it's been built in the first place. This is why there has to be a shift in the food culture in these communities.

Changing the food culture in a community means knowing how to get people from Point A to Point B, which involves, first and foremost, knowing where they're starting from. In the case of the communities where I work, the vast majority of people haven't even been exposed to the idea that there are other food choices they could be making that are healthier, kinder, and more sustainable. For so many low-income folks who have been working multiple jobs, living paycheck to paycheck, and struggling to keep a roof over their heads, exploring alternative food choices is fairly low on their priority lists.

It's for these reasons that activism at the community level fills such an important role in reaching these overlooked populations. By bringing this information directly to communities in the form of festivals, classes, cooking demos, workshops, and other events, community activists are providing people with the resources and support they need to begin making real, lasting changes in their lives. I have no doubt that it's because of the vegan activism being done at the community level across the US that African Americans are one of the fastest-growing vegan demographics in the country.

Effective vs. Impactful

As far as the effectiveness of community-based vegan activism, there may never be a magical equation for quantifying the "number of animals saved" based on the number of people who attend a vegan festival, class, or food tasting, but since there's a personal component to our engagement, community activists are able to gauge much more precisely the effect we're having on communities than activists engaging in drive-by activism. By tracking people's progression through our classes, workshops, festivals, and other programming, we can get a clear picture of the impact of our activism.

The combination of personal interaction and regular follow-up communications creates an environment where participants in our classes (500+ people every year), food tasting events (5,000+ people every year), and festivals (tens of thousands of people every year) feel comfortable inviting coworkers, family members, and friends to participate in our events. In this way, our sphere of influence expands through word-of-mouth and personal recommendations and isn't solely dependent on us going out and doing all the legwork to promote our events and programming. This fact challenges the commonly held idea that community-based activism reaches such small numbers of people that it's not worth funding.

So what would I say to that prominent animal rights movement donor who said he would never fund my work? I would tell him that it's not only his loss—since he's missing out on an opportunity to support valuable, groundbreaking work to shift food culture in marginalized communities—but it's a loss to the animals and the planet he claims to hold so dear. I would also point out that refusing to support work being done by a Black activist in Black communities is upholding white supremacist ideas about which communities are worthy of support and which ones aren't. In other words, it's racist, plain and simple.

2

Effective Altruism's Unsuspecting Twenty-First-Century Colonialism

Simone de Lima

I first became aware of the Effective Altruism movement when I met some of its enthusiasts during NYU's Center for Mind, Brain, and Consciousness's *Conference on Animal Consciousness* in 2017. As a foreigner, and often the outsider, returning to an academic space after time off in the nonprofit world, I was happy to interact with what seemed like a kind and earnest group of young people, who, after identifying with a question I had asked in a plenary session, struck up conversations during breaks.

I was curious to learn more about EAs, as they called themselves—an interesting identity they seemed to uphold, to mark a distinction. Altruism—who could possibly be against it? Effectiveness? I hesitated with the idea of effectiveness, as if it was a stand-alone value, decontextualized from history, culture, and worldviews. This reminded me of the many times I had been asked—by students, friends, and the press—about the "efficacy" of certain teaching methods. "Is it effective?," people would ask me about a new educational fad, such as the importation of a program promising to teach toddlers to read and write. My answer would always be to ask new questions: "Effective for what? What is your vision of education? What is your concept of childhood? What is, in your mind, the role of reading? Do you equate speed with quality?" These are the questions one needs to entertain when one asks about efficacy. And by that, I mean that any measure of efficacy is ideological.

Simone de Lima, *Effective Altruism's Unsuspecting Twenty-First-Century Colonialism* In: *The Good It Promises, The Harm It Does*. Edited by: Carol J. Adams, Alice Crary, and Lori Gruen, Oxford University Press.
 DOI: 10.1093/oso/9780197655696.003.0002

It's been three years since first coming into contact with this group of Effective Altruists, and I have since realized that they wanted less to make my acquaintance than to engage in the very US-based practice of networking—perhaps because of my role in a nonprofit at the time. Looking further into what Effective Altruism has brought to the movement has brought me up short, and I started to reflect on the movements' role, especially in the advocacy for animals in the Global South. This is because what I noticed in the following years was nothing short of a deluge of these ideas into advocacy for animal rights, and into my native country, Brazil.

The expansion of large US- and UK-based animal rights organizations into other countries, especially those in the Global South, was not exactly new. A large UK-based organization (then WSPA, rebranded as World Animal Protection) had been active in Brazil since the late 1990s, initially functioning as a federation, followed by a fallout with many of its member grass-roots organizations when it insisted on establishing a "model farm" to showcase "animal welfare." With Brazil consistently ranking as one of the world's largest producers and exporters of flesh from cows, chickens, and pigs, and soy for animal feed, with systems imported from the US and Europe, its strategic relevance in the world of farmed animal advocacy became clear. In 2010, a large US-based international organization, Humane Society International, set up shop in the country, followed by at least five other US- and Europe-based funded others (Mercy for Animals, Animal Equality, Veganuary, GFI, and Sinergia Animal).

These organizations didn't encounter a vacuum in terms of animal rights activism and campaigns. By 2003, when I founded ProAnima,[1] in Brasília, the capital, the country already had a burgeoning, if mostly volunteer and grass-roots, movement dedicated to the defense of animals. Granted, most of the tens of

[1] I left ProAnima in 2016, so am not responsible for current views.

organizations and collectives around the country focused on domestic animals (sometimes including those exploited for entertainment and experimentation), but ignored the plight of animals exploited for food. Awareness of a broader picture, however, was growing. There were two influential and professionalized organizations promoting veganism or vegetarianism. On the legislative front, animals had been recognized to some extent in anti-cruelty laws since 1938 and attained constitutional protection from cruelty in 1986. In 1998, mistreatment, mutilation, or injury of any animal—whether wild, exotic, or domestic—was recognized as a crime under the Environmental Protection Law, largely thanks to the work of historic animal rights activists.

In the meantime, vegetarianism had been slowly but surely growing in popularity, mainly from health-based or spiritualist perspectives. This was followed by the beginning of the vegan movement, with some of the seeds in the rock/straight-edge music scene, others in the more academic debate of philosophical extension of consideration of rights for nonhuman animals, and from the extension of awareness from those who had started off focusing on companion animals. The origin of veganism in Brazil was—as is the case in other countries—largely politicized and anti-establishment, even though it lacked a developed awareness of intersecting oppressions. Over the years, vegan collectives, knowledge sharing, demonstrations, organizations, campaigns, social media outlets, eateries, and products emerged. (I am proud to have been a partner in Brasília's first vegan establishment, Café Corbucci). Of course, these movements and orientations intertwined, collaborated, clashed, merged, bifurcated, and developed. My main point is that none of the incoming international organizations were responsible for "bringing the light" to my country.

As the branches of international organizations become established in Brazil—and I daresay, in other countries in the Global South—they no doubt have specificities peculiar to each of them. But there are some common dynamics that concern me, most of which get rehearsed in how Effective Altruism has come to be applied to animal rights issues.

First, the organizations tend to operate with a top-down, rather than collaborative, approach in their "branch" countries. Goals and standards for success are increasingly established by the organizations' central HQs, removed from an understanding of local sociocultural, historical, and political factors. This, in turn, is driven by a return-on-the-donation-dollar approach increasingly required by donors, which is one of the tenets of Effective Altruism: the quest to optimize "lives saved per dollar." As noted by lauren Ornelas in her *Reclaiming Our Grassroots* talk at the 2019 National Animal Rights Conference, this leads to homogenized campaigns and the impoverishment of activist creativity and connection to their culture. This happens even though locals are hired. Often members of the highly educated, English-speaking elite, these activists are lured by the promise of a wealthy, professionalized organization where their commitment to the cause can be turned into a paying job. However, on-the-ground staff are seldom in a position to question headquarters' directions. As the great Brazilian educator and philosopher Paulo Freire ([1970] 2005) explains, in the absence of education for freedom, the oppressed harbor the oppressor within. I would know—living since my childhood between countries of the North and South, it took a long time before I started to critically examine the introjected pressure to assimilate, blend in, and be recognized by colonized standards.

When an international organization sweeps into another country bringing in top-down goals and methods, it often disregards that country's history in activism and the cultural and legislative advancements gained by the movement before the establishment of these new "foreign" organizations. In my interactions with US animal rights organizations, I frequently met people who assumed animal-related legislation was backward in Brazil (it is, in fact, quite comprehensive, although enforcement is obviously an issue), or even doubted my assertions that, for example, hunting was illegal.

I was also met with resistance when explaining a different cultural view of so-called euthanasia of stray animals, with the practice of shelters in the United States being treated as the default, "civilized" option from which all we had to do was learn. (Brazilian animal rights activists have long fought for and introduced legislation in several states prohibiting the killing of treatable stray animals, as well as establishing rights to protection for community animals. This is based on the notion of lives not being expendable just because they happen to be lived on the streets.) Another frequent point of tension was the Brazilian labor legislation—a victory of decades of the workers' movement—which international organizations often met with surprise and disappointment, since they expected that hiring "in the Third World" would be cheap and devoid of employer obligations.

The pressure to "show work" to donors provokes a race to the bottom to identify easy campaigns that can score a "win" regardless of any real impact in advancing awareness, improving the lives of animals, or tackling the root causes of their exploitation. A case in point involves the ubiquitous cage-free campaigns across the world led by international organizations. Much has been elaborated on the questionable impact of cage-free egg production on the actual lives of chickens and public understanding of the exploitation of hens used in this industry. But nowhere has this become more salient to me than in the disconnect of these campaigns in Brazil, where governmental and institutional instability has increasingly become the norm and enforcement of and compliance with legislation is in frank erosion—even by the government, let alone by private enterprises. Despite this reality, what do these "effective" organizations do? They engage an army of organizational employees working on long-term commitments from the industry to go cage-free, announcing commitment after commitment with great fanfare in animal advocacy forums. However, as the movement itself recognizes, out of 130 businesses that committed to such changes, only 20 companies even deemed to answer follow-up questions from Fórum Animals' Egg Radar website ("Egg Radar," 2020), a few have blatantly ignored preestablished deadlines, and so far only one has met its commitment and turned its production to cage-free. In their turn, companies start using the commitments as propaganda tools almost immediately upon signing intentions for a distant future, leading the public to think they are purchasing less cruel eggs. Who exactly is winning here?

Another ubiquitous, depoliticizing, and homogenizing trend has been to associate veganism with what is deemed by Effective Altruists as the palatable, nonthreatening prototype of human: the lifestyle influencer. Stereotypically white, youthful, thin, and able-bodied, they avoid any messaging that connects veganism to other causes, sell a message of health and fitness, and even eschew the word "vegan" itself, going so far as trying to popularize the cumbersome and foreign term "plant-based"—in English! A scroll through the social media feeds of the organizations most openly espousing the tenets of Effective Altruism in the country shows the omnipresence of graphics and messaging portraying white US- and European-based celebrities.[2] Also omnipresent are each organization's Brazilian "brand ambassadors"—mostly blonde and White models and actresses, with an occasional nod to "diversity" here and there. Needless to say, this "average" and "neutral" person is neither representative of average Brazilians—even if our racist, classist, and colonialist structures establish them as parameters of attractiveness—nor do they promote a lifestyle that is accessible. It is with a heavy heart that I see a movement originally rooted in a critical analysis of oppression becoming equated with body shaming, ableism, and sexism, and the message of the dismantlement of harming other beings becoming diluted into lifestyle tropes. And as with activists who become bureaucratized

[2] Animal Equality showcases Kat Von D and Moby on its website's home page; Mercy For Animals showcases Leonardo de Caprio; while SVB quotes Paul McCartney, Woody Harrelson and Bryan Adams, among others.

by positions in organizations, social media creators are often homogenized into producing messages that are almost indistinguishable from those from other countries—and heavily affiliated with the organizations they have ties to and corporations for whom they market products.

This brings us to the central issue—the barrage of messaging brought by "Effective Altruism" and its moniker in the animal rights movement, "pragmatic/strategic veganism," that the popularization of diets not reliant on products stolen from the lives of animals will come about through the introduction of industrialized plant-based alternatives by large corporations into the market. As problematic as this market-based approach is in the United States, it brings added layers of problems in the Global South, and that has to do primarily with the different politics and geography of our food systems. Whereas access to foods in the United States is influenced by winter weather, the geography of urban areas, and the normalized culture of industrialized and fast food, Brazil—and other countries in the Global South—is not influenced by these forces in the same fashion.

Brazil is one of the most biodiverse countries in the world, and, except for a few areas, it is able to support local, year-round crops of vegetables, legumes, grains, nuts, and fruit; produce markets featuring fresh produce are abundant even in poorer neighborhoods in most of the country. Fast food is neither financially nor geographically accessible, and although specialists have recently started to study the existence of potential food deserts in the country, they constitute a different phenomenon from the urban, fast-food stricken neighborhoods in the United States, and are harder to pinpoint.[3] Add to that the fact that the food traditions

[3] The Brazilian Ministry for Social Development and Fight Against Hunger (MDS), extinguished by the Bolsonaro government, published an extensive report (CAISAN/MDS 2018) on the challenges of pinpointing food deserts in Brazil. The report points to the widespread presence of fresh food markets and outdoor stalls, as well as supermarkets throughout the country, with unclear patterns as relates to wealth. In an interview, Paula Martins, a researcher on the subject at the Universidade Federal de São

derived from Native peoples, enslaved peoples, colonizers, and immigrants compose a rich kaleidoscope of Brazilian heritage dishes, and that many of these are originally plant-based or can be adapted as such. Of these, some are present daily in family meals, while others are being lost due to the homogenizing pressures of globalization. Meanwhile, farmers receive subsidies for common ingredients in industrialized foods, such as soy and corn, and those foods are in turn marketed heavily, replacing more traditional local foods. The occupation of vast swaths of the country by monocultural, commodity crops that feature as ingredients in much of the industrialized, ultra-processed foods comes at the cost of biodiversity (Colli, Vieira, and Dianese 2020). As an example, even though corn is a traditional South American staple with an astounding original diversity of types, Brazilian corn crops are currently reduced to four "optimal" types, and it is a challenge to find corn products that aren't transgenic.

Burgers do not have the central role in the Global South diet that they do in US culture—a difference that became even more apparent to me when I read Carol Adam's *Burger* (2018) which situates its importance in the US food culture. It is appalling that the transposition of the logic that plant-based burgers would "revolutionize" Brazilian consumption of animal-based products was allowed to be naturalized in some sectors of the animal rights community through the action of these organizations, which brought

Paulo (UNIFESP), states: "The issue of food deserts is more complex than the simple presence of stores. Some interventions aimed at promoting access to healthy food used in developed nations have proposed the allocation of supermarkets in food deserts. This may not be a good solution (for Brazil), since the presence of these establishments may favor the consumption of ultra-processed foods even more" (Carnaúba 2018). In sum, it seems that fresh food availability—and its consumption, as opposed to ultra-processed foods—is much more widespread in Brazil than it is in the US, even though the phenomenon of food deserts is beginning to be investigated there. No doubt huge income disparities remain the fundamental issue for food security, aggravated by the pandemic. In 2020, 59.4 percent of households were shown to be food insecure, up from 36.7 percent in 2018 (Galindo et al. 2021) their unquestioned Northern and limited perspective on the burger to Brazil.

A quick look at different versions of vegan starter guides used by these organizations in Brazil reveals a range of writing and recipes that goes from the frankly US-centric (showcasing mainstream US meal and product choices) to an attempt to integrate culturally appropriate dishes,[4] but which still rely heavily on expensive, industrialized ingredients, found mostly in large urban centers, and the promotion of plant-based products produced by large corporations whose mainstay is factory farming. In fact, what the Effective Altruism movement has dubbed "strategic" or "pragmatic" veganism has invested heavily in praising, promoting, and even certifying as "vegan," food produced by some of Brazil's and the world's largest agribusiness complexes, companies that thrive on the exploitation of other animals, workers, Indigenous lands, and natural resources. This is all done in the name of "mainstreaming" veganism, but let's take a closer look at some of these companies and their practices.

A case in point is Burger King's much-heralded launch of the plant-based "Rebel Whopper." The second-largest burger company in the world, acquired by a Brazilian group in 2010, Burger King has a history of labor rights infringements in the country, having repeatedly been slammed with fines and settlements due to problems ranging from inadequate conditions for employees to sexual discrimination in the workplace. On the environmental front, a report by the nonprofit Mighty Earth (Bellantonio et al. 2017) found Burger King to be the worst fast-food company in terms of lack of accountability and responsiveness to measures to

[4] To give credit where it is due, Animal Equality Brazil's blog features quite a lot of culturally appropriate foods and traditions. Contrast this with MFA's veg starter guide, which suggests meals that are not part of Brazilian culture (such as the idea that a hot dog qualifies as "lunch") and places industrialized products prominently. Also of note is a blog promoting Effective Altruism in the animal rights movement (veganismoestrategico.com.br), which repeatedly sings praises of plant-based, industrialized products, with titles like "Ades [a Coca-Cola subsidiary] launches a new of vegan products and this is a good thing."

mitigate the presence of deforested areas in its supply chain, especially regarding the destruction of the biodiverse Brazilian Cerrado for soy, destined for animal feed. Its recently announced solution to the issue of GHG emissions by cattle? It is investing in changing the cows' diet of cows so they allegedly produce less gas, and marketing this as "sustainable" (Mock 2020).

The Rebel Whopper itself is produced by agribusiness conglomerate Marfrig—the world's second-largest beef producer, killing over 21,000 cows per day just in South America. The company is repeatedly cited in human rights and environmental nonprofit reports (Campos 2019; Human Rights Watch 2019; Mano 2019) as one of the conglomerates most unable to detach its supply chain from the beef purchased from illegally deforested areas in the Amazon, and the associated violence and destruction of Indigenous communities that goes along with the deforestation.

Although logging and mining play secondary roles in the Amazon's deforestation, it is important to highlight that close to 80 percent of deforested areas in the Amazon were cleared for animal-based cattle grazing (Global Institute of Sustainable Forestry 2020). *Grazing the Amazon* (2018), a documentary produced by investigative journalism agency O Eco and the nonprofit Imazon, explains the difficulty faced in the enforcement of environmental protection laws in the region, especially due to the many "cattle-washing" tactics employed to legitimize cattle raised in illegally cleared areas, not to mention the power of the agribusiness caucus at all levels of Brazilian politics.

Not coincidentally, another company being promoted by "pragmatic vegans" as "revolutionizing" the eating landscape on behalf of animals is the world's largest meat processing company, JBS, which launched a plant-based burger through its subsidiary, SEARA, the "Incrível Burger." This same JBS graced international headlines for a 2017 corruption scandal involving the bribing of meat inspectors and doling out of hush money to politicians. (De Lima 2017). JBS, which operates slaughterhouses in the Amazon, the Cerrado biome, and other areas of the country, has been implicated in the purchase of meat derived from illegally deforested areas by several reports released by those Greenpeace (n.d.), Mighty Earth (Hurowitz et al. 2019) and Amazon Watch (2019). The company has been featured in the list of Brazilian corporations engaging in labor practices analogous to slavery, and it paid one of the highest labor infringement fines in the country's history ("TST impõe multa," 2014) for forcing employees to work in conditions so frigid they sustained frostbite. In this instance, the workers were denied sick leave; instead, the company provided painkillers to ensure the workers would keep working despite the pain they were in. During the COVID-19 pandemic, a JBS plant was directly tied to the contamination of the Indigenous community in the state of Mato Grosso do Sul with the novel coronavirus, devastating the community (Oliveira 2020).

As the vegan cook and food autonomy educator Renata Octaviani (personal communication, 2020) points out, it's unfortunate that in a country with an abundance and variety of affordable plant-based proteins, vegan burgers produced by the world's largest meatpackers are presented as a breakthrough for veganism. This alienates an important part of the population, who come to identify veganism as a movement dependent on expensive, highly processed foods that are detached from our food traditions.

What have we come to when we call a diversification of business portfolios by these companies—which are involved, through their caucus in Congress, in the dismantlement of environmental laws, human rights, and animal protection laws—a success for the animals, and even going as far as to offer "vegan" certifications to a Unilever product?

In sum, the actions of supposedly "effective" organizations acting in the Global South have resulted in:

1. campaigns for welfarist measures, (mainly cage-free eggs),
2. the promotion of plant-based products produced and distributed by mega corporations and chains,

3. heavy investment in influencer/celebrity culture, and
4. the fostering of a belief in the self-regulation of a benign market.

To advance these supposedly effective interventions, a colonialist tactic could not be absent: that of convincing the public that this is *the* superior, tried and tested, science-based approach to animal advocacy. The result is that international lecturers engage in talk tours and workshops "teaching" "efficacy and pragmatism," popular social media groups promoting veganism are vied for and even taken over by this "pragmatic" ideology, and organizations that previously represented diverse voices and approaches become almost exclusively market-oriented.[5] They claim for themselves, and for themselves only, the word *strategy*, coining "strategic veganism," a rhetorical move to portray those who invest in community and alliance-building, politicized and contextualized activism, and the fight for food sovereignty and autonomy as devoid of strategy. Part of this rhetoric also uses an appeal to science and data while clinging to the most positivistic traditions in psychology and the social sciences—which thrive on the myths of objectivity—and ignoring critical and culturally and historically anchored scholarship.

Brazil now hosts an effective altruism/pragmatic veganism website, Veganismo Estratégico (www.veganismoestrategico.com.br), with many of its posts seemingly dedicated to portraying critical voices as unreasonable, adversarial, and alienating—building a straw-man argument of the "irrational, purist vegan" who must

[5] A case in point is SVB, the Brazilian Vegetarian Society, which once congregated diverse viewpoints on veganism, as reflected in its choice of speakers in annual conferences and the variety of initiatives in local chapters. It then became increasingly hostile to critical and anti-oppressive approaches while at the same time turning into a focal point for Effective Altruism trainings in the country through an ongoing collaboration with the Center for Effective Vegan Advocacy.

be defeated in order to allow veganism to go mainstream. While they present themselves as voices of balance, with reasonable arguments that vegan activism should focus on nonvegans and be inclusive, they use such arguments to promote the idea that a self-regulating, market-based solution is not only viable but the *main* strategy vegans should pursue. "Awareness is overrated" is a recurrent theme: if we convince corporations to give us vegan options, veganism will become mainstream.

Of note is a blog post that attempts to characterize awareness of injustice as an emotional and therefore inferior response, entitled "The meat industry is not our enemy" (Alvarenga 2019):

> Governments with corrupt systems, companies which place profit above all else and societies in which people place their interests above any sense of collective responsibility trigger our sense of injustice and leave us vulnerable to our emotions, leading us to favor emotion over reason. Seeing them [the meat industry] as the opposition is easy, intuitive, and, at the same time, not efficacious. The meat industry is not our enemy. Our cause's biggest enemy is the natural difficulty we, as activists, exhibit when dealing with those who think differently. Judgment and attacks create distance, rather than inspiring the change we want to inspire.

It's interesting that the same group of people who declare awareness to be overrated, urging activists to turn their efforts to changing corporations, themselves use language about *inspiring* change—as if inspiration, not profit, were a driving force for these corporations. Also of note is the dualistic thinking that establishes a necessary and insurmountable contradiction between the realms of emotion and rationality—one that has been so aptly questioned in the ecofeminist ethic of care. This line of thought promotes a dissociation between activism and the interests of animals being exploited by these industries, and it reveals such confusion between the dynamics of personal interactions and the structural organization of a society and its economy that it seems disingenuous.

I write this in 2020, in the midst of the COVID-19 pandemic. We wake up each day to a nightmare, a barrage of tragedy. Daily, we are met with the mismanagement of the crisis by governments; the disproportionate number of deaths in communities of color and migrant and Indigenous communities; the worlds' reliance upon and disregard for its poorest workers; the lack of access to health-care; the massive rates at which meatpacking workers—both in the US and Brazil—have been affected; the shattering mass killing of millions of "excess," "unmarketable" farmed animals; the acceleration in their exploitation in laboratories for medications and vaccines; the mass killing of mink; and the sheer mind-blowing scale of human and nonhuman deaths. All the while, according to a report from Americans for Tax Fairness and the Institute for Policy Studies Program for Inequality, US billionaires' fortunes have increased, to date, by $434 billion.

With the dysfunctionality of capitalism exposed like an oozing wound, if there is one thing that is made clear it is that the local, small-scale, personal connections that make up community support networks—precisely those that the Effective Altruism playbook looks down on as "ineffective"—are what are supplying literal lifelines for communities. Especially in countries where governments have attacked the scientific community, destroyed public health systems, and retreated from multilateral organizations, large systems are clearly failing us, and it is the ingenuity of closeness, generosity, and the ethics of care that are keeping the most vulnerable afloat. It's the community organizers countering fake news and doing outreach in different languages to immigrants; it's the mutual aid networks popping up; in Brazil, it's the Movimento dos Sem Terra (Landless Workers' Movement) providing thousands of tons of produce to those unemployed and disenfranchised by the pandemic; it's the Indigenous communities and allies working to protect their lands from miners, land grabbers, and the virus; it's the communities in the favelas self-organizing and sharing knowledge, food, and aid. Last but not least, it is the sustenance provided by art: a case in point is the phenomenon of the musical social media live events that have become a lifeline for millions in my country. Again, these are exactly the kinds of initiatives Effective Altruists would frown upon, with their "objective" calculations of lives saved per dollar.

In these days, in which we frequently feel gaslit by authorities, hope is hard to come by. Yet, in these closing notes, I'd like to say that I am hopeful that international collaboration is possible if we commit to decolonizing our perspective on how to work for justice for human and nonhuman animals across borders.

For international work to happen in a decolonized manner, it is vital that the power structures that accompany the interactions between US- and European-based organizations, initiatives, and individuals and those in the Global South are acknowledged. Being willing to scrutinize the history of North-South relations, how they impinge on the institutional and personal relations being actualized in the present is a first step.

To those interested in building international solidarity, I say: bring with you a spirit of legitimate interest in the history and dynamics of the other country—ask questions, more than offer guidance, be prepared to be corrected, elaborate your understanding, and ask for honest, critical feedback—and be prepared to re-route and re-elaborate. Additionally, ask what you could do in the United States and Europe to change structural forces that impinge on the Global South—an easy example is denouncing and working to dismantle corporations that thrive on the exploitation of pillaged natural resources from the Global South. Understand what partnerships could advance global causes from a collaborative approach, rather than a top-down one.

I see reason for hope in the animal rights activism in my country. Countering the naive, superficial, digital influencer-driven, commercialized culture, there is a burgeoning movement of activists who are discovering (or rediscovering) the wealth of our complex heritage of foods, rooted in the complicated history of a country rich in biodiversity but threatened by commodity monoculture. They celebrate and experiment with culinary traditions—avoiding the whitewashing of a "melting pot" narrative. They discuss and promote food autonomy and sovereignty, and investigate a vegan praxis that is affordable, diverse, culturally connected, inventive, resourceful, joyous, delicious, critical, and creative. They build bridges with the movement for agrarian reform, which tilts heavily toward restorative, ecologically grounded family agriculture. They engage with the necessary and hard conversations, such as when Afro-Brazilian vegan activists denounce the racist elitism in the movement. These activists, many organized in collectives through União Vegana de Ativismo and the Afro-Brazilian Vegan Society, are doing the hard work of forming actual alliances with different social justice movements.

The forces of Effective Altruism and "high-impact" professional activism in my country—and, I suspect, many others in the Global South—are heavily reliant on the companies that produce monoculture commodities. Not coincidentally, this has led to a Monoculture of the Activist Mind, if I may bring Vandana Shiva's concept into play here. But this is what I envision with hope:

Imagine what international solidarity could look like: organizations across the world dialoguing with, elevating, and supporting these diverse voices, with a radical respect for the groundedness of their activism in their territories, their cultures, and their histories, sharing resources and skills, finding common ground, recognizing different perspectives, deepening their knowledge, and impacting lives, livelihoods, and systems.

References

Adams, C. (2018). *Burger*. New York: Bloomsbury Academic.

Alvarenga, L. (2019). "Não devemos enxergar a indústria da carne como inimiga" [We shouldn't view the meat industry as our enemy]. Veganismo Estratégico. https://www.veganismoestrategico.com.br/postagens/nao-enxergar-a-industria-da-carne-como-inimiga/.

Amazon Watch. (2019). *Complicity in Destruction 2: How Northern Consumers and Financiers Enable Bolsonaro's Assault on the Brazilian Amazon.* Oakland, CA: Amazon Watch. https://amazonwatch.org/news/2019/0425-complicity-in-destruction-2.

Bellantonio, M., G. Hurowitz, A. L. Gronlund, and A. Yousefi. (2017). *The Ultimate Mystery Meat: Exposing the Secrets behind Burger King and Global Meat Production*. Norway: Rainforest Foundation. https://www.mightyearth.org/wp-content/uploads/2016/07/MightyEarth_MysteryMeat.pdf.

CAISAN/MDS. (2018). *Mapeamento dos Desertos Alimentares no Brasil.* Brasília: CAISAN/MDS. https://aplicacoes.mds.gov.br/sagirmps/noticias/arquivos/files/Estudo_tecnico_mapeamento_desertos_alimentares.pdf.

Campos, A. (2019), "JBS, Marfrig e Frigol compram gado de desmatadores em área campeã de focos de incêndio na Amazônia." São Paulo, Brazil: Repórter Brasil, August 31. https://reporterbrasil.org.br/2019/08/jbs-marfrig-e-frigol-compram-gado-de-desmatadores-em-area-campea-de-focos-de-incendio-na-amazonia.

Carnaúba, V. (2018). "Deserto Alimentar faz soar alarme no Brasil." *Entreteses*, July. https://www.unifesp.br/edicoes-anteriores-entreteses/item/3521-deserto-alimentar-faz-soar-alarme-no-brasil.

Colli, G.R., C. R. Vieira, and J. C. Dianese. (2020). "Biodiversity and Conservation of the Cerrado: Recent Advances and Old Challenges." *Biodiversity and Conservation* 29: 1465–1475.

De Lima, S. (2017). "JBS Parent Company to Pay $3.2 Billion for Bribery in Brazil." *Compassion Over Killing* (blog). https://animaloutlook.org/jbs-parent-company-pay-3-2-billion-bribery-brazil/.

Egg Radar. (2020). Available online: https://www.brasilsemgaiolas.com.br/egg-radar.

Freire, P. ([1970] 2005). *Pedagogy of the Oppressed.* New York: Continuum.

Galindo, E., M. A. Teixeira, M. De Araújo, R. Motta, M. Pessoa, L. Mendes, and L. Rennó. (2021). *Efeitos da pandemia na alimentação e na situação da segurança alimentar no Brasil* [Effects of the pandemic on nutrition and food security in Brazil]. Food for Justice Working Paper Series, no. 4. Berlin: Refurbium.

Global Institute of Sustainable Forestry (GISF). (2020). *Yale Global Forest Atlas 2020: Cattle Ranching in the Amazon Region.* New Haven, CT: Global Institute of Sustainable Forestry. https://globalforestatlas.yale.edu/amazon/land-use/cattle-ranching.

Iseense e Sá, Márcio, dir. (2018), .

Greenpeace. (n.d.). *Como o desmatamento e a criação de gado têm ameaçado a biodiversidade brasileira* [How deforestation and cattle farming have threatened Brazil's biodiversity]. Amsterdam: Greenpeace. https://www.greenpeace.org/brasil/biodiversidade/como-o-desmatamento-e-a-criacao-de-gado-tem-ameacado-a-biodiversidade-brasileira.

Human Rights Watch. (2019). *Rainforest Mafias: How Violence and Impunity Fuel Deforestation in Brazil's Amazon*. New York: Human Rights Watch. https://www.hrw.org/report/2019/09/17/rainforest-mafias/how-violence-and-impunity-fuel-deforestation-brazils-amazon.

Hurowitz, G., M. Jacobson, E. Higonnet, and L. von Reusner. (2019). *The Companies behind the Burning of the Amazon*. Washington, DC: Mighty Earth. https://stories.mightyearth.org/amazonfires.

Iseense e Sá, Márcio, dir. (2018). *Grazing the Amazon*. Brazil: O Eco & Imazon.

Mano, A. (2019). "Brazil Prosecutors Push Soy, Cattle Moratorium to Protect Natives." Reuters, November 14. https://www.reuters.com/article/us-brazil-agriculture-indigenous-exclusi/exclusive-brazil-prosecutors-push-soy-cattle-moratorium-to-protect-natives-idUSKBN1XO2JN.

Mercy For Animals. (n.d.). *Guia Vegetariano Para Começar*. Los Angeles: Mercy For Animals. https://file-cdn.mercyforanimals.org/mfa/files/GVPC.pdf.

Mock, S. (2020). "Less Windy Whoppers? Low-Methane Burger King Still Involves Some Hot Air." *Guardian*, July 22. https://www.theguardian.com/environment/2020/jul/22/less-windy-whoppers-low-methane-burger-king-still-involves-some-hot-air.

Oliveira, A. (2020). "Contaminação de indígenas em Dourados partiu de frigorífico da JBS" [Contamination of indigenous people started from JBS meatpacking plant in Dourados]. *Pública*, June 10. https://apublica.org/2020/06/contaminacao-de-indigenas-em-dourados-partiu-de-frigorifico-da-jbs/).

"TST impõe multa de R$ 10 milhões à Seara por danos morais coletivos" [Superior Labor Justice Court rules for a fine of R$10 million for collective moral damages]. (2014). Rede Brasil Atual, November 25. https://www.redebrasilatual.com.br/trabalho/2014/11/tst-impoe-multa-de-r-10-milhoes-a-seara-por-danos-morais-coletivos-4555/.

3

Anti-Blackness and the Effective Altruist

Christopher Sebastian

Writing for Bitch Media in spring 2012, UCLA associate professor Safiya Noble identified a troubling trend in commercial search engine results. A simple Google search for the phrase "Black girls" returned dozens of pornographic results depicting Black women and children in an overtly sexualized way (Noble 2012). Searches for the phrases "Latina girls" and "Asian girls" produced similar results. Searches for the phrase "white girls," however, returned no suggestive terms at all.

Google's search process is based on identifying and assigning value to various types of information through web indexing. Many search engines, not just Google, use the artificial intelligence of computers to determine what kinds of information should be retrieved and displayed, and in what order. When made aware of this discovery, Google reacted quickly to correct it. But while Google framed this incident as an unfortunate bug in the system, Noble asks the public to consider the idea that this incident illustrates something that is not a bug at all, but rather a feature.

This is not to suggest that Google programmers and stakeholders are mustache-twirling racists, but rather that their ignorance of racism makes it almost impossible for them to spot when racial bias is present. Such is the case with Effective Altruism (EA). The inability to recognize systemic racism, or the unwillingness to confront it, creates a space in which EA supports a racist system.

Christopher Sebastian, *Anti-Blackness and the Effective Altruist* In: *The Good It Promises, The Harm It Does.* Edited by: Carol J. Adams, Alice Crary, and Lori Gruen, Oxford University Press.
 DOI: 10.1093/oso/9780197655696.003.0003

Effective Altruism started around the 2000s as a philosophical and social movement based on reason and evidence. Instead of asking *how* to do good, this community chose to focus on how to do the *most* good in an impartial manner. Efficiency is the name of the game.

Effective Altruist leaders like William MacAskill or Peter Singer seek to identify the most efficient global problems to focus on based on the magnitude of effect on well-being, how neglected the topic is, and how practical or solvable the issue. Proponents of EA claim to encourage cause-neutrality (i.e., detachment of personal interests with a certain issue) and supposedly follow whichever path the evidence decides is the "most worthy" cause, thereby minimizing biases that can be introduced by factors such as race. EA also claims to identify the best charities through analyzing interventions by their perceived cost-effectiveness (i.e., cost per disability-adjusted life years) (Chung 2021).

In the abstract, it is easy to see the appeal of EA for idealistic people who want to change the world. Superficially, it is an alluring prospect. But in its application, this approach exploits adherents' desires for simple, quantifiable outcomes by promising evidence-driven solutions that it cannot necessarily deliver, and it abdicates responsibility for global inequality by papering over how the inequality originated. A reductionistic mindset permeates the EA community, a mindset that understates the complexity of social determinants of inequality. In addition, EA promotes top-down intervention programs that center Western thought and have the potential to do more harm instead.

Plainly stated, EA is mind-blowingly white—and this is not conjecture. Data compiled from EA sources illustrate the whiteness of the community. According to the *EA Survey 2019 Series: Community Demographics & Characteristics*, the EA community struggles to attract people of color. A total of 87 percent of survey participants were white, 10 percent were Asian, 5 percent Latin American or Spanish origin, 1 percent were Black, and 4 percent were of other racial identities (Dullughan 2019). The survey also indicated that at the Center for Effective Altruism's (CEA's) EAGxVirtual 2020 event, 68.7 percent of registrants were white, 16.7 percent Asian, 3.8 percent Latin American or Spanish origin, 1.3 percent Black, and 2.8 percent other racial identities (Dullughan 2019).

The EA movement also is not just white in terms of physical representation. Normative Whiteness[1] is cooked into the ideological foundation, because it focuses on maximizing the effectiveness of donors' resources, which entrenches power in the hands of donors and further reinforces a power imbalance (Saunders-Hasting 2015). This contributes to donor-defined effectiveness and reduces the experiences, preferences, and views of EA recipients (Wisor 2011). The sheer homogeneity of donors, their approaches and strategies that are deemed to be most "effective," merely reflects their own highly subjective definition of "good." This is white benevolence and white paternalism at their finest.

Systemic global injustice is rooted in historical and institutional contexts. As such, there is something fundamentally condescending and dishonest in believing that the solutions to it can be conceptualized by people who largely have profited from such injustice (Ross-Oliver 2021). Locating all the power and influence with donors also can lead to selecting causes and approaches that have the potential to produce immediate successes (Mills 2012). This diminishes involvement by recipient communities in decision-making and implementation (Gabriel 2017). In this, Whiteness is represented not only in the presumably majority of donors who are

[1] "Normative Whiteness," as used here, does not refer to skin color. Historically, colonialism and imperialism involved imposing the values of white-skinned Europeans onto others by force. These entrenched European social, legal, and political systems that privileged white Europeans and their descendants over all others were (and are) rigorously enforced (Hamad 2015). In this sense, normative Whiteness is about those who most benefit from their proximity to Whiteness and reproduce it accordingly. Correspondingly, "people of color" are those who are most excluded and most frequently bear the consequences of that normativity.

white, but also in the acceptance of the idea that the racial makeup of EA doesn't matter.

This has consequences for people of color, especially people who identify as Black. Why should Blackness be made explicit? Because the worst outcomes for people of color globally are experienced by people who are Black. In the United States, Black people are more likely to be arrested for drugs offenses, although they are not more likely to use or sell drugs, and thus represent a disproportionate amount of the prison population (Alexander 2012). The UK government's race disparity audit indicated that Black defendants were more likely to be remanded into custody relative to white and Asian defendants (Cabinet Office 2018). Also, Black people in Britain were approximately ten times more likely than white people to experience stop and search by police, and three times more likely than Asians. Black people are also more likely to be unemployed and homeless than *all* other racial minority groups (Cabinet Office 2018).

In South America, Black people have equally poor experiences. Approximately 56 percent of Brazilians identify as Black—the largest population of African descent outside of Africa. But Black people make up only 18 percent of the National Congress (Zarur 2019), 4.7 percent of executives in Brazil's 500 largest companies (Castro 2020), and 75 percent of people killed by police (Grelet 2020). Brazilian president Jair Bolsonaro even compared Black people to cattle and said, "They do nothing! They are not even good for procreation" (Meredith 2018).

Even in majority Black South Africa, RTE reported in 2019 that 72 percent of the nation's private farmland is owned by white people, even though they only make up 9 percent of the population (Libreri 2019).

Lack of Black representation means that EA conversations about activism, practice, and theory occur uninformed by Black experience and insights. This conflicts with the notion of doing the "most good, most effectively," because it reveals a poverty of political and philosophical thought. There is a limit to what white philosophers can "know" if their Whiteness inoculates them from certain experiences and relieves them of interrogating their Whiteness because of its normativity.

In seeking an example of Black people as the ultimate racial other, look no farther than Effective Altruist Nick Cooney's 2014 book *Veganomics*. In his section on ethnicity, he wrote the following:

> Compared to Caucasians,[2] African-Americans eat 70 percent more fish, 55 percent more chicken, 39 percent more turkey, and 10 percent more pork. These numbers are even more striking when you consider that African-Americans have in general lower income and education levels than Caucasians—factors that should have led to lower meat consumption. . . .
>
> African-Americans kill a mammoth 46 farm animals each year. Caucasians cause the death of 31 farm animals, Hispanics, 33, and other ethnicities—when combined into one group—also dispatch about 33 farm animals each year. So while Caucasians, Hispanics, and "others" slaughter about the same number of farm animals, African-Americans kill almost 40 percent more. (Cooney 2014)

Cooney's homage to the 2005 book *Freakanomics* by Steven Levitt and Stephen J. Dubner provides a dizzying array of statistics, but this passage doesn't provide much analysis. There is no obvious purpose in comparing African Americans to Caucasians,

[2] Use of the word "Caucasian" in this essay is strictly because of its use in the source text. Caucasian is an outdated and scientifically inaccurate term that originated from thoroughly disproven eighteenth-century European science of racial classification. German anatomist Johann Blumenbach popularized the term after a visit to the Caucasus Mountains, located between the Caspian and Black Seas, and proposed that the "Caucasian" people were created in God's image as an ideal form of humanity. According to the anthropologist Yolanda Moses (2017), "Blumenbach's system of racial classification was adopted in the United States to justify racial discrimination—particularly slavery. Popular race science and evolutionary theories generally posited that there were separate races, that differences in behavior were tied to skin color, and that there were scientific ways to measure race. One way racial differences were defined was through craniometrics, which measured skull size to determine the intelligence of each racial group." This flawed application of the scientific method led to an equally flawed system of racial classification that ranked races from the most primitive (Black and brown) to the most advanced (white, or Caucasian)

but it does establish for the reader a strict (although perhaps unintentional) binary between the two and, once more, creates a standard where white people are the template by which all other minoritized groups are compared. Also, it locates a greater burden on the shoulders of Black people for dead animals. His use of language also reinforces this—Black people "kill" while white people "cause the death of" farm animals.

When Cooney does make an analysis, he states that lower income and education levels should have led to lower meat consumption, according to research published in 2012. What he does not mention, however, are the policy decisions implemented by the US federal government as early as the 1960s that disproportionately littered low-income minority communities—especially urban African American ones—with poor-quality fast-food chains that relentlessly market animal products to those consumers (Jou 2017).

Cooney also neglects the fact that meat consumption is often associated with higher status, which may impel people lower on the social scale to consume it (see Chan 2018). Cooney certainly cannot be blamed for not citing research that didn't exist at the time of his writing, but this information isn't new, and it wouldn't come as any surprise to many economically disadvantaged Black consumers. Excluding this perspective can reflect a lack of due diligence in performing qualitative research. Absent any discussion about those economic and educational factors that explicitly create disadvantages for Black consumers in the first place, readers are left looking at Black people as drivers of animal suffering without any badly needed context. Cooney doubles down on this when he writes, "Keep in mind which groups eat the most animals. For example, African Americans eat far more animals than other ethnic groups" (2014, 157). These details may seem minor, but they serve to reinforce negative biases about Black Americans in the minds of every person who reads this book. It paints a target on Black bodies as the primary antagonists who commit acts of violence against animals.

In fact, Cooney concludes that "inspiring African-Americans to go vegetarian or cut back on meat should spare many more animals than getting Caucasian or Hispanics to do the same. Depending on how receptive they are to advocacy efforts, African-Americans might be a great group for vegetarian advocates to *target*" (emphasis added, see Brenda Sanders's chapter in this volume for the dangers here). To be fair, Cooney makes a good point. Paying attention to African Americans as a demographic might be tactically important (although it would be better to *support* rather than *target* them). In January 2020, the *Washington Post* reported that the fastest-growing demographic of people going vegan in the United States is African Americans (Reiley 2020). Unfortunately, that growth seems to have occurred *despite* the best efforts of the vegan movement. In the years since *Veganomics* was published, many Black-led efforts in the United States have stagnated due to lack of funding and support. In fact, Black vegetarian advocates report higher levels of burnout and emotional trauma specifically due to lack of resources and, at times, outright hostility from a movement that centers normative Whiteness (Gorski et al. 2018). Where are the donors who are led by reason and evidence?

Latent anti-Blackness also can be observed in Cooney's next section, about chickens. He states, "The reason men slaughter a lot more farm animals than women, and African-Americans kill a lot more than other ethnicities, is because they eat more chicken." Here, Cooney conceals Whiteness by conflating men (of all races) and African Americans as a whole, instead of speaking about the intersection of these identities.

He further conceals Whiteness by offering no historical context for the relationship between African Americans and chicken consumption, particularly fried chicken, which again is rooted in institutional anti-Blackness (Delap 2021). Not only was chicken not considered a proper meat by white people during US colonial times, but the Carolinas made it illegal in 1741 for enslaved Black people to own pigs, cows, or horses. Chickens, which were omitted, became increasingly important to Black people, some of whom traded their eggs, feathers, and meat.

Cooney does not address this or any other historical factors that contribute to present-day African American chicken consumption. His words scapegoat African Americans by burying the lead: the invisibility of white ownership in food production and distribution that strategically determines precisely the outcome that African Americans eat more chicken. As philosopher George Yancey (2004, 5) has stated, "Whiteness often does not speak its name, which is a function of both its power and its bad faith."

Cooney is, however, not alone. Other EA advocates don't think the vegan movement has a racism problem at all. When talking about the prevalence of racism within the vegan movement, EA adherent and self-proclaimed rational ethicist Stijn Bruers (2021) stated, "Racism is not allowed in the movement, so the victims of racism should not experience racism from the racists who are allowed in the movement. Racism can simply be punished." Bruers's hyper-focus on acts of individual racism gives cover to institutional systemic racism, despite the weight of the evidence that shows how pervasive institutional racism in the movement is.

In 2015, People for the Ethical Treatment of Animals (PETA) sent actress Pamela Anderson to congratulate anti-immigrant Maricopa County, Arizona (USA), Sheriff Joe Arpaio for serving vegetarian meals to immigrant detainees in an open-air jail (*Examiner* Staff 2015). This is a man who violated an injunction after a judge ruled that his office engaged in racial profiling, proudly compared his own outdoor tent cities (where temperatures sometimes rose past 120 degrees Fahrenheit [48 degrees Celsius]) to concentration camps, and was later convicted by a federal judge for criminal contempt before being pardoned by President Donald Trump (Dwyer 2017; Liptak et al. 2017). Yet, somehow, one of the biggest and most well-funded vegan organizations in the United States thought that promoting him was good for the movement. Flying in the face of Bruers's claim that racism is not allowed in the movement, it is, in fact, rewarded. Some might argue that this does not reflect racial antagonism on the part of PETA itself. But the organization's choice to promote Arpaio demonstrates a willingness to cynically engage in racism to further an agenda. And this is not a one-off incident.

In the previous year, PETA was criticized for offering to pay the water bills of poor Detroit, Michigan (USA), residents who faced shut-off because of nonpayment. Social media users observed that this offer was tantamount to veganism by extortion. Amanda Levitt wrote, "Water is a human right. Period. Holding it out like a prize proves PETA doesn't value human life" (NBC 2014). Given that 78 percent of Detroit's population identifies as Black (World Population Review 2021), it would be more accurate to say that PETA does not value Black human life.

And if these examples are not recent enough, PETA fanned the flames of racism again in February 2020 when it released a one-minute animated Super Bowl advertisement that showed a series of animals taking a knee to the tune of the US national anthem. The gesture was popularized by Black US football player Colin Kaepernick, who knelt during the anthem before games as an act of peaceful resistance to disproportionate police violence in US law enforcement. Dartmouth professor Dr. Joshua Bennett said on Twitter, "Given PETA's history of appropriating symbols of black social and political struggle, I guess I shouldn't be shocked by this" (Calma 2020). According to their publicly released financial reports for 2020, PETA's total revenues are in excess of $66 million (PETA 2020). That is the so-called punishment for racism.[3]

Bruers (2020) also argues that allowing explicitly racist animal rights activists into the community can be a net positive because they have a higher likelihood of being confronted with antiracist

[3] While PETA is not an organization based on Effective Altruism, it is one of the most well-known organizations advocating for animals, and its racist campaigns affect perceptions of animal advocates.

ideas, and that can in turn diminish racist attitudes. Conversely, he offers no insight into how many Black or Brown people are driven away by the presence of those who engage in explicit racism, despite the evidence that suggests a positive relationship between increased racial diversity and organizational outcomes (Kovvali 2018). This speaks very literally to the astronomical value placed on white identity and normative Whiteness when faced with reason and quantitative evidence. Far from being colorblind, it can be said that the EA community only sees one color—white, the color that (again) George Yancey declared dare not speak its name.

Most troubling, however, is the popular EA notion that being race-neutral is of value in a world that is rooted in racial capitalism, the notion popularized by Cedric Robinson that racialized exploitation and capital accumulation are mutually reinforcing. To be neutral about race is to ignore how race is being used to perpetuate animal oppression, and if the goal of EA is to reduce or eliminate animal suffering, it is thus undercutting that goal.

A clear illustration of this occurred in early 2019, when legislation was introduced in New York City to ban the sale of new fur within the city limits. This measure was relatively uncontroversial, in part because it was specifically limited to the sale of new (not used) fur. Controversy, however, ensued when Harlem preacher Reverend Johnnie Green poured a considerable amount of time and resources into filling buses for multiple rallies at City Hall to fight for the right to buy new fur coats.

Senator Jabari Brisport (2019), representing New York's 25th State Senate district, wrote an op-ed for the *New York Daily News* in response. In it, Brisport argued that this constituted a manipulation of Black voters. He brazenly accused the fur lobby of a tactic known as "astroturfing," which is the practice of masking the sponsors of a message or organization (e.g., political, advertising, religious or public relations) to make it appear as though it originates from and is supported by grass-roots participants. Brisport accused fur industry insiders of using Black voices as a collective mouthpiece to reproduce their message on their behalf, and using racial identity as a weapon to perpetuate an industry built on normative Whiteness. His argument was bolstered by the fact that a Mason-Dixon poll found that 77 percent of Black New York City voters supported the City Council bill to ban the sale of new fur (Mason-Dixon Polling & Research 2019). He was further supported by images circulated online that showed white organizers allegedly passing out homemade signs to the Black protestors and then retreating to the periphery, where they could maintain a modicum of professional and physical distance.

From this, it is clear that those who profit from animal exploitation have figured out how to weaponize racial identity, while the Effective Altruist works overtime to divorce race from animal rights and liberation. It is in this way that EA realistically astroturfs for the industries themselves, as well as for philanthropists. By diminishing the role that race plays, Effective Altruists run interference for the class of monied people who drive inequality by producing racist and anti-animal outcomes. Incidentally, it is that same class of people who engage in philanthropy. Far from changing the world, these groups work together to keep the world mostly as it is.

As it stands, EA pays little attention to questions of justice, especially racial justice, which hinders its ability to do good. The idea that EA removes racial bias is categorically untrue. Colorblindness or race neutrality are not shown to be objectively "effective." And centering altruism over solidarity ensures that the mechanisms of power that created the very inequality it seeks to address remain firmly in place. Overall, EA *performs* "goodness" by reducing complex social issues to quantifiable measures that are mostly valuable in the eyes of normative Whiteness, and it disguises this reductionism under a veil of faux sophistication that is as unscientific as it is intellectually dishonest. There is nothing wrong with using reason and evidence; the problem is a failure to follow the evidence where it goes.

References

Albala, K. (2019, October). *Interview with T. L. Sebastian.*

Alexander, M. (2012). *The New Jim Crow: Mass Incarceration in the Age of Colorblindness*. New York: The New Press.

Brisport, J. (2019). "Using the Race Card against Animals: African-American Opponents of the Proposed Fur Ban Are Being Cynical." *New York Daily News*, June 1. https://www.nydailynews.com/opinion/ny-oped-using-the-race-card-against-animals-20190601-xjdektuvubbolbqneprzqhztxm-story.html.

Bruers, S. (2020). "Reflections on Intersectionality in the Animal Rights Movement." Retrieved from Stijn Bruers, April 24, at https://stijnbruers.wordpress.com/2020/04/04/reflections-on-intersectionality-in-the-animal-rights-movement.

Bruers, S. (2021, February 18). Facebook comment in response to a post by Christopher Sebastian, Retrieved from https://www.facebook.com/photo/?fbid=3715568471843795&set=a.145577608842917¬if_id=1631961857292457¬if_t=feedback_reaction_generic&ref=notif.

Cabinet Office. (2018). "*Race Disparity Audit: Summary Findings from the Ethnicity Facts and Figures Website.*" London: Cabinet Office, March 2018. https://assets.publishing.service.gov.uk/government/uploads/system/uploads/attachment_data/file/686071/Revised_RDA_report_March_2018.pdf.

Calma, J. (2020). "PETA Compared 'Speciesism' to Racism in Allegedly Banned Super Bowl Ad." *The Verge*, February 3. https://www.theverge.com/2020/2/3/21120970/peta-banned-nfl-super-bowl-ad-colin-kaepernick.

Castro, E. G. (2020). "The Necessary Measures to Accelerate the Fight against Racism in Brazil." *Veja*, December 1. https://veja.abril.com.br/brasil/as-medidas-necessarias-para-acelerar-a-luta-contra-o-racismo-no-brasil/.

Chan, E. Y. (2018). "Jerkies, Tacos, and Burgers: Subjective Socioeconomic Status and Meat Preference." *Appetite 132*: 257–266. https://doi.org/10.1016/j.appet.2018.08.027.

Chung, D. (2021). "When Doing Good Goes Wrong: Reimagining Effective Altruism Using Equity- and Justice-Based Approaches in Global Health and Development Aid." *IMMpress Magazine*, May 12. https://www.immpressmagazine.com/when-doing-good-goes-wrong-reimagining-effective-altruism-using-equity-and-justice-based-approaches-in-global-health-and-development-aid/.

Cooney, N. (2014). *Veganomics*. New York: Lantern.

Delap, J. (2021). "American Fried Chicken Has Its Origins in Slavery." *Economist*, July 2. Retrieved from https://www.economist.com/1843/2021/07/02/american-fried-chicken-has-its-origins-in-slavery.

DiAngelo, R. (2018). *White Fragility*. Boston: Beacon Press.

Drew, A. (2010). "Being a Sistah at PETA." In *Sistah Vegan: Black Female Vegans Speak on Food, Identity, Health, and Society*, edited by B. Harper, 61–64. New York: Lantern.

Dullughan, N. (2019). "EA Survey 2019 Series: Community Demographics & Characteristics." Rethink Priorities. *Effective Altruism Forum*, December 5. https://forum.effectivealtruism.org/posts/wtQ3XCL35uxjXpwjE/ea-survey-2019-series-community-demographics-and.

Dwyer, C. (2017). "Ex-Sheriff Joe Arpaio Convicted Of Criminal Contempt." *NPR*, July 31. https://www.npr.org/sections/thetwo-way/2017/07/31/540629884/ex-sheriff-joe-arpaio-convicted-of-criminal-contempt?t=1633006261862.

Examiner Staff. (2015). "Pamela Anderson Helps Controversial Sheriff Joe Arpaio Introduce Vegetarian Jail Food." *San Francisco Examiner*, April 16. https://www.sfexaminer.com/entertainment/pamela-anderson-helps-controversial-sheriff-joe-arpaio-introduce-vegetarian-jail-food/.

Gabriel, I. (2017). Effective Altruism and Its Critics. *Journal of Applied Philosophy* 34 (4): 457–473. https://doi.org/10.1111/japp.12176

Gorski, P., S. Lopresti-Goodman, and D. Rising. (2018). "'Nobody's Paying Me To Cry': The Causes of Activist Burnout in United States Animal Rights Activists." *Social Movement Studies* 18 (3): 364–380. https://doi.org/10.1080/14742837.2018.1561260.

Grelet, F. (2020). "Blacks Account for 75% of Those Killed by Police in Brazil, Report Points Out." *UOL*, July 15. https://noticias.uol.com.br/ultimas-noticias/agencia-estado/2020/07/15/negros-sao-75-dos-mortos-pela-policia-no-brasil-aponta-relatorio.htm.

Hamad, R. (2015). "'Whiteness' Is More Than Just Someone's Skin Colour." *Daily Life*, September 17. http://www.dailylife.com.au/news-and-views/dl-opinion/whiteness-is-more-than-just-someones-skin-colour-20150916-gjo66b.html.

Jou, C. (2017). *Supersizing Urban America: How Inner Cities Got Fast Food with Government Help*. Chicago: University of Chicago Press.

Kovvali, P. G. (2018). "The Other Diversity Dividend." *Harvard Business Review*, July–August. https://hbr.org/2018/07/the-other-diversity-dividend.

Libreri, S. (2019). "'Let Us Share The Land'—Land Ownership Dominates South African Election Debate." *RTE*, March 19. https://www.rte.ie/news/world/2019/0319/1037200-south-africa/.

Liptak, K., D. Diaz, and S. Tatum. (2017). "Trump Pardons Former Sheriff Joe Arpaio." CNN, August 27. https://edition.cnn.com/2017/08/25/politics/sheriff-joe-arpaio-donald-trump-pardon/index.html.

Mason-Dixon Polling & Research. (2019). "*Mason-Dixon Polling & Strategy.*" Jacksonville, FL https://static1.squarespace.com/static/5ca8b23865a707e04

a9a1299/t/5cd5c1bb24a694961ea76eb9/1557512635922/Mason-Dixon+Fur+Poll+5.10.2019.pdf.

Meredith, S. (2018). "Who Is the 'Trump of the Tropics?': Brazil's Divisive New President, Jair Bolsonaro—In His Own Words." CNBC, October 29. Retrieved from https://www.cnbc.com/2018/10/29/brazil-election-jair-bolsonaros-most-controversial-quotes.html.

Mills, P. (2012). "The Ethical Careers Debate: A Discussion between Ben Todd, Sebastian Farquhar, and Pete Mills." *Oxford Left Review* 7 (May 12): 4–9. https://oxfordleftreview.files.wordpress.com/2012/07/issue-7.pdf.

Moses, Y. (2017). "Why Do We Keep Using the Word 'Caucasian'?" *Sapiens*, February 1. https://www.sapiens.org/column/race/caucasian-terminology-origin/.

NBC. (2014). "PETA to Detroit: Go Vegan for a Month, We'll Pay Your Water Bill." *NBC*, July 30. https://www.nbcnews.com/news/us-news/peta-detroit-go-vegan-month-well-pay-your-water-bill-n168896.

Noble, S. (2012). "Missed Connections: What Search Engines Say about Women." *Bitch* 12 (54): 36–41. https://safiyaunoble.files.wordpress.com/2012/03/54_search_engines.pdf.

PETA. (2020). "PETA Financial Reports." https://www.peta.org/about-peta/learn-about-peta/financial-report/.

Reiley, L. (2020). "The Fastest-Growing Vegan Demographic Is African Americans. Wu-Tang Clan and Other Hip-Hop Acts Paved the Way." *Washington Post*, January 24. https://www.washingtonpost.com/business/2020/01/24/fastest-growing-vegan-demographic-is-african-americans-wu-tang-clan-other-hip-hop-acts-paved-way/.

Ross-Oliver, A. (2021). "How Helpful Is 'Effective Altruism' as an Approach to Increasing Global Justice?" *e-International Relations*, April 5. https://www.e-ir.info/2021/04/05/how-helpful-is-effective-altruism-as-an-approach-to-increasing-global-justice/.

Saunders-Hasting, E. (2015). "Response to Effective Altruism." *Boston Review*, July 1. https://bostonreview.net/forum/logic-effective-altruism/emma-saunders-hastings-response-effective-altruism.

Singer, P. (2015). The Logic of Effective Altruism. *Boston Review*, July 1. https://bostonreview.net/forum/peter-singer-logic-effective-altruism.

Sousa, M. S. (2019). "AP Explains: 75 Percent of those killed in Brazil Are Black. *Associated Press*, June 5. https://apnews.com/article/2de3404e7e8e4eae9807edc5355ef356.

Wisor, S. (2011). "Against Shallow Ponds: An Argument against Singer's Approach to Global Poverty. *Journal of Global Ethics* 7 (1): 19–32. https://doi.org/10.1080/17449626.2010.548819.

World Population Review. (2021). "Detroit, Michigan Population." https://worldpopulationreview.com/us-cities/detroit-mi-population.

Yancey, G., ed. (2004). *What White Looks Like: African-American Philosophers on the Whiteness Question*. New York: Routledge.

Zarur, C. (2019). "Only 17.8% of Congressmen in Congress Are Black." O Globo, November 21. https://oglobo.globo.com/politica/apenas-178-dos-parlamentares-no-congresso-sao-negros-24091144.

4

Animal Advocacy's Stockholm Syndrome

Andrew deCoriolis, Aaron S. Gross, Joseph Tuminello, Steve J. Gross, and Jennifer Channin

It's time for Effective Altruists in the farmed animal protection movement to expand their strategic imagination, their imagination of what is possible, and their imagination of what counts as effective.

Effective Altruism has been a powerful way to help funders and influencers see the immense potential to do good by supporting farmed animal causes. We recognize that Effective Altruist support has brought new respect and tractability to the neglected plight of farmed animals, and we who have devoted our lives to this cause and worked in it for decades are grateful. But Effective Altruist thinking is also being used to guide strategies *within* the farmed animal space, and it is in this regard that it has—at least in practice—proven to be a woefully inadequate framework.

We write this essay as allies. Like us, Effective Altruists are especially animated by the immense and multidimensional suffering caused by factory farms. We share a profound concern, not only with reducing suffering, but also with reducing farmed animal suffering in particular. We even share a concern to impact as many animals as possible per dollar, and thus for more than a decade have focused our own advocacy energies on the plight of broiler chickens, especially their genetically induced suffering (anticipating Effective

Andrew deCoriolis, Aaron S. Gross, Joseph Tuminello, Steve J. Gross, and Jennifer Channin, *Animal Advocacy's Stockholm Syndrome* In: *The Good It Promises, The Harm It Does*. Edited by: Carol J. Adams, Alice Crary, and Lori Gruen, Oxford University Press.
DOI: 10.1093/oso/9780197655696.003.0004

Altruist-funded campaigns that also seek to change broiler genetics). But as Effective Altruist donors have settled into the farmed animal space, the sheer size of Effective Altruist funding relative to the farmed animal movement as a whole has generated a new gravitational force with troubling consequences that, while known to activists on the ground, have gone largely unnamed.

Under the influence of Effective Altruist funding driven by narrow metrics, advocates are taking our eyes off the prize (or at least one prize): the end of factory farming.[1] Advocates are simultaneously underestimating our enemies—those who profit from the exploitation endemic in industrial animal farming—and underestimating our own power. At worst, the farmed animal movement is getting gamed: it is being transformed from a serious threat to factory farming into its unknowing servant. Industrial agribusiness and the retailers that depend on its products have become skilled at creating arrangements whereby the groups that begin by attacking them are quickly turned into unwitting allies that bizarrely function to improve the reputation of factory farming.

It's Not Incremental Change versus Systemic Change

We agree with Effective Altruists that incremental suffering reduction work is crucial, but such incremental efforts are of at least *two kinds: suffering reduction that entrenches the status quo, and suffering reduction that makes industrial farming more vulnerable to challenge*. Effective altruist donors do not presently appear to have a

[1] "Factory farms (including all legally designated concentrated animal feeding operations, or CAFOs) are characterized not only by the concentration of animals—usually indoors, and often with tens of thousands of animals in one building—but also by structures of corporate ownership that incentivize the externalization of costs and the convergent use of intensive genetic manipulation, feed with pharmaceuticals added to it, and environmental control of temperature, light, air quality, and so on to maximize the profitability of a business model predicated on selling large quantities of inexpensive meat" (Gross 2015).

good way of distinguishing which one they are supporting—and at this point the factory farm industry knows this.

Presumably, we all would prefer the latter—change that promotes more change—but, in fact, our movement often supports the former, especially in Effective Altruist-funded strategies like global corporate campaigns. So eager are activist organizations to generate particular kinds of statistics attended to by donors (like pledges to go cage-free or counts of animals impacted) that, in the service of these aims, everything else is pushed to the sidelines—including actual resistance to factory farming.

Helping a retailer require that a factory farm they purchase from make tweaks to standard factory farming practices that cost the producer little and benefit animals, like confining hens in barns instead of cages, is, assuming for a moment all other things are equal, a good thing. But this kind of collaboration with corporations should not be mistaken for *activism that aims at meaningful social change.* It is not the best use of rare funding dollars. At times it may even amount to free consulting for companies profiting from industrial farming. Effective Altruists are sincerely trying to ask activists to pursue strategies that maximize suffering reduction, but what they have functionally asked of activists is to lower expectations about what kind of change is possible, thus limiting the imagination of change to the kinds of dubious improvements that massive, abusive corporations who are putting real farmers out of business around the globe have requested.

If we had "good data" showing that there is no way to end the factory farm, it would make sense not to waste our time. However, we have no such data, because the tools simply don't exist to answer such questions.[2] To assume from the get-go that ending the

[2] In a paper prepared for the Gates Foundation in 2008, Melinda T. Tuan summarizes the limitations of "integrated cost approaches" to measuring social value in philanthropy—that is, approaches that attempt to calculate numerically the social returns on philanthropic "investments" in order to identify what methods work. "Overall, these limitations point to the fact that the field of social program evaluation—the process of collecting social impact and social outcome data [evaluating projects with

system is not worth pursuing is not to be prudent and pragmatic, but precisely to give into an untested assumption. The future is open. We don't need to accept the factory farm as an inevitable evil and content ourselves with making it what we perhaps too blithely call "more humane." We could, perhaps with more or less the same resource investment, work toward ending it and still see suffering reduction advance in the course of marching toward the larger goal. Instead, we have, for example, cage-free campaigns that achieve suffering reduction in a way that turns "cage-free" into a value-added marketing term and creates the public appearance of an industry undertaking serious reform. That is better for animals than a kick in the face, but why not a campaign designed to achieve short-term change *and to weaken the factory farm system*?

The Necessity of Vision

Suffering reduction always matters, and to forget its value for lofty ideals is to forget what it is like to suffer.[3] Equally, however, suffering reduction is not a strategy for social *change. Oppressors will always be willing to reduce suffering, even by reducing profits, to secure a greater victory: the right to endlessly exploit.* In this way, a narrow focus on suffering reduction can open one to manipulation by industry. Our enemies in the factory farm industry know how to sacrifice a pawn. At its worst, the activism that Effective Altruism has supported not only accepts the pawn sacrifice, but declares it a

social missions]—and the methods of calculating the costs of social program delivery are not very well developed or established in the social sector. Despite these limitations, some people expect to be able to compare the social value of various social programs similar to how they compare the financial return on investment (ROI) of various companies. This is not a reasonable or realistic expectation given that the infrastructure necessary to calculate social value creation for social programs is virtually non-existent" (Tuan 2008).

[3] Bernard Rollin, who helped establish veterinary ethics as a field, has thoughtfully emphasized this point throughout his career. See Rollin 1999.

victory while industry basks in the glow of advocates' praise.[4] What are portrayed as win-win strategies, where both the corporation profiting from animal exploitation and the animal advocacy groups demanding incremental reform win, may in reality be the animals losing.

There is nothing wrong with building a campaign around an incremental change so long as one retains—and is accountable to—a larger vision. All large-scale social change has an incremental element. Our fear, however, is that because the immensity of factory farming can make it feel like an impossible problem to confront *systemically*, Effective Altruist dollars are not taking it on at all. The end of factory farming *appears* unrealistic and unpragmatic, and so it is abandoned in favor of a focus on a victory that is perceived as possible and measurable. This is both a failure to understand the real long-term vulnerability of factory farming and a failure of moral imagination.

[4] This is arguably true, for example, in cage-free campaigns, and can be particularly tragic in a global context—take India, for example. Farm Forward's allies in the south of India report the good news that, in recent years and for the first time since most Indian egg production was taken over by factory farms, a small segment of consumers are making efforts to avoid the cruelty of factory-farmed eggs and are instead seeking out and paying a premium for branded cage-free eggs. What is tragic is that, in many of the contexts where these cage-free eggs are sold, the consumer is not simply choosing them over standard factory-farmed eggs, but choosing them over eggs produced using more traditional methods where birds freely roam their whole lives and a larger percentage of the profits go to small farmers. The conscientious urban, middle-class Indian consumer cannot see that there is a minor difference between the cage-free egg and the standard factory-farmed egg, and a massive gulf separating both of these from the traditionally produced egg for a simple reason: the animal protection groups the consumer is relying upon are pointing to the (factory-farmed) cage-free egg instead of alternatives to industrial farming. It doesn't matter if the fine print of the animal group's website indicates that cage-free is still dismal, because it is the group's high-profile cage-free campaign that receives all the funding and thus commands public attention. In the worst case, animal advocacy is literally helping factory farms (albeit, farms one inch above the absolute worst) out-compete traditional farmers. This can be harder to see in the US context where small traditional egg farms have been all but wiped out by factory farms, but in India and many other countries traditional farming remains a *viable* alternative to factory farming. Whereas, in the United States, campaigns that applaud cage-free factory-farmed egg producers may merely entrench an already dominant system, in other parts of the world they may be hastening the factory farm's eradication of ethically superior traditional farming.

The structure of Effective Altruist funding has unintentionally made the next step the *telos* instead of the increment. *Better has become the enemy of the good, or, worse, mistaken for it entirely.* We forget that to end the factory farm would be in everyone's interests except the factory farm companies themselves. We forget that the factory farm is a late modern invention of a small elite that is both deeply entrenched and precarious. To point to just one aspect of its precarity, how long can the factory farm distract the public from the fact that it is almost certainly the central global driver of new infectious diseases?[5] We forget that, unlike questions about vegetarianism and veganism, opposition to the factory farm is something that unites the so-called radical vegan and the conservative carnivore. We forget our own strength.

Who Is Playing Whom?

The enemy has taken note of Effective Altruists' desire to declare corporate victories and the unsophisticated nature of the metrics now available to measure success. The industry is, we fear, effectively bartering modest—sometimes even simply *pledged and unspecified*—improvements in exchange for insulation from real threats. Animal groups and their donors are gladly trading away our true leverage. We are like a union that has won improvements for its workers on the condition that the union itself be shut down.

From where we stand, it looks a bit like a variation on Stockholm Syndrome. The industry has told advocates that any change to factory farming must follow a certain path. In practice this has meant corporate refusal to negotiate with nonprofits for changing practices unless these negotiations essentially guarantee no disruption to their exploitative business model. Industry has, for example, demanded from animal advocacy organizations campaigning

[5] For discussion see Foer and Gross 2020.

against them a "unified ask" for specific improvements (instead of facing diverse and changing demands from many fronts); they have asked for unprecedentedly long timetables for change; they have demanded our public praise for even the smallest and least costly changes; and, above all, they have asked that we advocates keep focused on the next "low-hanging fruit" and not focus our campaigns on more systemic problems. Rather than recognizing these demands and others like them for what they manifestly are—rules that prevent factory farming from actually being challenged—these rules of engagement are often functionally enforced by Effective Altruist funders upon activist groups that would never otherwise proceed in this manner. In an understandable desire to constrain thoughtless, undisciplined campaigning, Effective Altruist funding has enforced a rule book written by the enemy.

In part as a result of numerous single-issue campaigns—the most visible of which is the movement for cage-free eggs[6]—the farmed animal movement has some knowledge about how they could potentially achieve suffering reduction.[7] Yet calculations about this suffering reduction are complicated today by an important factor given too little attention: *the industry is already responding to massive shifts in public concern about animals.* We live at a time when, even if every animal activist organization were swept up in some animal rights rapture, we could still expect a steady stream of promises for more humane animal products from a sector of the meat industry itself. If we take into account that a certain degree of change is all but foreclosed, it complicates our analysis of what a victory for farmed animals looks like.

[6] In practice, groups advocating for cage-free are usually requiring a small package of changes, not just pledges to remove birds from cages. Still, as we use the term, this is a single-issue campaign and fundamentally different from campaigns that center systemic change.

[7] Tuan specifically cautions against applying a single metric as a "silver bullet." See Tuan 2008.

We may not be far at present from a dysfunctional strategy where animal groups make requests of industry that are essentially consistent with the industry's own plans, where these groups declare victories (genuinely believing them) when the corporations make the inevitable changes, and where Effective Altruists are unwittingly counting as social change something close to its opposite. Take an example like controlled atmosphere stunning and killing (CAS and CAK) in the broiler industry, which has been championed as a more humane method of slaughter. Once this technology is cheaper than the status quo methods, it will be adopted. It's only a matter of time. If we can speed the rate of change, that matters, but it is rather difficult to know if we are doing so. Why does it then count as a victory if a company commits to CAS if the industry itself agrees it's a better technology? In reality, the company may have simply committed to improve their bottom line and won some undeserved praise in the process.

Let us clarify again that we do not criticize the overreliance on a certain kind of corporate campaign as outsiders to these efforts, or without knowledge of how powerful corporate campaigns can be. Some of the writers of this essay are still involved in aspects of corporate campaign work or played a substantial role for years. Steve Gross led negotiations for what are arguably the first successful corporate campaigns to improve the lives of farmed animals, and which became influential models for today's movement. As a pro bono consultant to PETA in the late 1990s and early 2000s, Steve led successful negotiations first between PETA and McDonalds, and then between PETA and Burger King, Wendy's, Safeway, and others.[8] As PETA's inaugural campaign against McDonalds was declared a victory at the turn of the millennium, Dr. Temple

[8] The activist Henry Spira deserves credit for, a full decade earlier in 1989, having launched a high-profile campaign targeting Purdue with, among other tactics, full-page ads in the *New York Times*. In some important ways, this is the first farmed animal campaign that resembles today's farmed animal corporate campaigns and that is widely known among old-timers in the animal protection movement. PETA's early corporate campaigns in part drew inspiration from Spira's tactics by incorporating a robust pre-public-campaign negotiation element, but, in other ways, PETA's approach differed considerably and adopted a more antagonistic stance toward the industry it was

Grandin argued that she saw more change to reduce animal suffering as a result of the pressure from the McDonald's decision than in her entire thirty-year career.[9] It was this previously unrealized level of short-term change—which we note appears to have been catalyzed by PETA's creative experimentation with diverse tactics, but which was also influenced by other factors—that soon inspired virtually every large animal group to adopt corporate farmed animal campaigns.

We agree there are good reasons to think corporate campaigns can be powerful indeed. But, as often happens, the sequels are not always as impressive as the original that inspired it. In a 2020 interview, Grandin reaffirmed that, twenty years later, no similar bump of progress has been achieved for farmed animals—she still points to the turn of the millennium as the great leap forward (see Clancy 2020). Thanks to Effective Altruist funding, the farmed animal movement has more investments than ever going into corporate campaigns, but we suspect a careful historical analysis would reveal that returns have been diminishing for decades, even as reports of numbers of animals impacted have increased. Especially in recent years, industry has figured out how to benefit from contact with animal groups and adapted to our tactics, but it is these same musty tactics that seem to attract the most Effective Altruist funding.

Obviously, corporate campaigns do some real good, and we'd want to see them continue in some form—*but in their current form* they are not clearly more effective than other approaches. The overconfidence in current corporate campaign methods—and the

working to change. Indeed, Ingrid Newkirk's criticism of Spira at the time echoes some of the concerns expressed in this essay. In a *New York Times* interview, she argued: "He is hobnobbing in the halls with our enemy. Six or seven years ago, we had a lot in common. Everything he did then was putting gravel down for other people to pave roads, which was crucial. But I think Henry was deceived by the industry response. Henry was unable to cut himself loose from the mire of having become an industry mediator. The search for alternatives is a quite transparent ploy to maintain the status quo" (Quoted in Feder 1989, 6).

[9] Grandin stated this in a 2003 interview with Nation's Restaurant News. For discussion, see Foer 2009.

"quantity over quality" logic that drives them—is, in fact, a substantial harm. The overconfidence in single-issue corporate campaigns that aim exclusively to address the most egregious and visible problems seems to have often led to a lack of serious consideration of other methodologies, even corporate campaign work that seeks more systemic change or that aims to push the ceiling as well as raise the floor of animal welfare. Methodologies like community organizing, educational efforts, movement building, public policy, religious outreach, shelter and rescue work, film and books, and more are overlooked entirely or dismissed with an unreflective "we can't measure that" or "you can't fund everything." While Effective Altruists strive to be constantly reevaluating effectiveness, we see instead a dangerous and unjustified narrowing of vision.

Consider Community Organizing

Effective Altruists may not even realize what they are missing out on. Consider the example of community organizing to fight factory farming and build alternative foodways. We choose community organizing as an example because it is a strategy we admire but that is not our own. If more dollars go to community organizing strategies aimed against factory farming—and we are arguing here that they should—they should go to activists other than the authors of this chapter. Effective Altruists have more or less decided that community organizing is "not effective," and that has put a chill on support for certain organizations even when they could, if given the right opportunity, empirically demonstrate high levels of effectiveness. We would agree that, indeed, if all you count as metrics are things like corporate pledges, community activism looks like a messy and unsafe bet for social change. Indeed, part of the reason our own activism didn't focused on alliances with community organizers until recently was because it looked to us like it seems to still look to many Effective Altruists—that community organizing involves too many conflicting values. And how on earth would one measure its effectiveness? Better, or so it seems, to focus on efforts where we can be sure that our hours or dollars are well spent, right?

Well, let's think again. Let's ask why, in the first place, we think we know less about what makes community activism effective. It is true that there are profound limits to the ability to precisely quantify effectiveness in community organizing, but are those limits really greater than the ambiguities and uncertainties that abound when trying to measure the actual difference a corporate campaign has made for animals? Even if it is easy to quantify the impact on animals of a particular corporation changing from policy A to policy B, how easy is it to be certain the move from A to B was the result of activist interventions?

The most salient reason that we who write this essay—and, we suspect, the Effective Altruist allies we here hold to account—know less about how to evaluate the impact of community organizing is because we are firmly located in a white social world, whereas community activism has been a, perhaps *the*, primary tool for social upliftment in communities of color. It doesn't take a professional race theorist to start deducing that maybe the reason so many of us, Effective Altruists and others, were so primed to see corporate activism as "easily measurable" and community organizing as "unmeasurable" is because of our whiteness, not the actual facts on the ground.[10]

We're not claiming this is the whole story, but *think about it*: Current campaigns supported by Effective Altruists often focus on winning corporate *pledges* to make changes years and years later on the basis of studies that have not yet been published. Is it really

[10] For example, the "quantity over quality" thinking that in part undergirds the preference for corporate campaigns is identified by Kenneth Jones and Tema Okun in their workbook, *Dismantling Racism: A Workbook for Social Change Groups*, as among a cluster of common "characteristics of white supremacy culture which show up in our [social justice] organizations." For discussion, see "The Characteristics of White Supremacy Culture," Change Works, 2001, https://www.showingupforracialjustice.org/white-supremacy-culture-characteristics.html.

so easy to measure impact in this case? If we said we have achieved a big victory in, say, Baltimore, and a community there has pledged to do something in seven years that will benefit animals on the basis of a yet-to-be-produced study, would that sound like an easily measurable achievement? We assume not.[11] Yet this is precisely what counts as "most effective" in corporate campaigns currently supported by Effective Altruists. Our point is that a too-eager desire for metrics has not led us to challenge our assumptions, but rather, like the very philanthropy Effective Altruists have rallied against, led us into familiar ruts limited by our immediate social circles' values.

There is in fact no grand and clear evidence that it is easier to measure real change in anti-factory-farming efforts that pursue corporate campaign strategies than in community organizing strategies.[12] One can try to make that case, but the aporias are bigger than the solid conclusions. The strategies simply have different kinds of uncertainties. They proceed from different intuitions and different cultural locations. To obfuscate these differences and pretend that there is a scientific basis for asserting a neat hierarchy where one can objectively declare corporate campaigns more effective is a disservice. To pretend, for example, that radically simplified, abstract metrics like "animal years saved" is a serious way to compare different methodologies and a reasonable ground

[11] We use Baltimore as our example because the city has been the site of the most extraordinary local community organizing outcomes by vegan activists we have ever seen—particularly the work being led by activists Brenda Sanders and Naijha Wright-Brown to address community health and justice issues through vegan nonprofit and for-profit entities like Baltimore's Vegan Soulfest, Thrive, Black Vegetarian Society of Maryland, A Greener Kitchen, Land of Kush, and the Afro-Vegan Society. These entities have each impacted the diets of tens of thousands of Baltimore residents *directly*, and for a pittance compared to what is spent annually on corporate animal welfare campaigns.

[12] Ranghelli observes, "The increasing emphasis by funders on strategic grantmaking and measurable outcomes may be a disincentive to support policy and advocacy work, because of the perception that outcomes can be difficult to assess," but then goes on to argue that appropriate methods for evaluating community organizing do exist and often demonstrate high levels of impact (Ranghelli 2009).

for dismissing methodologies like community organizing is a curious form of witchcraft.[13]

The important point is that corporate campaigns, and other strategies favored by Effective Altruists, are perhaps more *familiar* than they are effective—particularly to funders who made their wealth working in the corporate sector themselves. In some cases, sticking with the familiar can be a good idea, but Effective Altruists are claiming they have empirical, scientific grounds for their funding decisions—and herein lies the danger. Serious evaluations of effectiveness are, per the Effective Altruist credo, the best basis for decisions, but these are not so easy to produce as Effective Altruist logics have suggested. A serious evaluation of effectiveness would at minimum begin by asking who is defining what it means to be effective in the first place, and by making sure that those involved in the definition include people from social locations that are not predominately white, male, or wealthy. To be uncertain how to tackle a complex social problem is challenging but workable. To be certain about the path to social change when one in fact does not know is comforting, not only to one's conscience, but to one's enemies as well.

Beyond Effective Altruism?

All this is to challenge Effective Altruism on its own ground—to suggest that its admirable focus on impact has misfired. We hope that some of what we said here will give Effective Altruists committed to that framework reasons to, at the very least, get more rigorous in their own commitments to evidence, especially recognizing the racial dimensions of how we think about *what*

[13] In using the metaphor of witchcraft, we follow activist and theorist Aph Ko (See Ko 2019).

counts as evidence in the first place. Perhaps Effective Altruist–style analysis could become a better version of itself.

But, perhaps, as other essays in this volume suggest, we don't really need the Effective Altruist framework at all to best evaluate strategies to fight factory farming. Effective Altruists have no monopoly on good metrics, and, in fact, we've argued that they have embraced highly dubious metrics for certain kinds of advocacy while not really giving the time of day to potentially game-changing approaches like the impressive community organizing work happening in several Black and Latinx communities that might not only be more effective, but would also tend toward diversifying the movement and allying it with other social justice causes like antiracism. These alliances could be enormously consequential, since factory farming thrives today in part because its most immediate human victims—exploited slaughterhouse workers and those suffering from environmental pollution—are disproportionately people of color. The political structures that promote the exploitation of vulnerable human communities are the same structures that support the factory farm.

Social movements toward justice are, regrettably, somewhat mysterious. They seem impossible before they happen and inevitable afterward.[14] The fight for farmed animals is fundamentally a fight for justice, and that means it has an unavoidable element of uncertainty. It is not a technical problem and cannot be reduced to one, even though, of course, particular efforts must have their operationalization.[15] Fights for justice can have only tentative roadmaps, and these must be constantly redrawn and refined. Effective Altruism seems to have been a useful map to bring donors to the growing territory of farmed animal advocacy, but that may be the extent of the map's usefulness at present.

[14] For discussion, see Jamieson 2020.

[15] For discussion of technical versus adaptive challenges, see Heifetz, Linsky, and Grashow 2009.

Our fear is that the metrics currently favored by Effective Altruists, especially those associated with corporate campaigns, are becoming idols rather than aides. The situation is analogous to designing a test to train pilots that encourages people to focus on how to pass the test rather than learn how to fly. People may pass the test, but when they get off the ground, accidents that could have been prevented are bound to happen.

We can learn to actually fly, but it will take a willingness to use metrics where they can be helpful while not overestimating what we can conclude on their basis. It means the messy work of listening to a wide range of strategic thinking to really suss out the limits and potentials of diverse forms of activism.[16] It means recognizing the biases that might lead us astray, especially the limits of vision created by race, class, and gender dynamics. It means building real partnerships with academics who can provide a more disinterested perspective over decades—not only scientists, but a diverse range of animal studies scholars as well. It means taking the utilitarian ethos that drives Effective Altruism seriously, while recognizing its immense limitations, which others in this volume address.

It means recognizing that, as tempting as it is, we cannot set the larger task of justice aside and just focus on "what works." If only we had the sort of cause, like curing Malaria, that is simple enough to approach more like a thing to be fixed instead of a justice to be won. We don't. Animal issues are different. Food advocacy is different. Both are tied to our personal and national identities in ways that make change in these areas particularly complicated. Thinking we can be effective while ignoring the larger issue of ending an

[16] In 2019, a team at Farm Forward researched and published a report that outlines sixteen diverse strategies being employed by farmed animal protection advocates, while acknowledging that just two of those strategies—corporate campaigns and food technology—receive the majority of Effective Altruist funding. See *The Farmed Animal Protection Movement: Common Strategies for Improving and Protecting the Lives of Farmed Animals*, by Andrew deCoriolis, Ben Goldsmith, Jennifer Channin, and John Millspaugh. The report can be found at https://www.farmforward.com/#!/publications.

oppressive food system or fundamentally changing how we think about animals and animality is simply a wish for a world that doesn't exist.

Without knowing the entire way forward, this much seems clear: we must hold together, always, the next step and the final goal. We must focus on reducing the suffering of chickens and sea animals, for example, and we must simultaneously focus on ending the entire exploitative factory farm system. Entrenching the entire factory farm system by giving it social legitimation at the very moment its reputation is coming apart at the seams is not an acceptable price to win some incremental improvements. Praising modest incremental improvements without clearly articulating the need for, at minimum, a shift in our default proteins from animal to plant sources will likely cause more harm than good. The incremental improvements we should pursue must be linked to a larger vision not just in theory but in their public instantiation. If corporations that could make such incremental changes balk and ask to "go slower," we could productively disagree, publicly and loudly. It is possible to pursue the incremental *and* keep our eyes on the prize, and we are suggesting that we would do well to do so.

There is so much to say, and this chapter is an opening and an invitation to future dialogue. We have not detailed the many examples we could cite to back up our arguments. Here it has seemed valuable to focus on the big picture, to lay out the concerns, rather than present all the evidence. The evidence, however, is there to be evaluated and critically examined; ultimately, it is the weighing of this evidence that we hope Effective Altruists will attend to with us.

Effective Altruist funders who first identified farmed animals as a neglected area that could benefit from funding are correct. Industrial animal agriculture has been, and is increasingly being, challenged from multiple directions. It is a statistical inevitability that new infectious diseases will continue to be traced in part to industrial farms. Pressures to address climate change will mount. And a new generation of consumers is raising ethical issues about race, animal abuse, and gender that will, in diverse ways, make life harder for factory farm corporations. In economies where the factory farm is not yet ubiquitous, like in parts of Africa and East and South Asia, there is the real potential to end the industry while it is still young and, compared to the North American and European context, politically weak. The upside potential of farmed animal work is enormous: nothing less than the transformation of the most basic act of material consumption, producing and eating food. The bet is extremely sound. It is rational and reasonable to assume that funds invested in competent organizations pursuing diverse strategies to mitigate and end industrial farming will likely contribute to the change, even if it can't be easily measured. There is a veritable small army of activists, many with decades of experience and, increasingly, with specialized degrees, ready to mobilize and capable of doing far more than single-issue campaigns.

Funding really has been the missing ingredient preventing the farmed animal movement from achieving more change, as every seasoned activist knows. Funders have an opportunity to do enormous good within their lifetimes, but only if simplistic metrics give way to a mature willingness to confront the complex social challenges we face. The movement needs more than Effective Altruists' funds and skill with metrics; it needs their fearlessness, their entrepreneurial spirit of experimentation, and their moral imagination.

Onward and forward.

References

"The Characteristics of White Supremacy Culture." (2001). Change Works. https://www.showingupforracialjustice.org/white-supremacy-culture-characteristics.html.

Clancy, Heather. (2020). "Animal Welfare Expert Temple Grandin: Creative Problem-Solving Takes Visual Minds." *GreenBiz*, January 28. https://www.greenbiz.com/article/animal-welfare-expert-temple-grandin-creative-problem-solving-takes-visual-minds.

Feder, Barnaby J. (1989). "Pressuring Perdue." *New York Times Magazine*, November 26: 6, 32.

Foer, Jonathan Safran. (2009). *Eating Animals.* New York: Little, Brown.

Foer, Jonathan Safran, and Aaron S. Gross. (2020). "We Have to Wake Up: Factory Farms Are Breeding Grounds for Pandemics." *Guardian*, April 20. https://www.theguardian.com/commentisfree/2020/apr/20/factory-farms-pandemic-risk-covid-animal-human-health.

Gross, Aaron S. (2015). "Factory Farming (Confined Animal Feeding Operations)." In *Encyclopedia of Food Issues*, edited by Ken Alba, 429–434. Thousand Oaks, CA: SAGE. https://www.academia.edu/36596069/Factory_Farming_Confined_Animal_Feeding_Operations_Encyclopedia_Entry_?auto=download&ssrv=nrrc.

Heifetz, Ronald, Marty Linsky, and Alexander Grashow. (2009). *The Practice of Adaptive Leadership: Tools and Tactics for Changing Your Organization and the World.* Cambridge, MA: Harvard Business Press.

Jamieson, Dale. (2020). "How to Change the World." Brooks Congress 2020, Miami, Florida. https://www.youtube.com/watch?v=h_jtHZrleY0.

Ko, Aph. (2019). *Racism as Zoological Witchcraft: A Guide for Getting Out.* Brooklyn, NY: Lantern Books.

Ranghelli, L. (2009). "Measuring the Impacts of Advocacy and Community Organizing: Application of a Methodology and Initial Findings." *Foundation Review* 1 (3): 16. https://scholarworks.gvsu.edu/cgi/viewcontent.cgi?article=1130&context=tfr.

Rollin, Bernard E. (1999). *An Introduction to Veterinary Medical Ethics: Theory and Cases.* Ames: Iowa State University Press.

Tuan, Melinda. (2008). *Measuring and/or Estimating Social Value Creation: Insights into Eight Integrated Cost Approaches.* Bill & Melinda Gates Foundation. https://docs.gatesfoundation.org/documents/wwl-report-measuring-estimating-social-value-creation.pdf.

5

Who Counts? Effective Altruism and the Problem of Numbers in the History of American Wildlife Conservation

Michael D. Wise

Numbering the lives of animals offers a tempting way to measure the efforts of wildlife conservation, but the indeterminate values of wild animals are difficult to comprehend, let alone quantify. Wild animals are strangers, creatures with whom human intimacies are fleeting and mediated through study or story. They are living embodiments of the gap between perception and deduction, their habits filtered to us in binary channels of anthropomorphic fable paired with empirical inconsequence, inscrutabilities that often elude even poetry, photography, and other domains of expression. All knowledges of wild animal lives are produced at a cost, some more appallingly so than others. While Aldo Leopold, for instance, was waxing in his *Sand County Almanac* about the American woodcock's "soft liquid warble that a March bluebird might envy" (Leopold [1949] 2020, 29), his colleagues were gunning them down from the sky to find out if only males performed the courtship vocalization, a hypothesis verified after killing fifty in a row (Duke 1966, 697). Later generations of wildlife scientists embraced remote sensing as a seemingly less intrusive form of data collection, as well

Michael D. Wise, *Who Counts? Effective Altruism and the Problem of Numbers in the History of American Wildlife Conservation* In: *The Good It Promises, The Harm It Does.* Edited by: Carol J. Adams, Alice Crary, and Lori Gruen, Oxford University Press. © Oxford University Press 2023.
DOI: 10.1093/oso/9780197655696.003.0005

as a more lucrative rationale for their research funding. Relying on radio telemetry, camera traps, and other technologies of surveillance, they organized a discipline based on survey methodologies from the social sciences, their panoptic aspirations and institutional review boards shrinking the gap between human and nonhuman subjecthood, if only inadvertently (Benson 2010; Mitman 1992).

Scaling wildlife to proportions of population, wildlife scientists largely relinquished their obligations toward individual animals as they reoriented their gaze from ethological studies of behavior toward the collection of quantitative data to support species-level management decisions. At the same time, filmmakers brought wild animals into ordinary peoples' living rooms through their television sets, using similar lenses as scientists, but with different focus and epistemological intention (Mitman [1999] 2009). Personified wildlife dramas on screen taught viewers more about themselves than the actual animals on camera, but the result was that audiences grew to love wild animals even more, supporting the cause of wildlife conservation more broadly than many other arenas of animal and environmental advocacy (Dunlap 1991). Bracketed by these paradoxes and intellectual ambiguities, the political and scientific work of wildlife conservation was long faced with the challenge of communicating its sophisticated goals and observations as crude metrics. And in that sense, the problematic indeterminacy of animal lives throughout the history of American wildlife conservation can help reveal the epistemic limitations of Effective Altruism's efforts to measure lives changed per charity dollar. The aggregation of wild animals into numbers has long structured wildlife conservation as an act of possession (Grove 1994; Worster [1977] 1994), and a historical appraisal of the relationship between quantification and conservation provides a critical glimpse at long-standing habits of transforming life into property of which Effective Altruism is just a recent manifestation.

Ownership has long dictated the terms under which animals can live or die in America, and so any effort to count animals—wild or otherwise—also entails considerations of which animals count, to whom do they count, and why they count. European colonists arrived in North America with their animal property as a possession of their individual households, representing a fundamental difference from the approaches of most Native American communities, who tended more toward models of kinship than ownership in their interactions with nonhuman animals, despite a wide diversity of specific practices (Anderson 2004; Bastien 2004; Harrod 2000; Jones 2003; LaPier 2017; Smalley 2017). Throughout the history of colonial America, questions of animal ownership expanded from the coastal barnyards and pastures of the individual household into the woods and mountains of the interior. From a European and particularly English perspective, one of the most marked differences between the "new" world and the old was the presence of wild game animals who seemingly had no lord—no individual claiming ownership over the lives or lands those wild creatures inhabited. In England, by contrast, a series of game laws passed during the same era effectively privatized wildlife as the property of large landowners. The infamous British "Black Act" of the eighteenth century also criminalized trespass by hunters as a capital offense (Hay 1975; Thompson 1975). In the colonies, however, wild animals had no documented owner and became anyone's and everyone's potential target. To a significant extent, this unregulated slaughter and exploitation of wildlife sustained North America's colonial export economy. It also produced rapid local extinctions of beaver, bear, and other fur-bearing mammals as early as the seventeenth century (Cronon 1983; White 1991; Witgen 2011). Moreover, this carnage brought Native communities across the continent into direct conflict with colonists as well as with one another, and the treaty proceedings that followed dealt both with debates over abstractions of land title as well as the issue of who held customary rights for hunting and fishing. These patterns continued long after the United States' independence from Britain. It was not until the decades after the Civil War that state and federal governments actively claimed wildlife as a "public resource" and took up systematic efforts for its conservation and management.

The public ownership of wildlife in America was largely a fiction, however, as race, class, and other social inequalities limited access to this supposedly communal resource. By the turn of the twentieth century, the historical emergence of American wildlife as a property of "the people" differed from the private ownership model of aristocratic Britain, but insofar as Americans understood all animals as *someone's* property, the logic of animal ownership was fundamentally similar. And far from rolling back presumptions of human dominion over animals, it updated them for a biopolitical era in which environmental governance emerged as a new technique for managing populations, one less reliant on the direct violence of killing or culling, and instead premised on legal structures that fostered some lives while disallowing others to the point of death (Foucault 1978, 138). Counting animals under these circumstances—both human and nonhuman—took on new significance. American political forces sparred over the extent to which populations of animals should be prioritized within hierarchies of property and ownership, implementing hunting quotas to systematize the "taking" of wild game and bounty-killing campaigns to incentivize the destruction of predatory carnivores who threatened domestic livestock. At the same time, they negotiated a politics of citizenship that adjudicated which human beings would and would not be beneficiaries of these public investments in animal control.

Between 1884 and 1924, for instance, Congress passed a series of federal laws that excluded Chinese Americans as well as other Asian Americans from US citizenship, and that adopted a quota system that severely restricted continued immigration from southern Europe, eastern Europe, and other parts of the world. Likewise, in 1924, Congress also passed an American Indian citizenship act that officially incorporated all Native people into the US body politic, whether they wanted to be or not (Lomawaima 2013). Early wildlife conservation advocates widely supported these social restrictions and exclusions (Powell 2016). Moreover, hunting regulations and a flurry of other state and federal conservation laws adopted during the era circumscribed traditional subsistence hunting and foraging activities so effectively that they forced entire communities into the market economy to sell their labor for wages (Jacoby 2001; Spence 1999; Warren 1999). At the dawn of the conservation era, then, all these efforts to manage human and animal populations were also efforts to transform America into a white possession streamlined for capital production, relying on a politics of counting human and nonhuman animals in ways that suggested the preexistence of all of nature as property (Harris 1993; Moreton-Robinson 2015).

From a practical standpoint, the public ownership of wildlife meant that counting wild animals was a convenient yardstick for measuring the necessity—as well as the success or failure—of wildlife conservation initiatives. Arguably the most important individual throughout the early history of American wildlife conservation was a taxidermist-turned-zoologist, William Temple Hornaday, who founded the American Bison Society toward the close of the nineteenth century, as well as the New York Zoological Society—forerunner of today's Wildlife Conservation Society (Dehler 2013). The success of these organizations was rooted in Hornaday's deployment of the ebb and flow of wildlife population numbers, which he used to solicit charitable donations by communicating a sense of imminent crisis as well as a confidence that by using reasoned analysis to distribute resources, his organizations would achieve results that could be measured using similar equivalencies as his wealthy donors used to value their business investments. In newsletters, annual reports, and a number of books and essays, Hornaday explicitly linked donation dollars to the number of animal lives that his organizations saved, much like the "life-units" that Effective Altruists today propose for measuring charitable giving (Isenberg 1997; Wise 2016). Several of Hornaday's works became instant classics, especially *The Extermination of the American Bison* (1889), a book that revolutionized wildlife science and conservation for decades to come with its demographic emphasis on counting the total number of living animals as the lowest common denominator of gauging a species' overall health.

Counting animals persisted as a methodological paradigm over the next century as the political and scientific work of wildlife conservation was professionalized. This fixation on numbers was driven in part by the easy communicability of population data, and in part by a powerful alliance of conservationists and sport hunters who sought to maximize the production of game animals on public and private lands to boost hunter success rates. Although the 1933 publication of Leopold's *Game Management* ([1933] 1987) is often used to mark the formal scientific maturation of the field, the population survey methods that Leopold espoused had already taken hold in American wildlife conservation at least a generation earlier. For instance, at the turn of the century the numerical data provided by Hornaday and others on the dire emergencies facing American bison and other game animals alarmed a generation of leisured American men, personified by Theodore Roosevelt, so-called "mollycoddles" who practiced sport hunting as a compensatory expression of their masculine virility in the face of a bourgeois exclusion they felt from the homosocial worlds of working-class manhood (Bederman 1995). Anxious already about the "passing of the American frontier," as the historian Frederick Jackson Turner observed ([1891] 1998), this cohort of sons of the eastern establishment saw wildlife conservation as a matter of their own manly salvation. In 1887, Roosevelt founded the Boone and Crockett Club with his friend, George Bird Grinnell, a fellow Long Islander and the editor of the magazine *Forest and Stream*, creating an organization devoted to representing the interests of this emerging class of sportsmen (Merchant 2016; Reiger [1975] 2001). These sportsmen-conservationists sought to preserve wild animals so that they could shoot them, and the close relationship they established between hunting and conservation structured the parameters of American wildlife policy over the next century.

Managing wildlife to boost hunter success rates relied on counting animals, and the federal government responded to the demands of sportsmen like Grinnell, Hornaday, and Roosevelt to use its interstate jurisdiction for the conservation of wild animals in ways that favored sport hunters by increasing populations of game animals while also imposing new hunting restrictions to curtail the killing of game animals for other purposes. In 1900, the Lacey Act first formalized federal law on the transport of wild animals (live or dead) across state lines. The law made it illegal to hunt or trap animals with the intent to sell their bodies or body parts in another state, criminalizing the work of professional hunters and trappers whom the *Forest and Stream* editors had popularly derided as "game hogs" ("Concerning an Epithet" 1899). Central to the bill's passage, however, was its reticence on any deeper consideration of animal protection other than ruling out the interstate commercial exploitation of animals owned in the public trust. Likewise, in 1918, congressional passage of the celebrated Migratory Bird Treaty Act—the first international wildlife agreement—criminalized the killing of hundreds of avian species, aside from those labeled "game birds," a category that included doves, ducks, coots, cranes, gallinules, geese, pigeons, plovers, and swans, among others. Both at the state and federal levels, an economy of duck stamps, hunting licenses, and trapping permits all emerged by the end of the 1920s to fund conservation activities focused on maximizing populations of game animals. And, in 1937, the passage of the landmark Pittman-Robertson Act further expanded and institutionalized the close relationship of American sport hunters and wildlife managers by instituting a federal excise tax of 11 percent on all firearm and ammunition sales, with the massive revenue apportioned to state wildlife agencies by the US Department of the Interior. With this political-economic infrastructure in place, wildlife conservation in America became about more than just limiting the kill; it was also about establishing *who* could do the killing and ensuring that adequate numbers of animals existed each year for the seasonal slaughter.

As the scientific sleeve of wildlife conservation matured into the midcentury, the importance of ecological paradigms shifted the field's counting focus from hunting to habitat, yet the overall goal of maximizing game populations for sport hunters persisted. In 1940, the creation of the US Fish and Wildlife Service (FWS) from the shell of the old Bureau of Biological Survey coincided with the agency's shift into its new role as a land manager, overseeing tens of millions of acres of the growing National Wildlife Refuge system. Several of these refuges traced their origins to acts of Congress passed during the Roosevelt era, such as the Wichita Mountains Forest and Game Preserve in Oklahoma (1905), the National Bison Range in Montana (1908), and the National Elk Refuge in Wyoming (1912). However, in the midst of dam building, the Dust Bowl, and so many other environmental upheavals of the 1930s and 1940s, a proliferation of new executive orders had transferred dozens of smaller tracts of state, federal, and privately owned lands in a major expansion of the refuge system, acquisitions that were funded through sporting revenues. These refuges were all essentially managed as pastures for wildlife, some more glaringly than others. At the National Elk Refuge, for instance, a feeding program where elk ate hay out of troughs ensured that enough of the animals would survive the Jackson Hole winter to sustain the sport hunting economies of Montana and Wyoming the following year. Likewise, in 1958, revisions to the federal Duck Stamp Act authorized the creation of two million new acres of refuges, dubbed "Waterfowl Production Areas," protected breeding grounds intended to provide hunters with a steady supply of airborne fodder (Sagsveen 1984). Funded with revenue from hunting fees and gun taxes, the National Wildlife Refuge system, as well as similar state-run programs, transformed into a kind of self-contained system of feedlots for game animals. The greater the production of animal lives, the greater the destruction of animal lives, and the greater generation of revenue for the system's expansion.

The Endangered Species Act (ESA) of 1973 challenged this sportsmean's grip on American wildlife conservation, yet as a tool it too revealed the ironies of using numbers as a measure for valuing wild animal lives. For all its good intentions of prioritizing the protection of endangered wildlife over game animals in environmental decision-making, the implementation of ESA rules often wreaked havoc on the lives of nonclassified species (Alagona 2013). In California and the Pacific Northwest, for instance, ESA rulings on endangered salmon species diverted water from FWS wetlands to increase downstream river flows for a few thousand fish, in turn subjecting millions of migratory birds to starvation, disease, and death (Wilson 2010, 141). Likewise, the controversial reintroduction of gray wolves to the northern Rockies under ESA protection helped restore a substantial population of these ecologically significant "keystone" carnivores at the cost of countless "predator-naïve" coyotes, deer, elk, and other wild animals whose numbers had trebled in wolves' absence (Berger 2008; Middleton 2014). Both of these episodes proved that the ecological effects of species restoration were complex and unpredictable, and that numbering target species alone was insufficient for measuring the success or failure of these efforts. And yet, as an heir to the long tradition of the production mentality in American wildlife conservation, the ESA was oriented around population recovery numbers in much the same way as Hornaday's American Bison Society had been eighty years earlier.

In one respect, the ESA did revolutionize wildlife conservation by enabling the pursuit of ecological objectives over the priorities of game production and revenue generation. In another respect, this simply translated to the production of *nongame* animals as a new fundamental numeric criterion for conservation. In 2002, for instance, just seven years after wolves returned to Yellowstone, FWS biologists determined that ten breeding pairs had survived in the recovery area for three consecutive years, meeting the numeric threshold established in the original recovery plan and triggering a reclassification review (US Fish and Wildlife Service and Northern Rocky Mountain Wolf Recovery Team 1987, 10). Seeking to preserve the credibility of the ESA, the FWS led the delisting process and worked with state agencies in Idaho, Montana, and Wyoming to develop their own state wolf management plans, none of which maintained protections for wolves. After defeating several legal challenges, the FWS removed northern Rockies gray wolves from the endangered species list in 2009. Once abandoned from federal and state protection, the state fish and wildlife agencies reclassified wolves as game animals, selling hunting permits and instituting wolf hunting seasons. And following the nationwide delisting of gray wolves by the Trump administration in 2020, the state of Wisconsin obstinately instituted a wolf hunt with a harvest quota of 2,000 wolves, even though its own population surveys indicated no more than 1,200 wolves existed within its borders (Smith 2021). Despite the intention of the ESA to prioritize ecological objectives over the desires of hunters, its emphasis on counting meant that the recovery of wildlife extended only to the point at which their populations could contribute surplus lives into a conservation economy funded by the "harvest," by the transformation of wild animals into private property, transactions that occurred at their moments of death. Under these circumstances, the ESA could only define wolf recovery as mere survival, a bare existence that is now once again threatened.

From his seat in the Roosevelt administration a century ago, the formative environmental bureaucrat Gifford Pinchot ushered in this new epoch of American conservation as a matter of counting, defining the goal of conservation as reconciling "the greatest good of the greatest number in the long run" (Pinchot 1905), a mantra that has structured the political ecology of American environmental discourse ever since, and one that could just as easily have been penned in our own time by advocates of Effective Altruism. In the dynamic and indeterminate ecological world in which we dwell, however, our historical experiences have revealed the ineffectiveness of wildlife conservation strategies founded on Pinchot's principle. Throughout the twentieth century, state and federal governments embraced an ethos of production in wildlife conservation oriented to serve the goals of sport hunters, who approached habitat management essentially as a task of creating open-range ranches for game animals. The political and ecological infrastructure that emerged in the service of this goal was so durable that it absorbed the impact of the ESA as well as other multigenerational efforts led by ecologists, environmentalists, and animal advocates to broaden the scope of wildlife conservation activities. For so-called nongame animals, conservation is mostly an incidental outcome of habitat programs developed for species targeted during hunting season. At best, it is an underfunded mission of NGOs and an afterthought of state wildlife agencies whose ambitions are merely to prevent extinction.

The solutions to this situation are not mysterious, but since they require uncomfortable readjustments in our human relationships with other animals, they are routinely dismissed. Foremost at stake is the presumption that all animals must exist as property, owned if not by a private individual or entity, then by the public trust. Assuming that wild animals are our public property is the unfortunate bedrock that underlies the biopolitics of counting, and that, in turn, limits the possibilities of wildlife conservation to move beyond metrics of life units that only imagine wild animals as peculiar species of livestock. But rejecting this ownership principle threatens the existing political economy of American wildlife conservation in ways that its dominant practitioners recognize. For instance, the Wildlife Society (the professional organization that publishes the *Journal of Wildlife Management* and that certifies wildlife biologists) has gone so far as identifying "an animal-rights world view categorically reject[ing] the concept of ownership of animals" as one of its main obstacles (Organ et al. 2012, 14). Rejecting the ownership principle also denies the right of the state to sell the lives of wild animals to hunters who effectively privatize these euphemized public resources upon their deaths, threatening not only a ritual of masculine performance as old as American wildlife policy itself, but also one upon which the preservation of wildlife has been rendered financially dependent. For these reasons and more, American wildlife conservation remains mired in an impasse where our ongoing efforts to count and number animals are disconnected from honest conversations about which wild animals count, to whom do they count, and why they count. These discussions also demand us to ask critical questions about how histories of race, gender, and other social inequalities have structured the production of knowledge in the wildlife sciences and then been naturalized across the American landscape.

Applications of Effective Altruism to wildlife conservation have entirely failed to address these structural problems, and not just because Effective Altruists have insufficiently operationalized their objective of doing "the most good" for wildlife, but also because their demands for quantitative measurements are cut from the same troublesome cloths that have costumed wild animals into human possessions for the last several centuries. Using the neologism of "welfare biology" to demarcate their seemingly novel approach, Effective Altruists at Animal Charity Evaluators (ACE), Wild Animal Initiative, and the Center on Long-Term Risk, among other organizations, have begun funneling funding toward projects that seek to minimize metrics of wild animal suffering, or simply "WAS" in the field's acronymous lingo. WAS presents a conundrum for Effective Altruists for the simple reason that "the number of wild animals vastly exceeds that of animals on factory farms, in laboratories, or kept as pets," as one Effective Altruist has put it (Tomasik 2016). Welfare biologists propose that they can minimize WAS using interventions like feeding wild animals to prevent starvation and vaccinating them against various diseases, only vaguely aware that conservation biologists have been using the same techniques for decades with problematic results (Horta 2015).

The history of wildlife conservation reveals how the imagined agonies of wild animals have long justified environmental interventions that have served powerful humans far more than the nonhumans they claim to have protected. Unlike the more modest ambitions of conventional conservation biology—a field tempered by the unexpected outcomes and ethical dilemmas of more than a century's worth of messy intrusions into the complex worlds of wild animals—the ahistorical aspirations of welfare biology neglect to even consider the ontological distance separating us from the lived realities of wild animals. Without this critical sensibility, murky assessments of wild animal suffering become just another set of allegories for justifying uneven social relationships, assuaging guilt rather than easing pain.

Setting aside even the naïve presumption that WAS exists as a category of experience that can even be effectively quantified at all, the emergence of welfare biology from discussions of *domestic* animal welfare already reveals the problem at its core: the assumption that all animals exist as human possessions, with the only difference between domestic and wild being that the former are owned by individuals and the latter by the public. The proposals of welfare biology not only demonstrate a severe lack of critical awareness about the scope, complexity, and unpredictability of environmental interventions, their efforts also indicate the extent to which the approach of welfare biology simply works as another self-serving act of possession that transforms wildlife into a kind of emotional livestock—animals of the imagination whose sufferings and salvations are parables for justifying human dominion.

Extending the demands of animal welfare beyond the barnyard does more to domesticate wild animals than it does to free them of any suffering. It further transforms them into a species of property, a special category of animal possessions whose living bodies may not be privately owned, but whose flesh, fur, and feathers are nevertheless expected to generate some type of social return—a quantification performed through public investments in conservation that have, for at least three centuries, intensified inequalities of gender, race, and class rather than ameliorated them. The prerogatives of Effective Altruism do nothing to challenge this problematic status quo of wildlife conservation that assumes all animals are property. Instead, they replicate a utilitarian and self-serving pattern familiar within the history of the movement that summons principles of efficiency, measurement, and ownership to funnel money in ways that help individuals master their answers to the now-classic question posed by William MacAskill (2015, 11): "How can I make the biggest difference I can?" In a paradigm requiring numeric measurement and accountability, the immeasurable wild lives of animals will never be fully counted, let alone articulated. However, their status as property will remain assured.

References

Alagona, P. (2013). *After the Grizzly: Endangered Species and the Politics of Place in California*. Berkeley: University of California Press.

Anderson, V. D. (2004). *Creatures of Empire: How Domestic Animals Transformed Early America*. Oxford: Oxford University Press.

Bastien, B. (2004). *Blackfoot Ways of Knowing: The Worldview of the Siksikaitsitapi*. Calgary: University of Calgary Press.

Bederman, G. (1995). *Manliness and Civilization: A Cultural History of Gender and Race in the United States, 1880–1917*. Chicago: University of Chicago Press.

Benson, E. (2010). *Wired Wilderness: Technologies of Tracking and the Making of Modern Wildlife*. Baltimore: Johns Hopkins University Press.

Berger. J. (2008). *The Better to Eat You With: Fear in the Animal World*. Chicago: University of Chicago Press.

"Concerning an Epithet." (1899). *Forest and Stream* 52 (11): 201.

Cronon, W. (1983). *Changes in the Land: Indians,* Colonists, *and the Ecology of New England*. New York: Hill & Wang.

Dehler, G. (2013). *The Most Defiant Devil: William Temple Hornaday and His Controversial Crusade to Save American Wildlife*. Charlottesville: University of Virginia Press.

Duke, G. E. (1966). "Reliability of Censuses of Singing Male Woodcocks." *Journal of Wildlife Management* 30 (4): 697–707.

Dunlap, T. (1991). *Saving America's Wildlife: Ecology and the American Mind, 1850–1990.* Princeton: Princeton University Press.

Foucault, M. (1978). *The History of Sexuality. Volume 1, An Introduction.* Translated by R. Hurley. New York: Pantheon.

Grove, R. H. (1994). *Green Imperialism: Colonial Expansion, Tropical Island Edens and the Origins of Environmentalism, 1600–1860.* Cambridge: Cambridge University Press.

Harris, C. I. (1993). "Whiteness as Property." *Harvard Law Review* 106 (8): 1707–1791.

Harrod, H. L. (2000). *The Animals Came Dancing: Native American Sacred Ecology and Animal Kinship*. Tucson: University of Arizona Press.

Hay, D. (1975). "Poaching and the Game Laws on Cannock Chase." In *Albion's Fatal Tree: Crime and Society in Eighteenth-Century England*, edited by D. Hay, 189–254. New York: Pantheon.

Hornaday, W. T. (1889). *The Extermination of the American Bison*. Washington, DC: Government Printing Office.

Horta, O. (2015). "Why the Situation of Animals in the Wild Should Concern Us." *Animal Charity Evaluators Blog*, January 5. http://www.animalcharityevaluators.org/blog/why-the-situation-of-animals-in-the-wild-should-concern-us/.

Isenberg, A. (1997). "The Returns of the Bison: Nostalgia, Profit, and Preservation." *Environmental History* 2 (2): 179–196.

Jacoby, K. (2001). *Crimes against Nature: Squatters, Poachers, Thieves, and the Hidden History of American Conservation*. Berkeley: University of California Press.

Jones, S. D. (2003). *Valuing Animals: Veterinarians and Their Patients in Modern America*. Baltimore: Johns Hopkins University Press.

LaPier, R. R. (2017). *Invisible Reality: Storytellers, Storytakers, and the Supernatural World of the Blackfeet*. Lincoln: University of Nebraska Press.

Leopold, A. ([1933], 1987). *Game Management*. Madison: University of Wisconsin Press.

Leopold, A. ([1949], 2020). *A Sand County Almanac and Sketches Here and There*. Oxford: University of Oxford Press.

Lomawaima, K. T. (2013). "The Mutuality of Citizenship and Sovereignty: The Society of American Indians and the Battle to Inherit America." *American Indian Quarterly* 37 (3): 333–351.

MacAskill, W. (2015). *Doing Good Better: How Effective Altruism Can Help You Make a Difference*. New York: Penguin.

Merchant, C. (2016). *Spare the Birds! George Bird Grinnell and the First Audubon Society*. New Haven, CT: Yale University Press.

Middleton, A. (2014). "Is the Wolf a Real American Hero?" *New York Times*, March 9. https://www.nytimes.com/2014/03/10/opinion/is-the-wolf-a-real-american-hero.html.

Mitman, G. (1992). *The State of Nature: Ecology, Community, and American Social Thought, 1900–1950*. Chicago: University of Chicago Press.

Mitman, G. ([1999] 2009). *Reel Nature: America's Romance with Wildlife on Film*. Seattle: University of Washington Press.

Morton-Robinson, A. (2015). *The White Possessive: Property, Power, and Indigenous Sovereignty*. Minneapolis: University of Minnesota Press.

Organ, J. F., V. Geist, S. P. Mahoney, S. Williams, P. R. Krausman, G. R. Batcheller, T. A. Decker, et al. (2012). *The North American Model of Wildlife Conservation*. Technical Review 12-04. Bethesda, MD: The Wildlife Society and The Boone and Crockett Club. https://wildlife.org/wp-content/uploads/2014/05/North-American-model-of-Wildlife-Conservation.pdf.

Pinchot, G. (1905). "James Wilson to the Forester, Forest Service, February 1, 1905." In *The U.S. Forest Service Headquarters History Collection*. Durham, NC: Forest History Society Archives. https://foresthistory.org/research-explore/us-forest-service-history/policy-and-law/agency-organization/wilson-letter/.

Powell, M. A. (2016). *Vanishing America: Species Extinction, Racial Peril, and the Origins of Conservation*. Cambridge, MA: Harvard University Press.

Reiger, J. F. ([1975] 2001). *American Sportsmen and the Origins of Conservation*. Corvallis: Oregon State University Press.

Sagsveen, M. G. (1984). "Waterfowl Production Areas: A State Perspective." *North Dakota Law Review* 60 (4): 659–692.

Smalley, A. L. (2017). *Wild by Nature: North American Animals Confront Colonization*. Baltimore: Johns Hopkins University Press.

Smith, P. A. (2021). "Forced to Hurry to Come Up with Details for a Wolf Hunt, the DNR Will Present Its Plan Monday." *Milwaukee Journal Sentinel*, February 13. https://www.jsonline.com/story/sports/outdoors/2021/02/13/wisconsin-wolf-kill-target-200-proposed-dnr/6729173002/.

Spence, M. D. (1999). *Dispossessing the Wilderness: Indian Removal and the Making of the National Parks*. Oxford: Oxford University Press.

Thompson, E. P. (1975). *Whigs and Hunters: The Origin of the Black Act*. New York: Pantheon.

Tomasik, B. (2016). "The Importance of Wild-Animal Suffering." London: Foundational Research Institute, April 22. https://longtermrisk.org/the-importance-of-wild-animal-suffering/.

Turner, F. J. ([1891] 1998). "The Significance of the Frontier in American History (1891)." In *Rereading Frederick Jackson Turner: "The Significance of the Frontier in American History" and Other Essays*. Edited by J. M. Farahager, 31–60. New Haven, CT: Yale University Press.

US Fish and Wildlife Service in cooperation with the Northern Rocky Mountain Wolf Recovery Team. (1987). *Northern Rocky Mountain Wolf Recovery Plan*. Denver: US Fish and Wildlife Service.

Warren, L. (1999). *The Hunter's Game: Poachers and Conservationists in Twentieth-Century America*. New Haven, CT: Yale University Press.

White, R. (1991). *The Middle Ground: Indians, Empires, and Republics in the Great Lakes Region, 1650–1815*. Cambridge: Cambridge University Press.

Wilson, R. (2010), Seeking Refuge: Birds and Landscapes of the Pacific Flyway, Seattle: University of Washington Press.

Wise, M. D. (2016). *Producing Predators: Wolves, Work, and Conquest in the Northern Rockies*. Lincoln: University of Nebraska Press.

Witgen, M. (2011). *An Infinity of Nations: How the New World Shaped Early North America*. Philadelphia: University of Pennsylvania Press.

Worster, D. ([1977] 1994). *Nature's Economy: A History of Ecological Ideas*. Cambridge: Cambridge University Press.

6

Diversifying Effective Altruism's Long Shots in Animal Advocacy

An Invitation to Prioritize Black Vegans, Higher Education, and Religious Communities

Matthew C. Halteman

Effective Altruism (EA) has a snappy brand and a compelling project. When it comes to two-word phrases that are bound to generate enthusiasm, it'd take big guns like "free pizza" and "TikTok famous" to do better than "Effective Altruism." And beyond the promising name, the act of doing well at being good is an attractive prospect, too. When you add in nuances like the fact that the *way* we do well at being good is by using *reason* and *evidence* to do the *most* good possible, the prospect looks even better. When it is clear that we can do more good rather than less, all things being equal, who wouldn't choose to do more?

As much as I resonate with the animating spirit of EA, this last question conceals two reservations that keep me from thinking of myself as a card-carrying member, especially where EA approaches to animal advocacy (my main focus here) are concerned. I'll italicize a couple of key phrases to highlight my two reservations:

Matthew C. Halteman, *Diversifying Effective Altruism's Long Shots in Animal Advocacy* In: *The Good It Promises, The Harm It Does*. Edited by: Carol J. Adams, Alice Crary, and Lori Gruen, Oxford University Press.
 DOI: 10.1093/oso/9780197655696.003.0006

When it is clear that we can do more good rather than less, *all things being equal*, who wouldn't choose to do more?

My first reservation is that it isn't always *clear* that we really *can* do more good by supporting EA-preferred causes, and that in some cases in particular—even where some of the most highly funded EA projects are concerned—the prospect of actually doing more good seems dim.

My second reservation is that all things are *not* in fact equal, and that in some cases—even if it were possible *clearly* to do *more good* on the aggregate by giving to some EA-preferred cause—the opportunity cost of doing so would be to further entrench systemic injustice, gaining more good on the whole at the expense of groups that already face significant disadvantages.

In what follows, I'll explain each of these reservations and then suggest some exciting new initiatives—institution-building in Black vegan advocacy, higher education, and religious communities—that could mitigate these reservations, energize and diversify the movement, and remain true to the EA method of supporting underexploited but potentially high-impact causes that produce nonfungible goods otherwise unlikely to be funded.

Let's start with the reservation about lack of clarity—that it isn't always clear that giving to EA-preferred causes will do more good than alternatives. "Effective Altruism," after all, is more an *aspirational expression* than it is a *success term*. In other words, it's much more like "best grandma ever!" or "world's greatest vegan sandwich" than it is like "Nobel laureate" or "three-star chef." It's a way of saying, "This is what we hope to accomplish!" or "This is what we're striving for!," but it doesn't guarantee that the aspiration is (or even can be) realized by those who adopt the name.

It's important to recognize, too, that—so far, anyway—the people who have adopted the name tend to share a great deal in common. Though the EA movement is not a monolith and is making strides into become more diverse,[1] Rethink Charity's 2019 EA Survey of 2,513 participants revealed a concerningly homogeneous culture: 71 percent male, 87 percent white, and 86 percent agnostic/atheist/nonreligious.[2] For some (and certainly for me), this homogeneity raises a concern that, among other worries, unchecked implicit bias, gaps in knowledge and understanding of certain demographics, and inadequately diverse methodology might compromise the vetting of preferred causes, despite best intentions. One might wonder, more concretely, how well suited the EA community is, given its current makeup and preferred methods for discerning evidence of impact, to make an accurate assessment, say, of the expected utility of investments in the Black vegan movement or in religious higher education. One might worry therefore that it is truly unclear—even by EA's own lights—what causes are really the most promising ones to fund.

Another clarity-related worry is that, as prominent Effective Altruists have acknowledged, any number of the most prized projects in the movement are "high risk/high reward." They may seem far-fetched or unlikely at first, but there's reason to believe they could pan out, and if they do succeed, it'd be huge. In short, EA is out there with some arguably effective stuff (like anti-malaria and anti-hunger campaigns), but there are some long shots in the mix too (like protecting us from asteroids and artificial intelligence). And the long shots are supposedly justified on the grounds that if they work, they'll work in a BIG way.

A more descriptively accurate phrase for the aspiration behind this diverse collective of causes, then, might be something like "Probably Effective Altruism" (PEA), or—where some of the

[1] The *Effective Altruism Forum* threads on Diversity and Inclusion show that awareness of the problems associated with demographic homogeneity and the value of a having more diverse EA movement are both very much under discussion and somewhat contentious among members of the EA community. See online at https://forum.effectivealtruism.org/tag/diversity-and-inclusion.

[2] For analysis and commentary on these numbers, check out Dullaghan 2019.

higher-risk projects are concerned—even "Possibly Effective Altruism, If Lucky" (PEAL). And where the application of EA methods to animal advocacy is concerned—especially now that EA money is flooding into food tech R&D for alternative protein in hopes of hastening the demise of animal agriculture—we might even need to consider something like "Venture Altruism" (VA). However promising tech miracles like "real meat without animals" may seem (full disclosure: I'm excited about their potential, support organizations that promote them, and am married to a person who works in the sector), the reality is that our ability to bring such products to scale is presently unknown and faces significant hurdles.[3]

Acronyms like PEA, PEAL, and VA, if perhaps more accurate, have decidedly less appeal than EA. But they call attention to something important: when enveloped by the confident aura that can emanate from seeing "Effective Altruism" as a success term, it's easy to lose track of the fact that aspiring to be maximally effective at doing good in this way is apparently compatible with taking *huge* risks—even long shots. And taking long shots always involves accepting significant opportunity costs.

In 2017, for example, the EA-based Open Philanthropy Project funded the mitigation of "potential risks from advanced artificial intelligence" to the tune of $43 million, second only to the $118 million awarded to global health and development projects.[4] The hope here is to mitigate important but often neglected "longtermist" concerns about "suffering risk," or "s-risk"—the risk of astronomical suffering and death that a future misaligned AI or other runaway technology could inflict on untold numbers of human beings, animals, potential sentient life from other galaxies, and potential sentient digital life.[5]

[3] For an overview of these hurdles, see Farm Forward 2020.

[4] This passage and the associated numbers are cited in Todd 2020 from an unpublished essay by Will MacAskill titled "The Definition of Effective Altruism."

[5] For a helpful FAQ on s-risk, see Baumann 2017. For engaging introductions to longtermist concerns about existential risk more broadly, see Bostrom 2014 and Ord

It's *possible* that this $43 million will play a catalyst's role in preventing the immense suffering of hundreds of billions of future sentients at the hands (artificial neural networks?) of a misaligned AI. But it's maybe just as likely—perhaps more likely, but who can say?—that this $43 million will make little difference except to the short-term career development of the grantees (most of whom, given the demographic realities of this sector, are likely to be highly educated, relatively affluent men). A reasonable person could be forgiven, it seems, for judging the opportunity costs associated with possibly foiling a misaligned AI in fifty years to be too high, and for suspecting that these millions of dollars could be better invested elsewhere. (I should add that the same reasonable person might simultaneously conclude that it is nonetheless wise to devote some resources to mitigating s-risk; my intent here is not to trivialize these serious risks, but to emphasize that significant investment in their potential mitigation, however important, is nonetheless a long shot, with present opportunity costs worth keeping in mind).[6]

The question of where such funding should go instead is made all the more acute by the second reservation noted above—that the folks most likely to bear these opportunity costs are those who already face disadvantages associated with systemic injustice.[7] One

2020. I am grateful to Dan Hooley, Caleb Parikh, Dominic Roser, and Zak Weston for helpful input on this topic.

[6] Thanks to Dominic Roser for helping me to see the complexity of this problem through the lens of intergenerational justice. Though it is tempting, given the pressing concern of inequitable cause prioritization, to weigh the opportunity costs of funding such tech long shots only in terms of the interests of *presently* disadvantaged communities, there are also the interests of *future* disadvantaged communities to consider. For a survey of the issues at stake here, see Roser and Seidel 2017; Part II of the book, titled "How Much Do We Need To Do? Intergenerational Justice" (pp. 55–96), is especially helpful.

[7] Saccoccio 2021 is a good starting point for considering the question of "how philanthropy in farmed animal advocacy reinforces white bubbles" (p. 53), and Graham 2021 approaches this general concern with EA explicitly in mind. For more input on how using data to guide funding decisions can inadvertently contribute to systemic injustice, visit the website of We All Count, an equity training organization which offers online workshops on the Foundations of Data Equity, at https://weallcount.com/workshop-landing-page.

might object that it is morally ill-advised—maybe even fanatical[8]—to invest tens of millions of dollars in tech long shots that *might someday* have a huge impact on the world at large while failing to combat intimately related systemic injustices *that are doing disproportionate damage right now* to already at-risk communities.

To make this worry more concrete in the context of the animal-focused applications of EA under discussion in this book, consider the disproportionate toll that the ascendance of industrial animal agriculture has taken on communities of color in the United States, and on Black communities in particular. These communities have been unjustly made to endure a system of food apartheid that treats them as second-class, having both much less access to the benefits of the system and much greater risk of being harmed by its costs.

Black farmers are much less likely to receive government subsidies (Castro and Willingham 2019). Black and brown workers disproportionately bear the burdens associated with the highest-risk jobs in slaughterhouses and processing plants (Pachirat 2011). Black neighborhoods are more likely to be food-insecure, with many more opportunities to consume animal-product-heavy fast food and many fewer opportunities to learn about and purchase affordable fresh produce. And Black people suffer disproportionately from diet-related illnesses like diabetes, obesity, hypertension, heart disease, and stroke, and generally have less access to affordable healthcare to treat these conditions (McQuirter 2010).

Notwithstanding this system of food apartheid, civil rights pioneers like Dick Gregory and Coretta Scott King were among the first to see the concerns of human and animal liberation as intertwined. Members of the Black Panthers were among the first to promote plant-based diets as the foundation of food autonomy and bodily health in their free breakfast programs (Mercer

[8] In an unpublished manuscript for the Global Priorities Working Paper Series titled "'In Defence of Fanaticism,'" Hayden Wilkinson acknowledges this problem but argues that the costs of abandoning expected value theory to avoid such fanaticism are too high to bear. See Wilkinson 2020.

2021). Black vegans like Nekeisha Alayna Alexis, Tabitha Brown, Christopher Carter, Breeze Harper, Aph and Syl Ko, Michelle Loyd-Paige, Christopher Sebastian, Tracye McQuirter, Brenda Sanders, Bryant Terry, and many others are doing what is, to my mind, some of the most holistic and provocative work in the food and animal justice movements. And Black celebrities and artists like Oprah Winfrey, Lizzo, KRS One, Wu Tang Clan, Beyoncé, and others have influentially centered these issues in their work. Given all this productive ferment, those paying attention won't be surprised to learn that African Americans are the fastest-growing vegan demographic in the United States, with 8 percent identifying as such (while just 3 percent of the general population do) (Reiley 2020).

To people who have become convinced that human and animal liberation are fundamentally intertwined (as I have been, in significant part by the work of Black vegans), it may seem morally dubious to allocate tens of millions of dollars to research and development for alternative protein (that may never come to scale) while influential Black vegans struggle to fund conferences and community events that seem poised to make a big impact on a variety of related fronts, from worker and environmental justice, to public health, to justice for animals. Moreover, though I focus in this chapter on EA's food tech long shots, it is important to observe that people concerned about inequitable cause prioritization may have similar reservations about EA support for incremental corporate campaigns within industrial animal agriculture (cage-free, Better Chicken Commitment, etc.), given unintended consequences for farmworkers and small farmers in the United States and throughout the Global South who are Black, Indigenous, or people of the global majority.

In such cases, skeptics might have one or both of two different worries: that EA has done the expected value calculations incorrectly (or maybe not at all) for lack of adequate understanding of the situation and potential of Black vegan communities and advocacy work; or that, even if they've done the calculus correctly, there is more than general goodness of outcome to consider where combatting entrenched institutional injustice is concerned. As Brooke Haggerty, executive director of Faunalytics, has written, "white animal advocates have an obligation to make the animal protection community an equitable space. This is our obligation not because the data tell us that doing so will increase our impact, but because our commitment to fighting oppression should not be limited to nonhuman animals" (2021, 131–132).

So though both alternative protein and Black vegan advocacy seem like high-priority causes that could be big winners from the standpoint of doing good, the latter may strike some as having a big advantage: even if the long-shot scenario doesn't obtain, the achievement of significant nonfungible good (including progress toward the great good of social justice) is a sure thing.

Let's say, for instance, that crack teams of Ivy League STEM grads get an EA cash infusion, with the hope—if they're lucky—of inventing amazing new alt-proteins that vastly reduce the carbon footprint of producing these foods and capture 30 percent of the market for animal products by 2050. And let's say they make some significant strides but ultimately cannot produce these proteins quickly and cheaply enough, or perhaps struggle to convince the public to get on board, and philanthropists stop funding their development before the products come to scale.

What will EA have accomplished in this scenario? *Some* good will have been done, as the exciting buzz around needed alternatives to animal agriculture and the rise of pioneering scientists and entrepreneurs in the sector will have energized elements of the movement. But it's not clear that the world will have become a significantly better place. This buzz and reputational gain are fungible, after all—there are other, similar ways those net positives could have been achieved. And the world will certainly *not* have become a more *just* place by virtue of this work, given that all these resources went, all too predictably, into the pockets or reputations of already relatively affluent and influential people, arguably at the expense of marginalized people with many fewer opportunities.

Consider, instead, that leading Black vegans get these EA philanthropic resources with the hope—if they're lucky—of spearheading a movement that makes going vegan fully mainstream, not just in Black communities but across the culture at large where the work of Black intellectuals, politicians, activists, athletes, and artists is increasingly ascendant. Let's say that these efforts make significant headway, but do not result in the hoped-for vegan revolution.

What will EA have accomplished? It'll certainly have made the world a better place, because the vegan ferment in Black communities will surely do *some* good, and likely even a *significant* amount of nonfungible good in the lives of the individuals reached (the relevant health benefits and expanded animal consciousness, for instance, are two significant goods that are not easily achievable by other means). But EA will also have supported Black vegan work that is often unfairly undervalued and excluded from the movement despite its significant originality, value, and promise, thus making the world a more just place, too.

My point here is that if EAs are comfortable with taking long shots—as efforts like foiling the extermination of humankind by a misaligned AI, avoiding obliteration by asteroid, and normalizing animal-free meat clearly seem to be[9]—then why not take some long shots in areas that have a fighting chance to make the world both much better *and* more just *even if they don't fully realize their seeming potential*? Supporting Black vegan efforts is one of the long shots that seems most promising now.

Two other long shots that seem well worth exploring are efforts to make food systems education mainstream in colleges and universities and efforts to engage and educate religious

[9] In a recent op-ed in the *New York Times*, Ezra Klein (2021) calls this effort a "moonshot," but suggests that it is one that should be launched by governments rather than philanthropists.

communities. These suggestions may seem counterintuitive, given the perception among some prominent EAs and EA sympathizers that education-based advocacy hasn't succeeded, despite four decades of effort, in bringing about the necessary food revolution. This perception has even driven some leaders in the movement to adopt a different theory of change altogether. The best way to end industrial farm animal production, on this new outlook, is not to educate people in hopes that they will boycott the system and push for better alternatives, but rather to transform the system from the inside using the mechanisms of technology and market capitalism to speed the obsolescence of animal products until they are supplanted by cheaper, better-tasting, more sustainable plant- or cell-based alternatives.

Though I find these matters intriguing, I am less interested than most of my EA friends in debating which theory of change is the right one. I'm of the persuasion that none of us knows what the right one is or even if there is just one. Letting a thousand flowers bloom in our approaches to advocacy (or at least a hundred reasonably well-tended ones?) can be a good way to meet folks where they are and get as many people into the movement (with their diverse outlooks, motivations, talents, and gifts) as we can. But I do think it is worth pointing out that there is a way to see *certain kinds* of education-focused advocacy work as deeply consonant with the EA method of looking for underexploited but potentially high-impact areas that produce nonfungible goods that are otherwise unlikely to be funded.

What I have in mind here by education-focused advocacy is not the typical model of sending a compelling vegan emissary from the outside into institutional spaces that are often culturally unfriendly to going vegan in hopes of generating a small percentage of converts. Once upon a time, when the ethics, science, and spirituality supportive of vegan commitments were less mainstream, this external approach to education-based advocacy was likely the best (and perhaps the only) way to go. But in an era of increasing ethical, scientific, and spiritual consensus among experts that a radical transition away from an animal-based food system is urgently requisite, it is now possible to imagine viable infrastructure-building for comprehensive vegan education *within* the relevant institutions, such that one cannot escape popular culture, college, or church without being thoroughly sensitized to and educated about these matters by one's own cultural heroes, teachers, and spiritual mentors.

Take higher education, for example. A recent study by Schwitzgebel, Cokelet, and Singer (2020) suggests that ethics classes can move students to eat less meat. And from surveying broader cultural trends in the evolution of public opinion on matters of gender, race, and other matters of justice, it seems intuitively plausible that views normalized in institutions of higher learning can have a profound shaping effect on the attitudes and actions of tens of millions of young people.

Those tempted to doubt the potential impact of higher education for transforming our food system need only reflect upon how successful the meat industry has been at shaping the values of generations of students at ag-funded universities. After graduation, their work as meat-friendly businesspeople, medical professionals, veterinarians, public health officials, and politicians has helped to build our animal-centric food system and shelter it from well-deserved criticism and reform.[10]

How many lives—human and other-than-human—might be changed for the better if wide access to cutting-edge instruction around the need to transform our food system became the educational air that college students breathe, precisely at the formative time when they are establishing the values and consumer habits that will govern their adult lives for decades to come?

[10] I am grateful to Jennifer Channin for calling to my attention this important example of higher education's profound ability to shape our food system (if not always for the better).

Most colleges and universities these days have existing faculty scattered throughout the arts and sciences who have both relevant scholarly expertise and pedagogical interest in teaching on food ethics and intermeshed disciplines such as animal ethics, animal law, climate science, nutrition science, public health policy, supply chain management, worker justice, gender studies, and antiracism. What these institutions often lack is the funding to empower such faculty to offer these courses regularly or, better still, to join forces as a collective to develop interdisciplinary centers, institutes, specialized majors, certificates, and graduate programs that could both thrust these issues into the educational mainstream and propel institutional changes in catering policy, dining hall food sourcing, and the use of animals in scientific research.

At a time when many institutions of higher learning are facing financial pressures that make them more receptive than ever to mission-targeted external funding, there is a real opportunity for the EA movement to make strategic institution-building gifts to colleges and universities that could influence the behavior of generations of students—gifts that, very importantly, are not likely to be made by traditional funders, who are often skeptical of or even opposed to such efforts, if they are aware of them at all.

The recent explosion of food studies programs at colleges and universities across the globe demonstrates that students want these courses, professors want to teach them, and universities want the prestige and market share they generate.[11] What's more, the causes of animal welfare and rights, especially explicitly vegan perspectives on them, still tend to be underrepresented within these programs, which gives animal advocates all the more reason to fund their

[11] For an ever-expanding list of opportunities to do food studies in higher education, visit Food Culture.Org, at https://www.food-culture.org/food-studies-programs/. For more on the rise of food studies programs in the United States, see Cosgrove 2015.

development.[12] EA should strike while the iron is hot for the best chance at shaping these trends.

Even more exciting is that there is nothing nefarious or manipulative about seeking such influence among students. Indeed, the kind of shaping influence I'm talking about here is just what an education is supposed to provide, according to most college admissions departments: exposure to and training within the best, most scientifically and ethically sound, most transformative curriculum for the purposes of grounding one's personal and vocational flourishing and contributing to the common good.

Outreach to religious communities is another important opportunity—one that is increasingly already understood within some ranks of the EA movement to have significant potential.[13] With 5.8 billion people on Earth self-identifying as religious, it's hard to imagine that the urgently needed global transition to a plant-based food system can be carried off without the aid of religious institutions. And as Sophie Ritchie (2015) has observed in the Effective Altruism Forum, there are surface indicators that a groundswell of enthusiasm for the cause among religious audiences could be influential, given the evidence that religious people tend to give more and more often to charitable causes.

Until recently, the big hurdle to achieving widespread influence among religious communities has been that the requisite institutional infrastructure for offering authentic *internal* food systems education has been lacking. Instead of receiving consistent, coherent spiritual formation from trusted authorities working within

[12] Thanks to Alice Crary for pointing out that the current underrepresentation of explicitly vegan perspectives in influential food systems programs is a feature rather than a bug when it comes to substantiating the need for funding such positions.

[13] Sophie Ritchie (2015) surveys this promising if complex nexus with reference to the specific prospects of engaging Jewish and Christian audiences. At the end of the post, she notes the existence of a Facebook group for "Christian effective altruists that has around 80 members, but isn't hugely participative or proactive beyond the online discussion space." Five years later, the group has 500 active members, a full-time director, three part-time staff, and a pending registration with the charity commission of the United Kingdom; read more about their work online at https://www.eaforchristians.org.

their places of worship and educational communities, adherents of faith traditions have had to rely on the honorable but inherently limited *external* efforts of activists beyond these hallowed halls, offering a humane society pamphlet here, a targeted video there, or a newsletter from the nearest affiliated vegetarian association.

I have supported and engaged in this kind of *external* advocacy work for the past fifteen years. As reading the annual reports of pioneering nonprofit organizations such as CreatureKind, Jewish Initiative for Animals, Sarx, and Shamayim confirms, these kinds of efforts produce groundbreaking and important results.[14] In my view, they well deserve our support. The hard work of committed advocates fighting uphill battles to engage religious cultures that can be quick to chasten new ideas and slow to adopt them deserve much credit for the fact that there is now more and more rapidly expanding potential than ever before for achieving widespread and lasting institutional headway in religious communities.

But at the same time, it seems likely that the kind of *internal* spiritual formation work I've done in collaboration with my colleagues and students at a Christian university and with leadership and fellow lay educators in local churches is more effectual (and more *potentially* effectual, if replicated on a grander scale in religious institutions generally) than external advocacy work could be. Spiritual formation work that is internal to religious institutions, after all, is not just about the disinterested adoption *à la carte* of this or that single-issue social cause. Rather, it molds the motivations and shapes the lives of adherents much more profoundly and lastingly than even the most compelling pamphlet, speaker series, or webinar ever could. What is at stake is nothing less than a rigorous,

[14] To learn more about CreatureKind, visit https://www.becreaturekind.org. To learn more about Jewish Initiative for Animals, visit https://www.jewishinitiativeforanimals.com. To learn more about Sarx, visit https://sarx.org.uk. To learn more about Shamayim, visit https://www.shamayim.us. For the sake of full disclosure, I should add that I am a member of the board of directors of CreatureKind and the advisory boards of Sarx and the National Interfaith Animal Welfare Initiative in partnership with Shamayim.

sustained communal endeavor to live out a holistic religious vision of the world through the adoption of concrete discipleship practices. And this ambitious task, it turns out, is one that the best readings of our sacred texts and religious ethics suggest cannot be done compellingly without profound changes in the way we view and treat animals, break our daily bread, and collectively feed the world.

Within my own religious tradition, Christianity, it is exhilarating to imagine what might be possible if already existing denominations and institutions of higher learning had the resources, infrastructural bandwidth, and personnel to start catechizing, teaching, and feeding their congregations, seminarians, college students, and day school children in harmony with the best already existing theological and ethical work.

What if a significant number of the world's 1.1 billion Catholics adopted the eating and consumer habits that follow from taking seriously the discipleship implications of Pope Francis's recent encyclical on care of creation, *Laudato Si'* (2015)? What if a good-sized swath of the 620 million evangelical Protestants on the planet adopted the attitudes and actions outlined in *Every Living Thing*, an evangelical statement on responsible care for animals signed by hundreds of church leaders?[15] What if interfaith collaboration among the many religious and spiritual traditions that promote peace and justice led to widespread changes in the attitudes and actions of adherents from many faiths?

Admittedly, such grand cultural transformations are long shots. But so are preventing the advent of misaligned AIs, averting would-be asteroid apocalypses, and supplanting industrial animal agriculture by making meat without animals. Some solid indications point to a reasonable hope that EA philanthropy can help to transform

[15] This statement's full title is *Every Living Thing: An Evangelical Statement on Responsible Care for Animals*, and it can be read in full and signed online at https://www.everylivingthing.com/sign-the-statement.

the meat industry by making targeted gifts to empower scientists and entrepreneurs who couldn't otherwise do so to discover and normalize the technology and markets that will power the alt-protein revolution and save untold billions of human and other-than-human lives.

Might EA philanthropy also reasonably hope to spur the transformation of religious attitudes and actions toward animals by making targeted gifts to empower denominations, universities, and religious leaders who couldn't otherwise do so to pioneer and normalize the religious visions and discipleship practices that will lead billions to support the transition to a plant-based food system? Might it reasonably hope to help foment similar revolutions in higher education more broadly and in the Black vegan circles whose gathering momentum seems poised to catalyze widespread cultural change?

If all goes well, EA's prioritization of the causes of alt-protein and institution-building in Black vegan advocacy, higher education, and religious communities could work in tandem to make the world a significantly better place. But even if the hoped-for long shots of total cultural transformation in these three arenas do not obtain, each nonetheless demonstrates *reliable* results in motivating people to change their diets and moving institutions to change their food policies—the problem is that we haven't invested enough to scale those results.

These institution-building efforts, after all, are not rocket science (or novel alt-protein science, as the case may be). They are matters of community organization (Black vegan advocacy and religious advocacy) and knowledge dissemination (higher education)—tried and true methods of achieving social change that are well researched and well understood. Let's see to it that they soon become well-funded, too, perhaps diversifying and expanding the EA movement and helping it to address some key weaknesses in the process.[16]

[16] I am grateful to Carol Adams, Nekeisha Alayna Alexis, JD Bauman, Andrew Chignell, David Clough, Alice Crary, Aaron Gross, Lori Gruen, Susan Halteman, Dan

References

Baumann, T. (2017). "S-Risk FAQ." *Effective Altruism Forum*, September 18. https://forum.effectivealtruism.org/posts/MCfa6PaGoe6AaLPHR/s-risk-faq.

Bostrom, N. (2014). *Superintelligence: Paths, Dangers, Strategies*. Oxford: Oxford University Press.

Castro, A., and C. Willingham. (2019). "Progressive Governance Can Turn the Tide for Black Farmers." Center for American Progress, April 3. https://www.americanprogress.org/issues/economy/reports/2019/04/03/467892/progressive-governance-can-turn-tide-black-farmers.

Cosgrove, E. (2015). "The Rise of Food Studies Programs." *Atlantic*, June 1. https://www.theatlantic.com/education/archive/2015/06/the-rise-of-food-studies-programs/394538/.

Dullaghan, N. (2019). "EA Survey 2019: The Community Demographics & Characteristics." Rethinking Charity, December 5. https://rethinkpriorities.org/publications/eas2019-community-demographics-characteristics.

Farm Forward. (2020). *The Farmed Animal Protection Movement: Common Strategies for Improving and Protecting the Lives of Farmed Animals*. San Diego, CA: Farm Forward Publications. https://res.cloudinary.com/hyjvcxzjt/image/upload/v1614024915/resource/farm-forward-publication-philanthropy-farmed-anima-3fd7.pdf.

Francis. (2015). *Laudato Si': On Care for Our Common Home*. Rome: The Vatican. http://www.vatican.va/content/francesco/en/encyclicals/documents/papa-francesco_20150524_enciclica-laudato-si.html.

Graham, M. (2021). "How Racism in Animal Advocacy and Effective Altruism Hinder Our Mission." In *Antiracism in Animal Advocacy: Igniting Cultural Transformation*, edited by J. Singer, 165–175. New York: Lantern.

Haggarty, B. (2021). "Using Research and Data to Create an Inclusive Animal Rights Movement." In *Antiracism in Animal Advocacy: Igniting Cultural Transformation*, edited by J. Singer, 128–139. New York: Lantern.

Klein, E. (2021), "Let's Launch a Moonshot for Meatless Meat." *New York Times*, April 24. https://www.nytimes.com/2021/04/24/opinion/climate-change-meatless-meat.html.

McQuirter, T. L. (2010). *By Any Greens Necessary*. Chicago: Lawrence Hill Books.

Hooley, Michelle Loyd-Paige, Caleb Parikh, Dominic Roser, Christopher Sebastian, Zak Weston, and Megan Halteman Zwart for helpful conversations on these topics and/or feedback on drafts of this essay. I am especially grateful to Tyler Doggett, who read and offered very helpful feedback on several drafts, and to Jennifer Channin, whose extensive commentary significantly shaped the final product.

Mercer, A. (2021), "A Homecoming: The Imagery of Veganism Propagated by the Wellness Industry Erases the Long—and Often Radical—History of Plant-Based Diets in the Black Diaspora." *Eater.com Longform*, January 14. https://www.eater.com/22229322/black-veganism-history-black-panthers-dick-gregory-nation-of-islam-alvenia-fulton.

Ord, T. (2020). *The Precipice: Existential Risk and the Future of Humanity.* New York: Hachette Books.

Pachirat, T. (2011). *Every Twelve Seconds: Industrialized Slaughter and the Politics of Sight.* New Haven, CT: Yale University Press.

Reiley, L. (2020). "The Fastest Growing Vegan Demographic Is African Americans." *Washington Post*, January 24. https://www.washingtonpost.com/business/2020/01/24/fastest-growing-vegan-demographic-is-african-americans-wu-tang-clan-other-hip-hop-acts-paved-way/.

Ritchie, S. (2015). "Effective Altruism and Religious Faiths: Mutually Exclusive Entities, or an Important Nexus to Explore?" *Effective Altruism Forum*, September 20. https://forum.effectivealtruism.org/posts/zY2jLwfdXENm6mGQP/effective-altruism-and-religious-faiths-mutually-exclusive.

Roser, D., and C. Seidel. (2017). *Climate Justice: An Introduction.* New York: Routledge.

Saccoccio, M. (2021). "How Philanthropy in Farmed Animal Advocacy Reinforces White Bubbles." In *Antiracism in Animal Advocacy: Igniting Cultural Transformation*, edited by J. Singer, 53–57 New York: Lantern.

Schwitzgebel, E., B. Cokelet, and P. Singer. (2020). "Do Ethics Classes Influence Student Behavior? Case Study: Teaching the Ethics of Eating Meat." *Cognition* 203 (October): 104397.

Singer, J., ed. (2021). *Antiracism in Animal Advocacy: Igniting Cultural Transformation.* New York: Lantern.

Todd, B. (2020). "Misconceptions about Effective Altruism." 80,000 Hours, August 7. https://80000hours.org/2020/08/misconceptions-effective-altruism/.

Wilkinson, H. (2020). "In Defence of Fanaticism." Global Priorities Working Paper Series. Oxford: Global Priorities Institute. https://globalprioritiesinstitute.org/hayden-wilkinson-in-defence-of-fanaticism/.

7

A Christian Critique of the Effective Altruism Approach to Animal Philanthropy

David L. Clough

In this chapter I present a Christian ethical argument against using Effective Altruism to guide donations to animal charities. First, I summarize Christian ethical concerns with the problematic oversimplification of utilitarian ethics, on which Effective Altruism is based. Second, I outline the problems with Effective Altruism that result from this dependence on utilitarianism. Third, I argue that there are specific problems with the application of Effective Altruism in the animals space. Finally, I outline an alternative starting point informed by a Christian ethical framework for guiding decisions about how best to donate money to improve the lot of animals. A Christian approach to this issue is likely to be of particular interest to members of Christian churches or those who otherwise identify with Christian traditions of thought and practice. The breadth and pluralism of the ethical approach I outline and the deficiencies of Effective Altruism it illuminates may also be helpful for readers.

David L. Clough, *A Christian Critique of the Effective Altruism Approach to Animal Philanthropy* In: *The Good It Promises, The Harm It Does.* Edited by: Carol J. Adams, Alice Crary, and Lori Gruen, Oxford University Press.
 DOI: 10.1093/oso/9780197655696.003.0007

Why Christians Have a Problem with Utilitarianism

I am a Christian ethicist. That means I see, as a part of my task, reconsidering the ethics of our practices in relation to other animals in the light of an appropriate Christian doctrinal understanding of animals. The two books I have written on this subject, *On Animals, Vol. I: Systematic Theology* and *On Animals, Vol. II: Theological Ethics* were motivated by the ethical question of what we should do in relationship to our fellow animal creatures.

For me, and for many Christians, Christian doctrine demands that we recognize in other animals fellow creatures that glorify God in their flourishing, fellow beneficiaries of God's work of reconciling all things in Jesus Christ, and fellow participants in the new creation. I believe the flourishing of animals matters to God, and therefore gives Christians reason to avoid actions that unnecessarily block their flourishing, and to take action where possible to promote it. This means, at the most basic level, that the lives and well-being of nonhuman animals have moral relevance in a theological ethics.

Christian ethics as it engages animals is necessarily pluralistic: it is interested in multiple perspectives on ethical questions and considers a complex weighing of relevant factors, which makes ethical thinking a difficult thing.

Utilitarianism shares with Christianity a concern about suffering. But utilitarian philosophers think they have found a system that cuts through the messy complexity of the moral life. As a Christian ethicist, I find utilitarianism shockingly neglectful of crucial insights from biblical and later theological ethical wisdom, including the sanctity of life.

Traditions of moral thinking include a wide range of different considerations: obedience to rules such as "Don't steal," fidelity to principles such as "Love your neighbor," the development of virtuous elements of character such as honesty, the value of moral affections such as compassion, the importance of your intention when you act, the role of stories in shaping the moral life, the significance of honoring prior commitments, and attention to the consequences of your actions. The question of whether there are particular norms that should never be transgressed, from a deontological ethical framework, is always going to be relevant in a Christian ethical understanding.

Christian ethical thinking also recognizes the value of attending to moral virtues. Virtue ethics focuses on the moral agent and does not base its evaluation on any judgment of interspecies similarity. In doing so, virtue ethics allows a different kind of moral thinking about animals than approaches based solely in claims about the characteristics and capabilities of animals. Virtue ethics directs attention to the ability of a moral agent to recognize and respond to the perceived need of other animals compassionately. Here it is the capacities of the moral agent that are most significant, rather than judgments about the capacities of the objects of their action. Training in character development and virtues and thinking about what it means to act as a virtuous person are crucial components of Christian ethical thinking. In nineteenth-century Britain, many Christians opposed scientists who thought they were entitled to conduct experiments on animals without regard for the suffering they caused. The arguments Christians used were not based on claims of human/animal equality, concepts of rights, or even fairness. Instead, they centered on the claim that since Christians worship an almighty God who condescends to care graciously for frail and vulnerable creatures, they saw clearly the wrongness of those who were strong selfishly using their power to exploit others. Christian opposition to vivisection was therefore based on a virtue ethics judgment that virtuous persons should not use their power over animals to gain knowledge by means that cause animals to suffer.

Christian ethics is also appreciative of a feminist ethics of care, which emphasizes morality as responsibility to care for others, as opposed to approaches that begin from the idea of morality as fairness. This approach to ethics is suspicious of abstraction and involves both attending to individual animals and attending to the causal systems that have placed specific animals in their situation. Christian ethics shares with a feminist ethics of care the concern for what it means to be in a relationship of care, to be attentive to the voice and needs of another.

These examples of different ways of thinking about ethical situations all belong in an adequate analysis of how to direct resources to address the problem of egregious, abusive, human treatment of animals. None on its own can do justice to the breadth and depth of the theological account of the place of animals.

Utilitarians are impatient with multiple moral considerations that may sometimes point in conflicting directions. In a utilitarian system, nothing apart from the consequences of an action matters. You decide what to do by working out which potential action will result in the best consequences. Utilitarians disagree among themselves about how you should decide what the best consequences are. Available options include the best balance of pleasure over pain, or happiness over unhappiness, or net utility, or satisfaction of preferences. They also disagree about whether people should follow rules that generally lead to the best consequences, or whether you should always do what you calculate will lead to the best results, no matter what the rules are. But they all agree that you should disregard all moral features of an action except its results. This leads to uncomfortable and counterintuitive conclusions, such as it being right to frame an innocent person if that will avoid some predictable negative consequences.

Why Christians Have a Problem with Effective Altruism

Effective Altruism is founded on utilitarianism, and utilitarianism achieves simplicity in its consideration of only one morally relevant aspect of a situation. That is problematic from a Christian point of view, because Christian ethics is much more diverse and complex than that and recognizes a whole range of other morally relevant features of ethical situations.

The heart of what's wrong with Effective Altruism is a fundamental defect of utilitarianism: there are important morally relevant features of any situation that are not reducible to evaluating the results of actions and are not measurable or susceptible to calculation. This makes it inevitable that features of a situation to which numbers can be assigned are exaggerated in significance, while others are neglected.

I appreciate what attracts donors to Effective Altruism. It promises a clear and simple system to tell us the most effective way of giving money. In the context of a bewildering variety of different kinds of projects that claim to be doing the most important work on behalf of animals, it would be great if a straightforward scheme like this could cut through the confusion and complexity and deliver clear guidance to donors about the most effective way of spending money. I'd be delighted if all this were the case. Unfortunately, it's not.

The problem is that Effective Altruism can't deliver on what it promises. It can develop metrics that measure aspects of the activity of particular animal-related projects. It can use those metrics in calculations and rank different activities according to those calculations. And it can issue recommendations to donors on the basis of this ranking. The workings of this system can look really impressive. It looks scientific. It looks rational. It looks objective. But the fact that a system uses numbers is no guarantee that it's telling us what it's telling us it's telling us. And it isn't.

Effective Altruism can accurately tell us the results of doing particular calculations on particular measurements about the activity of animal projects. But that's not the same as telling us the best way of spending money.

Effective Altruism can give donors answers about how to direct their money, but the important question is whether there is reason to believe that the answers it gives actually identify the best way to direct that money. There are good reasons to believe that it doesn't.

The key reason Effective Altruism fails to deliver on its claim to be the best guide to effective giving is that it shares in the defects of utilitarianism. The attractiveness of Effective Altruism is that it short-circuits all the complexity of ethical thinking by saying, "Here, let me give you some numbers for you to be able to measure how well you are doing in your goals of giving in order to sort out this animal problem." But this is a false claim. All it is doing is taking one measurable feature of a situation and representing it as maximal effectiveness. A Christian ethical analysis of making decisions about spending money, or anything else, would always be concerned to bring due attention to all the ethical moving parts.

The Problem of Effective Altruism Applied to Animal Philanthropy

If we turn to the question of giving money to try to improve things for animals, the relevance of the problem with the utilitarian basis of Effective Altruism should already be clear. How do you decide between supporting an animal sanctuary offering the opportunity for previously farmed animals to live out the remainder of their lives in comfort, or a campaign to require additional environmental enrichment in broiler chicken sheds, or the promotion of plant-based diets? Each is likely to have beneficial impacts on animals, but they are of very different kinds. The animal sanctuary is offering current benefits to the particular group of animals it's looking after.

If successful, the broiler chicken campaign is likely to affect many more animals, but with a smaller impact on each. If the promotion of plant-based diets is successful on a large scale, it could reduce the demand for broiler chickens together with other animal products, but it might be hard to demonstrate the long-term effects of a particular campaign.

In the comparison between a farm animal sanctuary and an initiative to improve broiler chicken welfare, the effectiveness of giving to a farm sanctuary looks negligible from an Effective Altruism perspective compared to an initiative that might impact on a large number of chickens. Effective Altruism is likely to prioritize the broiler chicken initiative on the grounds that the number of chickens affected is likely to be very high and the cause-effect relationship between the campaign and the change in practice is easy to demonstrate. But it is not obvious that this is reason to judge that it's a better use of money than funding animal sanctuaries or making efforts to change dietary practice.

So how might a Christian ethical analysis reflect differently on giving to a farmed animal sanctuary?

It would start by recognizing the complex range of things that are going on in the practice of animal sanctuaries. For example, the potential for education and moral formation among people visiting a farm animal sanctuary is very hard to quantify. People have the experience of coming to a farmed animal sanctuary and encountering animals that are not being used in production systems. They have an opportunity to recognize the particularities of the animals' lives, such as what it means for this kind of animal to flourish. This encounter might well be transformative in the person's understanding of their relationship with farmed animals. But it is not possible to quantify what the impact of that transformative encounter might be.

A Christian ethical assessment of a farmed animal sanctuary might also recognize the value of a symbol of noninstrumental mode of human beings relating to other animals—a symbol of a possible future in which the kinds of animals that are being looked after within the sanctuary are no longer held captive to particular human economic ends. It is possible to recognize the moral value of places enabling the imagining of an alternative, without being able to document exactly how that kind of realization of a different kind of relationality might be "effective."

In a moral context where we are thinking about what it means to be moral agents, we need to attend to how moral agents are formed. The insight of virtue ethics is that this is not merely a matter of rule and regulation, but a process of character development. We recognize people who act in ways that are virtuous in different respects. We shape our behavior through emulation of their example. We come to change the way we behave not only through adherence to rules, but also by coming to behave in different ways. Virtues are good habits. We learn to live in different ways, and that plays a part in the person we are becoming through our actions.

An attention to animal issues that took seriously the need for virtue development would be very strongly interested in the kind of educational opportunities that might have the potential to be vehicles for that kind of character development, and so might shape people in the future who might be attentive to the need to be compassionate to animals in all kinds of ways. It would be hard to measure the effectiveness of that kind of education and character development in Effective Altruism terms.

The temptation with a lot of animal activist projects is to take a shortcut that doesn't go through the really hard work of getting people to change their hearts and minds. If you do have an impact on changing people's attitudes, then those attitudes will shape virtuous behavior toward animals in all kinds of future situations that are not possible to predict. If you shape a moral agent who is compassionate and convinced that abuse of animals is wrong, that will guide their behavior in every context, not just in a particular decision about choosing what to eat for dinner. If instead you take the shortcut of just getting people to buy plant-based meat because it tastes good or costs less, as soon as either of those things change in a particular context and it becomes advantageous for people to behave in ways that result in bad treatment of animals, they have no reason to do otherwise.

It is tempting to make the decision to bypass the really difficult challenge of moral formation, and to prefer a strategy directed to quicker smaller wins. It's hard to make the case for the kind of long-term educative effort that might, over time, transform people's moral understanding, because you are always going to get more attention from funders, from media, from any direction, from campaigns with an immediate deliverable. Investing in moral formation is never going to look as persuasive.

Another particular problem arises with projects aiming to make incremental improvements within large systems involved with animals. Animal campaign groups have an interest in demonstrating to current and potential donors that they are effective in achieving successes for animals. Companies making use of animals have an interest in convincing their customers that they are treating animals well. So an animal campaign group asking for a small improvement in how broiler chickens are treated looks like a very good prospect on the basis of an Effective Altruism analysis, but might also be profitable for the company to implement because of the effect of building their reputation for good animal welfare. There is then the potential for a deeply unsettling common interest between a donor looking to use their money effectively to benefit animals, the Effective Altruism analysis that demonstrates that small changes that affect large numbers of animals should be prioritized, the animal rights group that can demonstrate campaigning success to its supporters, and the company that can respond positively to a high-profile campaign and burnish its animal welfare credentials for a change it already considered to be advantageous. In this scenario, the donor's funding has been ineffective, or even counterproductive, despite an Effective Altruism analysis showing it to be the most effective option.

Example scenarios such as this one do not demonstrate that all funds spent according to Effective Altruism analyses are being wasted. No doubt much of the funding is having benefits for animals. But it does indicate what might go wrong in taking an overly simplistic judgment of what kinds of projects should be prioritized by donors. It's important to be clear that this problem is not a one-off that could be fixed by appreciating an additional feature of this situation. If Effective Altruists agreed with my analysis of the scenario in the previous paragraphs, they could incorporate a different understanding of the likely consequences into their calculation. But such a revised calculation would still be missing key morally relevant features of the situation. It would inevitably be missing other important considerations, because Effective Altruism is based on the mistaken claim of utilitarianism that it can evaluate situations morally while ignoring all features of a situation except the potential consequences of actions.

Ethical thinking is much more complicated than utilitarianism and Effective Altruism allow. The idea that you could single-mindedly pursue a particular goal and measure the effectiveness of the goal and exclude all other moral considerations is profoundly morally inadequate from a Christian ethical perspective. It is not only wrong, but dangerously wrong in the harms it will inflict on others impacted by the decisions.

In my advocacy for animals among Christians, I've become convinced of the value of the hard work of changing hearts and minds, rather than just going for quick measurable wins. Shortcuts are tempting, but my goal is to encourage changes in understanding and attitude that will result in long-term and sustainable changes in practice. I think this is an effective strategy for change that accords with long traditions of Christian thinking about moral formation, but it's not one that's likely to score well with Effective Altruists.

The obvious question that follows from a critique of Effective Altruism in relation to giving to animal causes is what should replace it. The bad news is that there is no simple alternative Christian procedure for identifying the best options for giving. The reason there is no alternative simple system is that ethical decision-making is not simple.

A failure to recognize all the morally relevant features of a situation represents a serious misunderstanding of how people are motivated to care for animals, and therefore misjudges the effectiveness of campaigns.

If you were taking seriously norms that belong to particular ethical subjects, in this case animal subjects, and believe that respect for them means not treating them in particular ways, you might be highly motivated to participate in a project that was not affecting a huge number of animals but seemed to be treating a particular group of animals in seriously problematic ways. The campaign to change the practice of US military dogs being killed when they were no longer useful for service is a case in point. The number of animals is vanishingly small compared to farmed animals. But what led to the success of that campaign is that people were seriously convinced that something was owed to those dogs. They had done a job of work alongside human combatants, and to end their lives when they were no longer useful was a fundamental lack of respect and a lack of regard for what was owed to them. On a utilitarian basis, it made sense not to have to spend money on feeding or caring for them anymore. But what the campaign recognized, and what public support recognized, was that this was a fundamental injustice to those dogs that needed remedy. It was the recognition of them as moral subjects to whom something was owed that generated the force of the campaign, which argued it was an injustice to the dogs to not care for them in retirement. The public recognition of moral obligations toward these dogs is potentially transformative in many other contexts of animal exploitation. It is striking that it depends on recognition of a way of thinking about ethics that has no place in the utilitarian approach on which Effective Altruism is based.

I have suggested that Effective Altruism makes an attractive but false claim to provide clear, scientific, rational, objective guidance to donors about where their funds should be directed to achieve maximum effectiveness. Using Effective Altruism to direct giving can give an answer, but it is by no means clear that it's the right one. My guess is that donors are only prepared to be guided by Effective Altruism in their giving because it falsely promises to be able to resolve a complex decision with a straightforward calculation. But I doubt they would trust a numerical system to resolve other complex decisions, such as what career to pursue, what school to send a child to, or what candidate to vote for in an election. It is a similarly bad idea to use it to guide charitable giving.

An Alternative Starting Point for Thinking Ethically about Animal Philanthropy

I recognize that my position—that the whole business of making wise decisions about giving money for animals, not to mention the rest of moral decision-making, is difficult and complex—has the potential to cause donors to become discouraged. If the effectiveness of their giving is more difficult to ascertain than they had imagined, might it cause them not to give at all?

We're living in a time in which egregious wrongs are being done by humans toward animals in our use of them for food, textiles, labor, research experimentation, sport and entertainment, pets and companion animals, and through our destruction of the habitats of wild animals. Much of this mistreatment is tightly connected to egregious wrongs done to humans, too, who are disproportionately ethnic minorities, migrants, indigenous peoples, and the socioeconomically disadvantaged. And it is frequently connected to environmental destruction. None of this wrongdoing is necessary. Most of it is motivated by the narrow interests of wealthy elites who are enriching themselves at very great cost to others. It is sustainable only on the basis of the presumed consent of an under-informed public, the majority of whom would object to it if they saw clearly what was being done. All this means there are urgent reasons to work for changes that benefit animals together with humans and the planet, and an urgent need for donors who feel deeply the wrongness of what we're doing and the need for change.

Once you decide it is not easy or simple to decide how to give well, and are receptive to looking for something more grounded in the pluralistic reality of our lives, you might recognize that often the actual pressing practical question is choosing between good alternatives.

Here are three first thoughts about an alternative approach to giving to animal causes. The suggestions are informed by the ethically pluralistic Christian ethical framework I have drawn on in the course of this chapter, but I hope they are helpful whether or not one identifies with Christian ethical traditions.

First, you have more reason to trust your judgments than you assume. What motivates you to give to make things better for animals? What kinds of mistreatment of animals are you most concerned about? Of the many kinds of activities benefitting animals, which are you most drawn to? Reflect on your priorities as a starting point. Do not be tempted by claims of Effective Altruism or any other scheme to offer an objective rational basis for your decision. This is complicated stuff. It is much more complicated than any decision-making system can deal with. Your own commitments are likely to be a better initial basis for decision-making than any claimed objective system.

Second, be prepared to learn about what you do not yet see. It is easy to get the public to be concerned about big fluffy animals like pandas that they've seen in nature documentaries and who live far away. It is harder to get people interested in the farmed animals who live in warehouses not far away but hidden from view. Many of those profiting from the large-scale exploitation of animals are trying to operate under the radar so that their conduct is not the subject of public concern. Commit to reading up on how animals are being treated, and be prepared to have your priorities for giving reshaped by your widening sense of what you recognize to be most problematic in human practice toward animals, or most overlooked by current initiatives, and what might be done about it.

Third, accept that there are lots of good answers to where money should go to benefit animals. Farm animal sanctuaries, campaigns for improvements to farmed animal welfare, and the promotion of plant-based diets all merit support, together with conservation efforts to protect wild animals, care for abandoned companion animals, protests about laboratory experimentation, and so on, and so on. It is unhelpful to think that you are searching for the single most effective way your money can be used. Instead, you are looking for a good way to support a project that aligns with your priorities, is well-run, and looks like it has a good chance of achieving its goals.

8
Queer Eye on the EA Guys

pattrice jones

Imagine this: You live in an enchanted forest, but the forest is on fire. You have to decide what to do. As thickening smoke makes it harder and harder to see, your own rising panic makes it harder to think clearly. All around you, other animals are in similar predicaments. Flee? Where and with whom? Fight the fire? How and with what? The questions become even more befuddling when you try to take the interests of others into account rather than thinking only about your own skin and kin. Alarm cries and howls of pain surround you.

Out of the din and smog steps a hero with a shining sword. He once saved a whole village by giving them mosquito nets! Surely, he will know what to do.

He does know what to do, he assures you. It's merely a matter of using the magic sword to slice away superfluities and sentimentality in order to avoid wasting resources on anything other than what will bring the maximum benefit per unit of energy expended. You must be ruthless, he says. Pay no attention to the squirrel screaming in that tree! Stopping to save her will only detract you from what you need to do, which is to save the lives of five future squirrels by preventing future fires.

"You know how to do *that*?," you ask. "Yes!," he says confidently, but you notice that he mumbles the explanation and that nonhuman animals seem unmoved by his boasts. You feel uncertain too. In the midst of an emergency caused, in part, by the failure to

pattrice jones, *Queer Eye on the EA Guys* In: *The Good It Promises, The Harm It Does.* Edited by: Carol J. Adams, Alice Crary, and Lori Gruen, Oxford University Press.
DOI: 10.1093/oso/9780197655696.003.0008

think ecologically and respond multidimensionally, could there really be one best thing to do?

I asked you to imagine all of that, but in fact it's all true. You really do live in an enchanted forest. Life thrums all around you, whether or not you happen to be tuned into it. Your very life depends on trees, who converse with one another via underground networks of fungi as insects and other underground animals convert dead matter into life-giving soil nearby. The forest really is on fire, both literally and figuratively, as climate change sparks wildfires, floods, and other death-dealing catastrophes.

You really do need to decide what to do. With so many competing emergencies—did I mention the slow-moving collapse of consensus reality and the consequent upsurge in neofascism?—it can be hard to figure out how to expend your own finite time, energy, and other resources. And here comes our hero, calling himself Effective Altruism, to show you the way—if only you will agree to use his sword to slash anything and anyone he considers to be superfluous.

I want to encourage you not to follow him, even as I understand how emergencies can lead people to embrace decisive men offering simple solutions. I too long for clear answers that might be found by means of easy assessments. Alas, it is not so. Solutions that are at once frugal and significantly useful are vanishingly rare when solving even the simplest problems. The likelihood of decisively identifying such solutions for complex problems tends to be zero.

I said that you need to decide what to do, but I do too. When I jumped into activism as a queer teen in the 1970s, I already had an inkling that I was choosing to do what I was best suited and situated to do. Since the 1990s, when juggling urgent work on the AIDS emergency with long-term projects to undermine the structural inequalities that led that crisis to fall hardest upon people already disadvantaged by homophobia, racism, poverty, and disability, I have been urgently aware of an internal imperative to strategically make the most of my finite energies.

My own ways of reckoning are rather more queer than those of EA. I believe that effective activism begins with an accurate analysis of the problem to be solved, including the relationships among its causes as well as its relationship to other problems. Every problem is a *situation*, by which I mean a set of circumstances at a particular time and place. So, let's begin our assessment of EA by being sure to situate *ourselves* accurately, as great apes in the midst of unprecedented emergencies who urgently need to figure out what to do.

Here We Are

Here we are, on planet Earth, at the present moment. Of course, I can't know what will happen in the interval between the day I type these words and the day you read them, but what's happening as I write is that humans are coping with—or, rather, failing to adequately cope with—three interrelated emergencies: (1) the climate emergency, which becomes more catastrophic with each passing day; (2) a worldwide pandemic; and (3) cascading collapses in consensus reality, which make solving the other two problems seem impossible.

Who is this "we" of whom I speak? A species of great ape who, by virtue of exceptional behavioral plasticity, have dispersed across the planet, often wreaking wreckage along the way. Their ability to solve discrete problems via technology can be remarkable, but social and ecological problems tend to vex them. They fight with each other a lot, often over the sound symbols they call words and other metaphorical matters. Within their social groups, problems such as inequality or violence can persist for decades or even centuries despite steady efforts at amelioration. Until they ran out of planet, ecological problems tended to be solved by going elsewhere or sending some subset of the population elsewhere.

At present, despite decades of concerted effort by many of the most knowledgeable and politically powerful among them, they have collectively failed to make any substantial progress in confronting the escalating emergency of climate change—itself a result of lack of foresight among many of the most knowledgeable among them in past decades. Now in the midst of a pandemic that has killed millions, their experts are unable to convince enough people to take even the most self-evidently useful measures to protect themselves and their offspring. Of course, they cannot agree about what might be the cause of the breakdown of the social processes by which they used to be better able to agree about what reality might be.

Like all animals, humans are less rational than plants. Emotion, which evolved to motivate motion, infuses all of their cognitive processes. Jolted by fight-flight-freeze reactions, they can become confused. Driven by desire, they reach for happiness, safety, and each other.

A Question of Methods

We reach for each other. Because we are animals, we have wishes. We *want* to live and to be happy. Because we are social animals, we want and need to do this in the company of others, who also wish to live and to be happy. Our feeling good depends, in part, on the well-being of the social groups in which we participate. As social animals, we are physically predisposed not only to want to feel good but also to *be* good (or at least be *seen* as good), and that means we have to make some methodological decisions, whether or not we recognize them as such.

First, we must decide what we mean by "good." Next, we must decide how we will assess ourselves against that standard. So, in order to determine whether EA will be helpful to humans in the current context, we have a series of questions to answer. First, since EA is rooted in utilitarianism, we have to decide whether utilitarianism is the method of moral reckoning we want to use. If so, then we also need to decide whether EA's methods of assessing efficacy really do add up.

Methods of Moral Reckoning

I've had a number of conversations with young acolytes of EA, and those dialogues always seem to founder upon the same shoals. The problem turns out to be rooted in their presumption that the common-sense utilitarian precept of "the greatest good for the greatest number" is self-evidently the best goal of both moral and practical decision-making. Indeed, some seem not to realize that there are competing methods of moral decision-making, nor be able to imagine that there might be equally—or more!—valid ways of thinking about efficacy. In dialogue, this leads to mutual frustration: The EA acolyte cannot understand why I so stubbornly resist what seems self-evidently true to them. Meanwhile, I feel increasingly exasperated by what feels to me like discussing comparative theology with a fundamentalist.

So, let's avoid that impasse by making sure that we are working with the same ideas about the diversity of ways of thinking about ethics. While we begin from the same place at birth, as squalling bundles of sensation and emotion who feel good or bad in the physical sense and are highly motivated to win the favor of the adults upon whom we depend for survival, people can and do develop different ways of thinking about good and bad in the moral sense. Utilitarianism, as it is popularly understood, is one of those methods. It's popular because it is simple to understand, but that simplicity is also its downfall, as it falters in situations of ambiguity and when encountering the unquantifiable.

Understanding more about how moral reasoning develops may help us to situate utilitarianism as one among many options for deciding what to do. Moral reasoning skills develop over time. As youngsters we feel good or we feel bad. Being scolded or punished feels bad. In contrast, being praised or rewarded feels good. And so begins the process of association between *feeling* good or bad and *being* good or bad.

Notice that we use the same words—good, bad—for both physical sensations and moral evaluations. This association often carries over into adulthood, regardless of whether or not we consciously believe that riches are the result of virtue. You know what I mean, probably, because you've felt it yourself. Perhaps you have emerged from an aquatic workout refreshed and energized, your body brimming with endorphins, and felt not only physically well but somehow virtuous. This can go horribly wrong when people are shamed for ill-health or disability, so it's worth being aware of what seems to be a built-in bias.

Luckily, our bodies also seem to be primed to feel good when we do good. Presumably, that's because, for social animals like us, helpfulness, generosity, and even self-sacrificing altruism tend to maximize the survival of the group—and survival of the group is necessary for the survival of individuals. Whether or not I am right in that presumption, the fact remains that human toddlers appear to be predisposed to try to help those in need, and very young humans also consistently tend to both recognize and reject inequality (Callaghan and Corbit 2018; LoBue et al. 2011).

Over time, through the process of socialization, these building blocks evolve into adult methods of moral reasoning. Developmental psychologist Lawrence Kohlberg broke that process down into six stages, ranging from the most infantile (being good to avoid being punished or to get a reward), through the conventional (doing good so as to be seen as a good person or following the rules simply because they are the rules), to the ostensibly superior realm of self-chosen universal principles (Kohlberg 1964). Within that system, utilitarianism comes in at level 5—mature but falling short of what he considered to be ideal.

I don't share Kohlberg's Eurocentric esteem for abstract principles, but I do find it useful to reflect on the process by which embodied infantile experiences evolve into what often feel like purely cognitive processes of moral reasoning. Students of developmental psychology often find it enlightening to reflect on the factors that played a role in their own moral development, and I would encourage adherents of EA to do the same.

One of those factors is gender. Kohlberg did his initial research using only male subjects. Later, when his typology began to be used to assess the maturity of the moral development of individuals, girls and women consistently fell short. Carol Gilligan then performed a close analysis of the kinds of answers that were leading girls and women to be judged as immature in comparison to boys and men. She found that, probably due to the effects of socialization, girls and women tended to reason differently than boys and men, often trying to find a solution that made sure everyone's needs were met rather than focusing on abstract ideas about justice (Gilligan 1982). In Kohlberg's reckoning, this practical ethics of care was considered to be inferior to adherence to abstract principles without regard for actual consequences.

Like modern-day adherents of EA who do not *intend* for their prescriptions to disadvantage projects led by women, people of color, and people with disabilities, Kohlberg did not intend to disadvantage girls and women. Bias was built into his methods of data collection, analysis, and interpretation. At this late date in social science history, the potential for such biases to creep into research results by way of careless methodologies is well known. And so, if we do choose utilitarianism as our preferred method of moral reasoning, we still will need to be very careful in selecting methods of measuring "greatest," "good," and "number."

Methods of Measurement

I can't count the number of times I have stood at the back of an auditorium listening with escalating alarm as an animal advocate—sometimes a conman, sometimes a friend—spins numbers to "prove" that promoting veganism is *the* most effective way to help animals. Sometimes the numbers literally spin, in dramatic visual displays behind the speaker. The point is that farmed animals represent *the greatest number* of animals harmed by humans. But what about the billions harmed by climate change? Sometimes a word or phrase, such as "captive" or "under human control," erases them from consideration without explanation. More often they are simply ignored. Also unremarked is the reason why all farmed animals are lumped together. Even if we are only considering captive animals, it would be just as valid to break out the numbers by species, in which case we would learn that the number of rats used in animal experimentation is greater than the number of cows used in dairying. My point is not to suggest that those of us who work for cows ought to drop everything in order to focus on rats in labs or insects menaced by climate change, but rather to make clear the lack of transparency behind the numbers most often used by EA within animal advocacy.

It gets murkier. In presenting raw numbers of animals harmed as the reason why activists ought to focus all of their energy (and donors all of their money) on promoting veganism, EA adherents typically fail to offer any argument at all in favor of drawing that conclusion from the numbers. This is where my conversations with EA adherents have tended to go haywire, because it seems self-evident to them that of course promoting veganism will bring the *greatest good* to those large numbers. But it would be equally valid to use the same numbers to argue that the thing to do is to devote all time and energy to directly rescuing the animals *currently* captive—thereby surely ending their suffering—rather than focusing on suffering that hasn't happened yet.

But that would be impossible, you might be thinking, and that leads us to another way of imagining how to do the most for the billions of animals currently suffering in some way at the hands of humans: the theory of low-hanging fruit. Here, the argument is that it will be most effective to focus your energy on the things that you are most likely to succeed in doing. So many people tell me that they have not yet succeeded in convincing a single person to go vegan. Almost all animal advocates report extreme frustration at how hard it is to convince even the people they should be most able to persuade—friends, family, and neighbors sharing similar circumstances, identities, and worldviews —to go vegan. Multiply that difficulty by billions of people, factor in the resistance of the millions whose livelihoods depend on animal agriculture, and you've got an uphill struggle, to say the least.

In contrast, it's comparatively easy to convince people to forgo fur, circuses, and nonmedical products tested on animals. So some activists have argued that it would be most effective to organize the people (including not-yet-vegan people) who oppose those forms of cruelty in order to decisively end them. According to the kind of social psychology studies EA activists like to cite, it's easier to get people to make a big change after you've convinced them to make a small change. So, in addition to ending the suffering of all of the animals exploited in those ways (which in the case of product testing is considerable), this might make it easier to tackle animal agriculture going forward. From that point of view, the turn toward promoting veganism has been profoundly *ineffective* because it drew activists and donors away from efforts to reduce suffering that were more likely to succeed.

Another way to think about doing the most with your finite resources is to think about intensity or urgency of suffering. Of course, it is often impossible to make fine comparisons among varieties of suffering within even one species yet alone across several. Nonetheless, it is possible to imagine which animals might be experiencing the most intense suffering. This is a different way to conceptualize *greatest good* than counting numbers of animals.

I'm not arguing for either of these ways of thinking as a method of deciding how to expend one's resources (although I wouldn't be mad at anyone who chose to use them to guide their own choices about their own activities). I mention them merely as examples of the *many* different ways one might parse the well-known utilitarian precept. Different methods lead to different conclusions. It's simply not possible to say that this or that course of action will reduce the most suffering. And so the promise made by EA—we can show you how to most effectively expend your resources—is factually false.

The Fact of Fallibility

"To err is human," we say, but we don't really mean it. Even those of us who have consciously rejected human supremacy tend to see human irrationality and propensity for catastrophe as glitches rather than features of our profoundly fallible species. I have had experiences that have allowed me to glimpse myself from the vantage point of other animals, and these have tended to mute my own human hubris.

Once, while weeding my vegetable garden, I viscerally experienced myself as nearby insects might have experienced me: a giant lumbering lummox who might ruin everything at any moment. More than once, at the sanctuary I cofounded and currently direct, I have noticed ducks talking smack about me, clearly unimpressed. Once, when I was having a hard time convincing newly rescued turkeys to go inside for the night, a giant cow called Thunder all but rolled his eyes at my incompetence while gently showing me what I needed to do.

Such experiences have led me to adopt a stance toward myself and other humans that presumes we are more likely to be errant than otherwise. I also believe that we can learn from failure. So, I offer the following list of some of the many failings of EA not only as an antidote to EA's exaggerated claims, but also as an example of how far wrong we can go even when we are trying very hard to put the interests of other animals ahead of our own.

The Many Failings of EA

EA is incoherent. EA implicitly embraces care as a virtue by holding the reduction of suffering as a key value and by asserting that actual outcomes, rather than intentions or abstract principles, are what matter. On the other hand, EA encourages a kind of calculating dispassion that can lead to callousness. When EA adherents insist that the suffering of actual animals must be ignored in order to focus on reducing as much future suffering as possible, something has gone badly wrong with the reckoning.

EA encourages dishonesty. By setting themselves up as advisors to donors, acolytes of EA implicitly encourage activists to make outsized claims. In the realm of animal advocacy, EA's insistence that promoting veganism is *the* most effective way to help animals has not only drawn donors away from literally life-saving projects but also encouraged those who do promote veganism to make false claims.

EA cannot be blamed for the bad habit of claiming that vegans "save" a certain number of animals per year—that predated the rise of EA within animal advocacy. But EA has taken that hyperbolic way of talking to new heights by giving favored interventions credit for vegan conversions and then multiplying those conversions by numbers of animals ostensibly saved in order to come up with a number of animals saved per dollars spent.

The primary problem here is that, except in the unlikely event that an intervention was the first and only time that the new vegan ever encountered the idea of not eating animals, the most anyone can claim is that their intervention was the tipping point. Unless the person never met a vegan or vegetarian, never heard a relative at Thanksgiving explain why she wasn't eating turkey, never saw an anti-meat billboard or read a newspaper article about some stunt pulled by PETA, or never encountered even a single pro-vegan post on social media, the intervention didn't "make a vegan"—it simply closed the deal.

Even if an intervention had "made a vegan" all by itself, that doesn't necessarily mean that any animals were saved. As in the infamous case of "cheese-bombing" (wherein the dairy industry began loading more and more cheese into various premade products in order to make up for a decline in demand for liquid milk), animal-exploiting industries cleverly respond to any loss in their number of customers by inducing other customers to consume even more. And, of course, there is the matter of exports, as well as the common practice of governmental purchases of surplus, which means that—uh oh!—both leftists going to protests against the WTO and well-heeled lobbyists influencing the direction of trade and agriculture policies are also doing important work, even if they never directly promote veganism. Finally, even when we do succeed in reducing worldwide production of a particular animal product, we're not so much saving lives as we are preventing animals from being born into lives of captivity, suffering, and slaughter.

EA lacks rigor. Drawing inferences from data is a process of inductive reasoning that requires both honesty and rigor. Here are a few of the steps that EA usually skips:

- Considering how the framing of the research question may limit what can be concluded from the findings.
- Determining and disclosing the ways that the sample population may not be reflective of the population at large.
- Reporting any possible ways that the study's methods might have skewed the results.
- Imagining and fairly discussing alternative explanations for the findings.
- Putting the findings in the context of similar studies, especially those that have contradictory results.
- Answering Roberta Flack's perennial question, "But compared to what?"

EA can't cope with complexity. The situations in which a single variable can be meaningfully affected by a simple intervention are vanishingly rare in the real world, which consists of nested and interlocking systems of physical and social relationships. EA makes no effort to utilize the advanced mathematics used for systems analysis, preferring instead to use the numerical results of simple calculations (e.g., dollars per vegan, number of animals saved per vegan, very basic statistical analysis of survey data, etc.) to signal that something scientific is happening. Real data scientists know it's not that simple.

EA can't cope with ambiguity. Every day at a sanctuary is a case study in decision-making under conditions of uncertainty. People like me thus must become adept at making decisions in situations that are both ethically and factually ambiguous. Often, these are literally life-or-death decisions. From this standpoint, I can report that the rudimentary mathematics of utilitarianism are not at all utile. Even in simple situations, any quest to decisively identify the greatest good for the greatest number often proves impossible.

EA harms worthwhile endeavors. In planning this essay, I found myself asking, "Is EA evil?" By evil, I meant both immoral and malevolent. You may protest: Whether or not we agree on what is or is not moral, surely Effective Altruists do not mean to cause harm, and are therefore not malevolent actors. But is that true? First, doesn't EA itself insist that outcomes matter more than intentions? Secondly, has not EA set out deliberately to disadvantage some people who are trying to do good works? EA acolytes might argue that they seek only to advantage certain individuals and organizations by steering money and volunteers to them. But the very premise of the project rests on the fact that such resources are not infinite. More for those favored by EA equals less for everybody else. By seeking to advantage some charitable endeavors, EA seeks to disadvantage others. I can attest that EA has succeeded in that aim, causing both fiscal and emotional distress to activists engaged in truly useful work.

EA promotes callousness. It seems ludicrous that I should have to say this, but we will not awaken human hearts to animal suffering by becoming callous to that suffering ourselves. Yet EA insists that we harden our hearts to elephants in zoos—because there aren't that many of them. We must set aside any sympathy we may feel for ferrets or chimpanzees in order to focus our efforts on fishes and chickens. The loneliness, confusion, and terror felt by the last remaining members of an endangered species? Irrelevant! Unless saving that species will lead to lots of happiness for lots of other animals, we cannot waste our energy on them, and we must swallow our sorrow in order to be able to be as ruthlessly calculating as possible if we want to maximize our impact.

EA both enacts and encourages egotism. Everybody wants to do the most with what they have. But EA makes the self-centered wish to have an outsized impact the center of its project. Within animal advocacy, EA acolytes have done this by setting themselves up as the arbiters of the efficacy of the activism of others. Far from the muck and blood of animal rescue, they opine that such work is worthless while crediting themselves with saving thousands of lives. The hubris of this is so extreme that it seems I must be engaging in hyperbole myself by typing those words. But I have seen their websites with my own eyes and gaped at the numbers of animals some EA advocates have claimed to have saved—without ever once using their own muscles to actually save a single animal. Which brings us to classism and other forms of bias.

EA colludes with social injustice. Despite the fact that the majority of animal advocates, including the majority of organization founders, are women, the preponderance of organizations initially deemed highly effective by the self-appointed Animal Charity Evaluators (ACE) were founded by men. Until quite recently, ACE failed to acknowledge good work by even a single organization led by people of color. Even as of this writing, one of the four "Top Charities" highlighted on the ACE website was founded by a known perpetrator of sexual assault, and another was founded by a male friend of his who helped him evade consequences for many years. Coincidence? Maybe. A more likely explanation is that the sexism and racism are built into the evaluation criteria by favoring the kinds of simple and quantifiable single-issue tactics favored by white men and disadvantaging the kind of ecological, multi-issue, complex strategies favored by those who are committed to feminism and antiracism. Whatever the explanation, here is the fact: EA within animal advocacy has consistently steered funds toward organizations run by white men, thereby compounding the structural difficulties in raising funds faced by organizations run by people of color as well as by women-led organizations.

EA has vitiated the animal advocacy movement. In the process of further disadvantaging already disadvantaged activists, EA has discouraged all but the narrow sliver of potential tactics that it deems effective, thereby profoundly narrowing the strategic vitality of the movement. Long-term, multifaceted strategic plans often include actions that may not lead to any visible short-term gains. EA insists that such tactics not be funded, thereby forcing projects in need of funds to adopt a short-sighted approach focused only on near-term quantifiable results.

EA treats animals like objects. It is maybe not surprising that the overall effect of EA on animal advocacy has been to lessen overall efficacy, since EA does not and never has accorded due respect to animals, ironically treating them like numbers or tools in the same way that animal-exploiting industries do. Lately, some Effective Altruists have begun to concede that it might not be a complete waste of resources to care for animals at sanctuaries—but only if it can be proved that doing so promotes veganism. Within this is an implicit demand that sanctuary residents be put on display in some way that might motivate people to go vegan.

Queering EA

I have a confession to make: I sometimes give workshops on "Effective Activism," secretly hoping to divert interest in EA into more truthful and useful directions. In so doing, I bring my own queer history of tenant organizing, antiracist education, feminism, LGBTQ liberation, and animal rescue to students and grass-roots activists struggling with the question that leads many to EA (and which began this essay): In a world of harm and hurt of so many kinds, how can I be most useful?

I don't often quote Mao, but when I do, it's "Let a hundred flowers bloom." What I believe, based on extensive study (and practice!) of activism, is that significant social change is most likely to occur when a variety of people approach the same problem from a variety of angles using a variety of tactics—ideally, although not necessarily, in cooperation with each other. That makes sense: Big problems tend to be complex situations in which social, cultural, economic, and material factors all play causal roles. It will rarely be the case that a single intervention can make a big difference. Even comparatively smaller problems, such as the need for a simple change at the local level, will be easier to solve if agitators are marching in the streets while insiders are simultaneously proposing practical solutions behind closed doors.

And so I encourage workshop attendees to first inventory themselves—their skills, interests, standpoints, talents, and personality characteristics—and then look for existing projects that might need exactly those things. That's just one of many ways of doing the most: looking for the *best match* between what you have to give and the many different things that need to be done.

To go about that from another angle, I suggest choosing a problem and then listing all of the things that somebody should be doing about it right now. Which of those things aren't yet being done? Are you in a position to do one of them? Do that.

What is now VINE Sanctuary began when Miriam Jones and I found a chicken in a roadside ditch in the part of the United States where factory farming of chickens was invented and perfected. Right away, we saw that we were in a position, simply by converting a garage to a coop, to save lives. And so that's what we did. Twenty-plus years later, our multispecies community includes more than seven hundred nonhuman survivors of the war against animals, some of whom liberated themselves and others who were rescued by humans, often at significant risk to themselves. Along the way, we've seized every opportunity to do things we happened to be uniquely situated to do, from figuring out how to rehabilitate roosters used in cockfighting to helping LGBTQ people see the linkages between queer and animal liberation. We know we're not the only ones doing this work. We trust others to do the things they are better positioned to do.

Sometimes adherents of EA suppose that its opponents don't care about efficacy. For me, nothing could be further from the truth. It's just that my ideas about efficacy are more ecological, which is to say more queer. Animals are exploited (not to mention displaced and polluted) in a multiplicity of ways in a multiplicity of places, each of which is shaped by both material (physical) and social (economic and cultural) forces. That being the case, there's literally "something for everyone" in terms of things that need to be done.

We need people who are gifted with words or images to write and design leaflets, posters, websites, and other media. We need researchers with the patience to spend hours finding and compiling information. We need natural scientists to develop new and improved alternatives to vivisection, and we need computer scientists to implement those that involve computer modeling. We need botanists, economists, and agronomists to work out how to transition regions now dependent on animal agriculture to plant-based agricultural economies. We need lobbyists to convince state and federal government to quit subsidizing big "meat" and "dairy" and to pour that money into organic vegetable, fruit, nut, and grain cultivation instead. We need courageous people to engage in direct action of all kinds, whether it be undercover investigations or just walking in the woods with a booming radio during hunting season. And we always need artists and other creative thinkers to come up with new ways of awakening empathy, sparking imagination, and inspiring action.

An artist-activist in another country once told me that the multispecies community here at VINE Sanctuary exists in her mind as a source of inspiration, even though she's never visited. I want a way of thinking about efficacy that recognizes the value of that.

Four More Catastrophes Happened While I Edited This Essay

Seven to twelve additional calamities probably will have happened by the time you read these words. The world really is on fire. And here we are, together, unsure. Whatever we do or don't do will become part of the circumstances in which we and others exist. We must choose.

If you want to use utilitarianism to guide your own choices about what you will do to respond to the emergencies, that's fine by me. You do you. If tallying lives saved per unit of energy expended will motivate you to do your utmost, I will hand you a pad and pencil. All that I ask is that you refrain from deploying your own resources to try to stop others from doing good works.

If some people are doing something that seems less than maximally worthwhile to you, then don't join them. Do something else. Wish them well, understanding that they might see or know things of which you are unaware. Hope that you're wrong and that whatever they're doing will make a big difference. Especially now, when there is so much need and so little certainty, we all need to reject the injurious intolerance of Effective Altruism in favor of a more modest and generous mode of relating to the projects of others.

Remember the trees? Communicating with each other underground, exhaling the oxygen you need to breathe? They might have projects too. They need allies, not heroes, and so do the squirrels who (like us) depend on them for everything. If becoming more aware of the limits of human reason and more aware of perspectives other than your own leads you to become better able to perceive and work within the power of the larger-than-human world, then—by my reckoning—the time you spent reading this essay will have been effectively spent.

References

Callaghan, Tara, and John Corbit. (2018). "Early Prosocial Development across Cultures." *Current Opinion in Psychology* 20 (April): 102–106.

Gilligan, Carol. (1982). *In a Different Voice: Psychological Theory and Women's Development*. Cambridge, MA: Harvard University Press.

Kohlberg, Lawrence. (1964). "Development of Moral Character and Moral Ideology." In *Review of Child Development Research*, Volume 1, edited by Lois Wladis Hoffman and Martin L. Hoffman, 383–432. Thousand Oaks, CA: Russell Sage Foundation.

LoBue, Vanessa, Tracy Nishida, Cynthia Chiong, Judy S. DeLoache, and Jonathan Haidt. (2011). "When Getting Something Good Is Bad: Even Three-Year-Olds React to Inequality." *Social Development* 20 (1): 154–170.

9

A Feminist Ethics of Care Critique of Effective Altruism

Carol J. Adams

Permit me to introduce to you *rational-economic man,* a construct that drives capitalism. The rational-economic man is presumed to rationally analyze available outcomes and make decisions according to his rational self-interest. He is a utilitarian in economic theory, although mutually disinterested (which means doing what will promote his own interests without harming others' interests, supposedly). He is not going to actively promote the "most good"—the market is allegedly going to do that.

In this essay, I will explore the troubling legacy of rational-economic man, including the emergence of Effective Altruism (EA). I will consider the dismissal of caring and sympathy as valid sources of knowledge and motivation, and how this has influenced and limited the animal advocacy movement. I will show that the application of EA principles to evaluating animal advocacy organizations has done harm, and I will show how this is related to the issue of privilege. I offer a *feminist ethics of care* as an alternative philosophical approach that recognizes the importance, and inevitability, of situated decision-making.

Carol J. Adams, *A Feminist Ethics of Care Critique of Effective Altruism* In: *The Good It Promises, The Harm It Does.* Edited by: Carol J. Adams, Alice Crary, and Lori Gruen, Oxford University Press.
© Oxford University Press 2023. DOI: 10.1093/oso/9780197655696.003.0009

Rational Economic Man

While Genevieve Lloyd's *The Man of Reason* finds the association of the rational with masculinity going "back to the Greek founding fathers of rationality as we know it" (Lloyd 1993, 19), it was the economist Adam Smith who named "rational-economic man" in the eighteenth century. This naming seems to acknowledge the changes in Western society that accompanied the Scientific Revolution. Carolyn Merchant's classic book *The Death of Nature: Women, Ecology and the Scientific Revolution* describes how:

> Between 1500 and 1700 an incredible transformation took place. . . . Living animate nature died, while dead inanimate money was endowed with life. Increasingly capital and the market would assume the organic attributes of growth, strength, activity, pregnancy, weakness, decay, and collapse obscuring and mystifying the new underlying social relation of production and reproduction that make economic growth and progress possible. Nature, women, blacks, and wage laborers were set on a path toward a new status as "natural" and human resources for the modern world system. Perhaps the ultimate irony in these transformations was the new name given them: rationality. (Merchant 1980, 258)

An alternative view existed. Josephine Donovan (2007) identifies a Western philosophical tradition of sympathy that existed alongside the prizing of abstract reasoning as the preferred philosophical approach. Notably, Adam Smith also advocated sympathy (or empathy, as we now talk of it).

The rational-economic man construct gained ascendancy because it is authorized by and mirrors historic patriarchal fictions about gender: that a gender binary exists (man/woman), and that it is related to other binaries (rational/emotional; objective/subjective; abstraction/particularity). The gender binary, in its facilitation of other binaries, interacts with and is influenced by race, class, and disability status.

The division between reason and emotion, or rationality and sentiment, is—like the gender binary—a fiction, but acceptance of these binaries as accurate representations of reality has distorted philosophy. The result is a valuing of disembodied rationality and the devaluing of caring. Lori Gruen and I point out how abstract reasoning is also "the capacity that historically has served to justify the hierarchical ranking of beings" (Adams and Gruen 2022b, 10), establishing a legitimization of the oppression of those ranked lower, including the other animals. With the construction of political and moral discussion as rational and "manly," the role of "womanly" sentiment was seen as an impediment rather than an aid to engaging with the problem of what humans are doing to other animals.

The Abjection of Caring and Sympathy

Many people come to the animal advocacy movement motivated by sympathy. Peter Singer's *Animal Liberation: A New Ethics for Our Treatment of Animals* often influences people because of the sentiments evoked while reading his precise descriptions of animals' experience of oppression. But a central necessity for Singer was to dethrone sentiment and offer what he considered a rational approach to the issue of animals' status.

In fact, he saw sentiment, not abstract reasoning, as a major impediment to advocating for animals. He writes that "the portrayal of those who protest against cruelty to animals as sentimental, emotional, 'animal-lovers' has had the effect of excluding the entire issue of our treatment of nonhumans from serious political and moral discussion" (Singer 1975, ix). According to Singer, the problem is not the philosophical exclusion of sympathy, nor the misogyny that has caused the animal movement to be seen as feminized and abjected. It's the use of this disregarded sentiment and sentimentality to discuss animals' status—or its portrayal as such—that has caused the treatment of other animals to be neglected in serious political and moral discussions. He assumes that if sympathy, or its reception, is the problem, it cannot be the solution.

The book's subtitle suggests Singer offers a *new* approach, but instead he proposed a preexisting ethic—utilitarianism. By the time in the mid-1970s that Singer, and other philosophers writing in the tradition of the rational-economic man, brought their attention to the other animals, caring had been privatized and was seen as "weak" politically. In *The Way We Never Were*, Stephanie Coontz argues that the "the liberal theory of human and political citizenship did not merely leave women out. It worked precisely because it was applied exclusively to half the population. Emotion and compassion could be disregarded in the political and economic realms only if women were assigned these traits in the personal realm" (2016, 63).

If the rational-economic man acting in the public realm was not supposed to suggest sympathy motivated him, then such an expression of sympathy would be seen as de-masculinizing the person. Abjecting the "caring" person who identifies as a man polices the person straying from the norms of the gender binary, reinforces these symbolic gender norms as legitimate, and silences approaches other than the chosen, masculine-identified one. In national security discourse, for instance, Carol Cohn found that "there are things professionals simply will not *say* in groups, options they simply will not argue, nor write about, because they know that to do so is to brand themselves as wimps" (1993, 234).

When animal rights activists who identify as men are called "wimps," "sissies," or "pussies," or when jokes are made about whether they have a vagina, we see with clarity the functioning of patriarchal gender norms that assume fixed identities, and that body parts fix those identities. But, as Cohn points out, labels such as *wimp* or *pussy* foreclose a whole range of inputs and options from deliberation (235).

The tragedy of the animal liberation movement is that it contains the possibility of challenging rational-economic man's dismissal of sentiment. However, both personal and political reasons existed for those who identify as men to be disciplined in rejecting sentiment, and these influenced the ascendancy of solutions that adhered to the outlook of the rational-economic man.

The Rational-Economic Man's Solution to Abjection

How to discuss the status of animals when the public sphere distrusts sentiment and sympathy? Several responses subsequent to the publication of Singer's book appeared, all hewing to his rejection of sentiment (though, notably, not necessarily embracing utilitarianism). These include the following:

1. Differentiate yourself from those who went before, those whom you see as having feminized the animal advocacy movement, those "little old ladies in tennis shoes," according to a stereotype frequently evoked. After the March for the Animals in Washington in 1990, an activist explained to the *Washington Post* that "[p]eople used to think of animal rights supporters as a bunch of crazy old ladies in tennis shoes" (Harriston and Thomas-Lester 1990). In 2008, Wayne Pacelle, then executive director of the Humane Society of the United States (HSUS), declared to the *New York Times* that the animal activist movement was no longer made up of "little old ladies with sneakers" (Jones 2008).
2. Hypermasculinize the environment. The leaders who were white and identified as men telegraphed the message that their arrival in the animal rights movement was

going to correct the decades in which those stereotyped old ladies held back the movement. They did this through a hypermasculinization of the movement in which ideas of manhood were situated centrally within their activism. EA advocate Nick Cooney encouraged activists to "portray vegetarian men as very masculine in order to counter stereotypes" (2013, 157). The hypermasculinization nurtured a self-reinforcing dynamic of a "bro" culture (self-named by the participants) that emphasized centralized leadership over grass-roots movements, and in which these leaders adopted over-the-top-praise schemes for each other. By fetishizing authority, they diminished the role of entire teams that make significant events possible. These "bros" were and are banded together not only through institutional association, but through financial, personal, and affective ties (some calling each other "brothers of different mothers"). They became a class of elites, offering each other jobs, praise, book promotions, and investments in new not-for-profit and for-profit companies. Protected via their leadership position, some of these "bros" were also serial sexual exploiters, whose decision to exploit others was supported or overlooked by some of the other "bros" (Gunther 2018a).[1]

3. Clarify you don't personally care. The rational-economic man who is an animal advocate often makes a very public disowning of sympathy. Most recently, EA advocate and executive director of the Good Food Institute (GFI) Bruce Friedrich told the New York Times in 2019, "I didn't have a particular affinity for animals . . . I have a very German, logic-based temperament, for better and worse." This differentiated him from some activists because "he is not motivated by any

[1] On sexual exploitation in the animal rights movement see Anonymous 2018, Paquette 2018, Bosman et al. 2018, Kullgren 2018, and Gunther.

sentimental or emotional attachment to other creatures" (Popper 2019).

4. Keep the focus tight—on animals.

As the animal rights movement evolved, tension existed between those who argued "We must stay focused on animals, and we don't want to get distracted from that," and those who argued that the situation of nonhumans was related to the oppressive systems of gender, race, class, and ableism. HSUS executive director Pacelle asserted that the movement should imitate the National Rifle Association, urging activists to vote for legislators based only on the issue of whether they supported legislation on behalf of animals, regardless of any regressive positions on other issues.

The dominance of the "keep-the-focus-tight" rational approach distorted the entire field of action within animal rights. For approximately fifteen years or so, this small group of "bros" elevated their expertise as they settled upon the approach of gradual reform and working with the animal agriculture industry.[2]

Keep-the-focus-tight was also the response to those who came forward with reports of sexual exploitation. They were told the leaders who were identified as sexual exploiters contributed so much to the animal movement that this outweighed their unethical behavior. Survivors heard statements such as "'He just has a soft spot for women' or 'If it doesn't involve animal abuse, I don't want to hear about it' or 'You are lucky he likes you!'" (Anonymous 2018). Organizations pushed survivors and their advocates out, guaranteeing their silence through nondisclosure agreements (NDAs). A reversal of culpability evolved: survivors and advocates speaking out were seen as "hurting" the cause, not those who chose to be sexually abusive.

[2] See Chapter 4 in this volume, "Animal Advocacy's Stockholm Syndrome," by DeCoriolis, et al.

Effective Altruism and Privilege

For Effective Altruism (EA), the rational-economic man is the actor. According to EA, this actor is allowed to be individualistic and interested in maximizing the individual good. The individual actor, in doing what is in their best interest, also does good. This disregards how social reality is transformed.[3] EA also dismisses what was privatized by the culture and undervalued by the philosophical sources it relies upon: sympathy. Instead, it offers a new remedy for sympathy: the mechanism of metrics. The move to metrics is a pessimistic move that assumes the transformation of consciousness does not work or is too much work while perpetuating a keep-the-focus-narrow approach. It focuses on solutions without considering contexts.

Advocacy of Effective Altruism arises from the same privilege that undergirded the assumption that a small group of "bros" could determine the priorities and tactics of the animal rights movement. It is a privilege that permits a limited few to assume their social reality is an accurate basis upon which to draw conclusions and make recommendations about how to challenge animals' oppression. Yet activists, funders, and theorists are located somewhere, and that location influences their experience of oppressions.

In a controversial essay, the utilitarian philosophers Jeff Sebo and Peter Singer forwarded Effective Altruism as the best approach to animal activism. They do not surprise in terms of hewing to the utilitarian calculus at the heart of Effective Altruism. What *is* surprising is their response to a frequent criticism brought against advocates of EA—that "the history and demographics of the animal rights and EA movements might be limiting their perspective" (Sebo and Singer 2018, 41). They concede that "many EAAs

[3] See Chapter 15 in this volume, "Effective Altruism and the Reified Mind," by John Sanbonmatsu.

[effective animal activists] have relatively privileged identities and backgrounds" (42). This acknowledgment is notable because it suggests *context* might matter.

But they do nothing further with this insight except to ask, but not answer, "Does that [privilege] make them [EAs] more trusting of current social, political, and economic systems than they should be?" (42). They appear unequipped to examine what privilege consists of, the kinds of benefits it confers upon them as individuals, *how* their privilege influences their advocacy of EA, their choice of animal activist groups to recommend, or whether and how the privilege has resulted in harms to others. They presume that we share their social reality, or that the way they are situated is how we are—or wish to be—situated, or that how they are situated is unproblematic in their advocacy of their chosen approach. They seem unable to state how their own privilege allows them to situate themselves within a moral theory that instructs that their specific embodiment and any privileges that accompany it—their being members of the dominant gender, race, nationality, and class—are not relevant to considering the moral impact of actions. To do otherwise would require naming not just their whiteness, but their identifying as men; their Western, analytical philosophical training; and their location as professors at elite universities.

Sebo and Singer flourish as academics in a white supremacist patriarchal society because others, including people of color and those who identify as women, are pushed down. If Sebo and Singer were to name *why* they flourish—the privilege granted them within a white supremacist patriarchy—they might be prompted to examine how white supremacy and patriarchy structure animal exploitation.[4] This, in turn, would pull the rug out from their

[4] I won't rehearse here the many arguments showing how white supremacy and Western ideas about manhood inform oppressive relationships with animals. See Adams 1990, Deckha 2010, Harper 2010, Kim 2015, Ko and Ko 2017, Kheel 2008, Luke 2007, McJetters 2016, and the many ecofeminist writings appearing in and cited in Adams and Gruen 2022a.

arguments for Effective Altruism. Perhaps their trust arises not from a rational perspective but an irrational identification with and allegiance to the hegemonic norms and institutions of a white supremacist, patriarchal, capitalist system that continues to benefit them. This trust also prevents them from comprehending what their privilege allows them to do—to define social reality in a way that excludes the social reality of others.

The privileges Sebo and Singer fail to address are the same kinds of privilege that allowed sexual perpetrators in the animal advocacy movement to continue to operate without accountability for their individual actions. Uninterrogated privilege functions to reinforce a "keep the focus on what we deem is important" approach, accepting the status quo, and condemning those excluded from this privilege to be acted upon rather than actors. Absent an analysis of the entitlements of privilege, Sebo and Singer instead offer a new variation on the keep-the-focus-tight argument. They write that "people can disagree about strategy with other members of the same movement." But, they lecture, we should do so "at the appropriate occasions," and we should not "become so consumed by these differences that instead of focusing most of their limited resources on the exploiters of animals, they focus most of these resources attacking those who are, from a broader perspective, allies in the struggle for animal liberation" (44). That their statement hews to similar principles articulated by sexual exploiters and their enablers about not making public the sexual violations that took place by "allies in the struggle" is eerie and disappointing.

I know Sebo and Singer are not explicitly saying perpetrators are not a problem in the movement, nor that they should not be held accountable, but their failure to see any of the issues they discuss, especially this one, from a position other than the one their privilege grants, allows for a facile plea for unity, ignorant of what they are really asking.

Situated Decision-Making

At some point, substituting a mathematical formula for the harder work of living situated ethical lives in the midst of a variety of relationships with different demands will fail to provide an answer for the kinds of decisions that we have to make. But the rational-economic man is unwilling to acknowledge that how one is situated can legitimately be determinative in ethical decision-making, becoming a mythical nowhere man. What happens when a nowhere man finds themselves, by virtue of their social location, situated? For instance, one's mother has Alzheimer's disease and needs help. The vulnerability of someone with dementia is a very particular kind of vulnerability. There is no cookie-cutter template for the progression of the disease; it can erode one's memory and cognitive abilities slowly or more quickly; and environmental influences such as the presence of loved ones, or music, or being included in conversations and games can help, at times, hold the disease at bay.

In 1999, Singer was asked how someone who helped to shape the current theory and practice of utilitarianism explained financially supporting his mother when she needed caregivers because she had Alzheimer's disease. He replied it was "probably not the best use you could make of my money." He then suggested it did offer "employment for a number of people who find something worthwhile in what they're doing" (Specter 1999, 55). In that reply we hear the voice of rational-economic man reducing caregiving to a worthwhile employment opportunity.

Singer's predicament arises from the tendency of liberal capitalism to polarize "people's thinking between 'objective,' universal principles in the public sphere and 'subjective,' particularistic relationships in the private one" (Coontz [1992] 2016, 65). The feminist ethics of care challenges this division; Singer's philosophy arose from it.

The rational-economic man is unable to say, "I care about my mother and have a responsibility to help her as she suffers this disabling illness." Or to discuss the reciprocal nature of care: "My mother cared for me, and I want to return that care now." To respond thusly he would have to acknowledge the validity of the ethics of care in influencing decision-making about financial resources. Nothing in his philosophical system would allow for this; the very legitimate reason he could offer would not only expose the false logic of utilitarianism but also expose him to the abjection rational-economic man offers to those expressing sympathy. Singer chooses to be seen as inconsistent rather than caring because it is less problematic for his utilitarianism. If there is a reason to devote extra resources to one individual because of the responsibilities of care, why not other individuals needing care, including a specific animal at an animal sanctuary? Lost is the understanding that one's participation in the process of caregiving might transform or challenge one's epistemological presumptions, that others—besides those who already know caregiving is worthwhile—have something to benefit from the act of providing care (Adams 2017).

Singer might even have argued in the terms of economic exchange: "I owed my mother something." Or offered a critique of the healthcare system that requires he use his money: "A capitalist for-profit system has privatized healthcare, and my funds were needed to remedy this systematic problem in this particular case." But, having committed himself to a nowhere-man epistemological stance, he cannot budge from that.

The next year, he added that "he is not the only person who is involved in making decisions about his mother (he has a sister)" (Bailey 2000). Here, he reveals what Lori Gruen has called "entangled empathy." Gruen explains that we find ourselves situated in ways that our agency is constructed by the relationships we are already in. It was this entanglement that influenced his decision-making. Bailey, the interviewer, writes, "He did say that if he were solely responsible, his mother might not be alive today." Building on Gruen's theory of entangled empathy, it could be suggested that we deliberately entangle ourselves with people who make the decisions *we need them to make on our behalf.*

Twenty years later, again given the opportunity to articulate a defense of why—contrary to utilitarianism—some of his money went to support his mother, Singer answered, "The money that my sister and I spent on my mother, and keeping her comfortable, at that level—there could have been better things you could have done with that." To which I say, the money that my father, sisters, and I spent on our mother, who also suffered from Alzheimer's, and keeping her comfortable, stimulated, and among people whom she knew loved her, until her very last breath, was worth every cent (Adams 2017). Within utilitarianism, Singer could find nowhere to stand and say something similar. When challenged about finding himself situated in a very specific social location, the nowhere man finds his theory not only fails him in providing an explanation but *condemns him for what he did.* Another ethical theory existed that could help him out of this quandary: the feminist ethics of care. But acknowledging that would require him to reject utilitarianism. So he passes off caring to his sister, that other decision-maker, and justifies inconsistency with appeals to entanglement.

Effective Altruism and the Animal Advocacy Movement

During the first two decades of the twenty-first century—those years that intervened between the *New Yorker*'s first and second discussions with Singer about paying for caregivers for his mother—Effective Altruism as an approach to charitable giving, with Singer as a key formulator, took hold. The animal advocacy movement may have been especially susceptible to the promises of EA, because Singer is also seen as "father" of the animal liberation movement. The push to keep-the-the-focus-tight in the animal advocacy movement also made it receptive to EA. Dependent on theorists like Singer for its approach, EA is unequipped to work with an understanding of interconnected and overlapping oppressions.

The Problem of Animal Charity Evaluators

The creation of Animal Charity Evaluators (ACE) initiated a tremendously successful incursion by Effective Altruism into the animal advocacy movement. The same privilege Sebo and Singer leave unexamined allowed ACE to become a philanthropic gatekeeper.

The idea at its heart is that groups they evaluated highly would then be recommended to funders of all amounts. While ACE is an evolving institution—at this writing ten years old—its records reveal how the perspective of rational-economic man framed its methodology and presumptions. To begin with, it established the principle of not funding sanctuaries, sites of care. Meanwhile, during those early years, the organizations led by the "bros" and organized according to their principles, including the Humane Society of the United States, received high marks.

For the first several years, their evaluation practices involved reaching out to leadership, thus smoothly transferring the movement's bro culture to EA's emphasis on metrics and success. Once ACE started calling non-leadership individuals, "we were surprised and disheartened to learn about the extent of the sexual harassment problem within the movement, the many repeated allegations against the same individuals, and the apparent toleration of harassment *at multiple organizations*" (McAuley 2018 [my emphasis]). EA failed to consider that an "effective" organization might maximize (that is, exploit) the labor of nondominant humans "for the animals," while suppressing accountability for its leadership. Leaders accused of sexual exploitation who managed to suppress the information from becoming public continued to be seen as effective according to EA standards.

The importance of these early years is that those decisions became self-perpetuating; they helped to cement the importance of certain groups, including HSUS, Mercy for Animals, the Humane League, and, once it was founded, the Good Food Institute, over other groups. These groups benefitted greatly from increased visibility that insured success in raising funds. Their successes gave these organizations a fast track to performing in ways that EA would construe as favorable. This also catalyzed a consolidation of power in terms of determining the direction of the movement. During those early years, the emergence of EA principles in the animal rights movement made it harder to hold abusers accountable because their behavior was not considered in evaluating "effective" animal organizations. What EA deemed "effective" became "successful," reshaping reality.

It took several years after it was founded before ACE decided to consider workplace culture during its evaluation process. After information about the sexually exploitative behavior of Wayne Pacelle and Paul Shapiro, president and a vice president, respectively, of the Humane Society of the United States (HSUS), became public in early 2018, ACE found itself in a difficult position. The news about HSUS, an organization consistently rated highly by ACE, was so problematic they had to backtrack on their recommendations. At first, they simply removed praise of Shapiro and Pacelle. But then they decided "to formally rescind our 2016 Standout recommendation of The Humane Society of the United States' Farm Animal Protection Campaign" (Smith 2018).

One source told Marc Gunther that ACE had been "slow to look into allegations of sexual harassment in the movement, and timid in its response" (Gunther 2018d). Their executive director, Jon Bockman, referred to " 'the rumblings we've heard for a while' about issues of gender bias and sexual harassment in the movement" (Gunther 2018a). Just how long "for a while" continued without being attended to and why it took so long to respond is left unsaid.

ACE enhanced HSUS's success at fundraising by giving them the highest marks in their system. It could do so only by ignoring the social reality of the organization. This is how they contributed to the harm of exploitation while making it harder to fix the problem.

In the announcement that they were rescinding their recommendation of HSUS, Allison Smith admitted, "We've already seen evidence that these issues [of sexual harassment] have interfered with HSUS' work, probably for at least several years." Still, Smith emphasized, "we take seriously our commitment to provide evidence-based recommendations, and we prefer to conduct our own comprehensive investigations before making any important decisions" (Smith 2018).

But what is a "comprehensive investigation"? How is an investigation comprehensive when it did not uncover something that had been going on for years? Apparently, until then, they talked with very few people from an organization and focused on the leadership: "In the case of HSUS FAPC [Farm Animal Protection Campaign], the information provided by our contact focused primarily on leaders' reputations for effectiveness within the animal advocacy movement and on general organizational policies" (Smith 2018). Measuring effectiveness won't and can't uncover sexual exploiters. The proof of this is that their reviews did not uncover this information, even with the egregious cases of Shapiro and Pacelle that ACE acknowledges had been going on for a few years.

Those whose behavior as individuals was unethical continued to be rewarded at the institutional level for their success. This begat more success and recommendations for funding, then the following year brought further recognition in terms of positive rankings for their "effectiveness," begetting further success in an unending self-fulfilling cycle that perpetuated social oppression.

Once ACE began to take workplace culture into consideration, the bro-led organizations, as well as others, came under scrutiny. In 2021, ACE rescinded its recommendation of the Good Food Institute (GFI) because of its workplace culture. GFI had been highly rated for the first five years of its existence. ACE explained why they did not recommend GFI: "[W]e received several reports from current and former staff that alleged both retaliation and fear of retaliation by GFI's top leadership for voicing disagreements at the organization. We found the reports to be reliable and substantial enough in their severity to not continue recommending GFI in 2021" (Spurgeon 2021). Here was another case of a workplace culture issue difficult to uncover: staff fear of retaliation.

One might wonder how GFI rocketed to top charity ranking in its first year, 2016. That was the year EA advocates Nick Cooney and Bruce Friedrich founded it, with funds and support from ACE-endorsed Mercy for Animals. Being a new organization, it did not have a track record of accomplishments, nor could it, as a new organization, demonstrate "cost-effectiveness"—criteria ACE used for evaluating groups. Nathan Harrison (2016) raised this issue at the time of GFI's early funding, "The question should not be whether GFI has potential, but whether, as ACE claims, the evaluation process was rigorous. It obviously wasn't."

Harrison (2017) also suggested that ACE was "strongly biased toward a few nonprofit organizations, especially those in which [Nick] Cooney is involved." ACE responded with an inadequate defense: "[W]e do not feel that any of our staff members' relationship with Nick Cooney was so strong as to concern us. It's true that we regularly correspond with Nick, but not more often that we correspond with leadership from other animal advocacy groups" (Bockman 2016). Bockman, however, misstated Cooney's role with GFI, saying he was "on the board" of GFI, rather than, more accurately, "co-founder" and "board chairman."

Steve Hindi also raised the issue about ACE's claim to objectivity given its relationship with Nick Cooney:

> The most controversial problem for Animal Charity Evaluators (ACE) is that you have consistently placed organizations listed as "Top Charities" that are tied directly to Nick Cooney. This

> includes *The Humane League* (Founder, Board Chair) and *Mercy For Animals* (Executive Vice-President). More recently, *The Good Food Institute* (Co-Founder and Board Chair) was made a top charity. . . . You claim to deal with science, so you must understand that the odds that out of thousands of active animal protection organizations, only those where Mr. Cooney either directly profits from or is a board member are given Top Charity status is astronomical. It simply is not reasonable that there has been such an outcome. (Hindi 2017)

ACE became the institutional fulfillment of Effective Altruism in the animal movement, and in this illustrated EA's discrepancies, inconsistencies, and errors. They didn't apply their metrics to the world, they applied their metrics to their friends. They also blunted the radical arm of the movement in their endorsement of those organizations who directed the gradual reform wing of the movement.

How the Rational-Economic Man Got It Wrong

In "Ecofeminist Footings," Lori Gruen and I argue that perpetuating a reason/sympathy dualism and valuing an arid and limited understanding of reason is "a profound obstacle to making the world more just and compassionate" (Adams and Gruen 2022b, 10). The reason/sympathy dualism results in a misvaluing of the beings not seen as "rational," reinforcing the traditional hierarchical ranking of beings. It perpetuates a misunderstanding of how reason and emotion are co-constituted. Good ethical decision-making requires both.

The construct of rational-economic man obscures real structures of inequality and keeps the actual experiences of those who are oppressed at arm's length, while failing to account for ways that oppressions interconnect. This limited understanding of social reality may exacerbate the situation of the other animals. Why do we want to reproduce this construct with all the problems it causes for nondominant beings?

When effectiveness is considered through capitalist logic, animal rights campaigns are evaluated based on how likely they are to "save or spare multiple animals per dollars spent" (Sebo and Singer 2018, 39) thus reifying the commodity system of animal agriculture that considers animals' lives only within a cost-benefit system. It is telling that such a numerical approach ignores the role of pregnancy in animal agriculture, the kinds of suffering that attend frequent forced pregnancies (captivity and frequent prolapsed uteri for pigs; yearly pregnancies and forced separation of mother and child for cows), and the number of animals brought into existence through forced pregnancies. When EA counts pregnant animals as "one" in their number crunching, they commit both a mathematical and conceptual error.

The rational-economic man lurks behind and within the problems with Effective Altruism. It is to this capitalist, disembodied, mutually disinterested "nowhere man" that Effective Altruism appeals. Effective Altruism innovated new ways to protect a social reality arising from privilege and power, while degrading care and sympathy-based forms of activism. It was the case, as Shakespeare has Hamlet say, that there were more things in heaven and earth than are dreamt of in their philosophy.[5]

References

Adams, Carol J. (1990). *The Sexual Politics of Meat: A Feminist-Vegetarian Critical Theory*. New York: Continuum.

[5] Thanks to Nancy Adams, Bruce Buchanan, Alice Crary, Merv Fry, Lori Gruen, Krista Hiddema, pattrice jones, and John Sanbonmatsu who discussed these ideas with me and made important suggestions.

Adams, Carol J. (2017). "Towards a Philosophy of Care through Care." *Critical Inquiry* 43 (4): 765–789.

Adams, Carol J., and Lori Gruen. (2022a). *Ecofeminism: Feminist Intersections with Other Animals and the Earth*. 2nd ed. New York and London: Bloomsbury.

Adams, Carol J., and Lori Gruen. (2022b). "Ecofeminist Footings." In *Ecofeminism: Feminist Intersections with Other Animals and the Earth*, edited by Carol J. Adams and Lori Gruen., 2nd ed, 1–43. New York and London: Bloomsbury.

Anonymous. (2018). "#TimesUpAR: Guest Blog." In Carol J. Adams (blog). https://caroljadams.com/carol-adams-blog/timesupar.

Bailey, Ronald. (2000). "The Pursuit of Happiness, Peter Singer Interviewed by Ronald Bailey." *Reason*, December 2000. https://reason.com/2000/12/01/the-pursuit-of-happiness-peter/.

Bockman, Jon. (2016). "Responses to Common Critiques." Walnut, CA: Animal Charity Evaluators, December 21. https://animalcharityevaluators.org/blog/responses-to-common-critiques/#c.

Bosman, Julie, Matt Stevens, and Jonah Engel Bromwich. (2018). "Humane Society C.E.O. Resigns amid Sexual Harassment Allegations." *New York Times*, February 2. https://www.nytimes.com/2018/02/02/us/humane-society-ceo-sexual-harassment-.html.

Cohn, Carol. (1993). "Wars, Wimps, and Women: Talking Gender and Thinking War." In *Gendering War Talk*, edited by Miriam Cooke and Angela Wooltacott, 227–246. Princeton: Princeton University Press.

Cooney Nick. (2013). *Veganomics: The Surprising Science on What Motivates Vegetarians, from the Breakfast Table to the Bedroom*. New York: Lantern Books.

Coontz, Stephanie. ([1992] 2016). *The Way We Never Were: American Families and the Nostalgia Trap*. New York: Basic Books.

Deckha, Maneesha. (2010). "The Subhuman as a Cultural Agent of Violence." *Journal of Critical Animal Studies* 8 (3): 28–51.

Donovan, Josephine. ([1994] 2007). "Attention to Suffering: Sympathy as a Basis for Ethical Treatment of Animals (1994)." In *The Feminist Care Tradition in Animal Ethics*, edited by Josephine Donovan and Carol J. Adams, 174–197. New York: Columbia University Press.

Gruen, Lori. (2015). *Entangled Empathy: An Alternative Ethic for Our Relationships*. New York: Lantern Media.

Gunther, Marc. (2018a). "The Animal Welfare Movement's #Metoo Problem." Nonprofit Chronicles, January 26. https://nonprofitchronicles.com/2018/01/26/the-animal-welfare-movements-metoo-problem/.

Gunther, Marc. (2018b). "Humane Society CEO under Investigation for Sexual Relationship with Employee." *Chronicle of Philanthropy*., January 25. https://www.philanthropy.com/article/Humane-Society-CEO-Under/242342?cid=cpfd_home.

Gunther, Marc. (2018c). "The Latest: #Metoo and The Animal Welfare Movement." *Nonprofit Chronicles*, January 31. https://nonprofitchronicles.com/2018/01/31/the-latest-metoo-and-the-animal-welfare-movement/.

Gunther, Marc. (2018d). "Times Up: Wayne Pacelle." *Nonprofit Chronicles*, February 2. https://nonprofitchronicles.com/2018/02/02/times-up-wayne-pacelle-is-out-as-ceo-of-the-humane-society/.

Harper, A. Breeze. (2010). *Sistah Vegan: Black Female Vegans Speak on Food, Identity, Health, and Society*. New York: Lantern Books.

Harrison, Nathan. (2016). "Re-evaluating Animal Charity Evaluators: A Response to Jon Bockman." *Medium*, December 22. https://medium.com/@harrisonnathan/re-evaluating-animal-charity-evaluators-c164231406f7.

Harrison, Nathan. (2017). "The Problems with Animal Charity Evaluators, in Brief." *Medium*, August. 11. https://medium.com/@harrisonnathan?p=cd56b8cb5908.

Harriston, Keith, and Avis Thomas-Ledster. (1990). "Animal Rights Activists Boo Moderation." *Washington Post*, June 11. https://www.washingtonpost.com/archive/local/1990/06/11/animal-rights-activists-boo-moderation/2521598b-3051-4ca0-a11d-77f44f386c06/.

Hindi, Steve. (2017). "ACE Letter 1." Geneva, IL: SHARK, June 1. https://sharkonline.org/index.php/charity-cops/1731-ACE-Letter.

Jones, Maggie. (2008). "The Barnyard Strategist." *New York Times Magazine*, October 26. https://www.nytimes.com/2008/10/26/magazine/26animal-t.html.

Kheel, Marti. (2008). *Nature Ethics: An Ecofeminist Perspective*. Lanham, MD: Rowman & Littlefield.

Kim, Claire Jean. (2015). *Dangerous Crossings: Race, Species, and Nature in a Multicultural Age*. New York: Cambridge University Press.

Ko, Aph, and Syl Ko. (2017). *Aphro-ism: Essays on Pop Culture, Feminism, and Black Veganism from Two Sisters*. Brooklyn, NY: Lantern Books.

Kullgren, Ian. (2018). "Female Employees Allege Culture of Sexual Harassment at Humane Society." *Politico*, January 30. https://www.politico.com/magazine/story/2018/01/30/humane-society-sexual-harassment-allegations-investigation-216553/.

Lloyd, Genevieve. ([1984] 1993). *The Man of Reason: "Male" and "Female" in Western Philosophy*. London: Routledge.

Luke, Brian. (2007). *Brutal: Manhood and the Exploitation of Animals*. Champagne: University of Illinois Press.

McAuley, Roisin. (2018). "Sexual Harassment within the Animal Advocacy Movement." Walnut, CA: Animal Charity Evaluators, January 19. https://animalcharityevaluators.org/blog/sexual-harassment-within-the-animal-advocacy-movement/.

McJetters, Christopher Sebastian. (2016). "Exploring Connections between Black Liberation & Animal Liberation." https://www.youtube.com/watch?v=H_ebX07H4wM.

Merchant, Carolyn. (1980). *The Death of Nature: Women, Ecology, and the Scientific Revolution*. New York: Harper & Row.

Paquette, Danielle. (2018). "Humane Society CEO Is Subject of Sexual Harassment Complaints from Three Women, according to Internal Investigation." *Washington Post,* January 29. https://www.washingtonpost.com/business/economy/humane-society-ceo-is-subject-of-sexual-harassment-complaints-from-three-women-according-to-internal-investigation/2018/01/29/12c8961e-053b-11e8-94e8-e8b8600ade23_story.html

Popper, Nathaniel. (2019). "This Animal Activist Used to Get in Your Face. Now He's Going After Your Palate." *New York Times*, March 12. https://www.nytimes.com/2019/03/12/technology/bruce-friedrich-animal-activist.html.

Sebo, Jeff, and Peter Singer. (2018). "Activism." In *Critical Terms for Animal Studies,* edited by Lori Gruen, 33–46. Chicago: University of Chicago Press.

Singer, Peter. (1975). *Animal Liberation: A New Ethics for Our Treatment of Animals*. New York: New York Review of Books.

Smith, Allison. (2016). "Our Recommendations of the Good Food Institute and New Harvest." Walnut, CA: Animal Charity Evaluators, December 21. https://animalcharityevaluators.org/blog/our-recommendations-of-good-food-institute-and-new-harvest/.

Smith, Allison. (2018). "ACE's Decision to Rescind Our Recommendation of the Humane Society of the United States' Farm Animal Protection Campaign." Walnut, CA: Animal Charity Evaluators, February 2. https://animalcharityevaluators.org/blog/decision-to-rescind-our-recommendation-of-hsus-fapc/

Specter, Michael. (1999). "The Dangerous Philosopher." *New Yorker,* September 6, 46–55.

Spurgeon, Jamie. (2021). "Changes to Recommendation Status of the Albert Schweitzer Foundation and the Good Food Institute." Walnut, CA: Animal Charity Evaluators, December 10. https://animalcharityevaluators.org/blog/changes-to-recommendation-status-of-the-albert-schweitzer-foundation-and-the-good-food-institute/.

10

The Empty Promises of Cultured Meat

Elan Abrell

The world's first burger made from cow flesh grown outside the body of a cow debuted on August 5, 2013, in a televised tasting demonstration (Stephens et al. 2016; Wurgaft 2019). Created by the Dutch biologist Mark Post as a proof of concept for the use of cell culture techniques to grow edible meat without having to slaughter animals to harvest it, this $325,000 prototype cultured-meat burger consisted of salt, breadcrumbs, egg powder (for flavor), red beet juice and saffron (for color), and, most importantly, cow muscle cells cultured from cells collected by biopsy from a live cow. Extensive media coverage and intense industry hype have helped gin up billions of dollars of investment in over fifty cultured-meat start-ups around the world (Crosser et al. 2019), while also stoking excitement and hope among many activists in vegan and animal protection circles that cultured-meat products could help facilitate a rapid transition away from the global food system's increasing reliance on animal farming. Guided by cell-culturing techniques and technology originally developed in the biomedical industry, scientists and engineers at these start-ups endeavor to use cell cultivation tanks, or bioreactors, filled with a liquid growth medium to culture edible tissue from animal cells.[1] This tissue is referred to

[1] The most effective and commonly used growth medium is fetal bovine serum (FBS), a byproduct of cattle slaughter collected from fetuses of pregnant cows. Some companies claim to be working on non-animal-derived alternatives, and cultured-meat production

Elan Abrell, *The Empty Promises of Cultured Meat* In: *The Good It Promises, The Harm It Does*. Edited by: Carol J. Adams, Alice Crary, and Lori Gruen, Oxford University Press.
DOI: 10.1093/oso/9780197655696.003.0010

variously as cultured meat, cultivated meat, cell-based meat, clean meat, and in vitro meat by advocates and developers, and most commonly as lab-grown meat by journalists and headline writers.

Given the media hype, it's easy to understand why an average consumer might mistakenly think that cultured-meat products are already available at the local grocery store or gastropub, especially with the rising popularity and wide availability of new meatless burgers like the Impossible Burger and Beyond Burger that closely replicate the gustatory experience of eating burgers made of animal flesh (Adams 2018). However, other than a small number of portions of chicken made of "cultured cells bound together with plant protein, meat glue and fat" sold by one cultured-meat start-up at well below cost through a delivery service in Singapore (McCormick 2021), cultured meat is not available for sale anywhere in the world. And it is not clear when or even if it ever will be.

On September 22, 2021, an extensive article by Joel Fassler in *The Counter* (Fassler 2021) detailed the significant technological challenges to successfully producing cultured meat products at market scale. This article sent a ripple of doubt through the community of advocates, entrepreneurs, and investors in the cultured-meat space. Reporting on a thorough techno-economic analysis commissioned by Open Philanthropy and produced by chemical engineer David Humbird (2020), the article made a compelling argument that it will not be financially or technologically possible to produce commercial cultured products that could compete with conventional meat products at any significant scale in the next decade. In fact, Humbird's analysis predicts that at a production scale of 100 kilotons of cultured meat per year, the lowest prices the industry would be capable of achieving for a single-cell slurry product consisting of "a mix of 30 percent animal cells and

that continued to rely on FBS would in fact be too cost-prohibitive to ever be scalable. For decades the biomedical industry has been unable to develop a suitable alternative, and as of 2021 it remains a technical challenge that aspiring cultured-meat producers have yet to overcome.

70 percent water, suitable only for ground-meat-style products like burgers and nuggets," would be $17 per pound at the point of production, or—with current markups—$40 per pound at the grocery store and $100 per quarter-pounder at a restaurant (Fassler 2021). Whole cut products like steaks and filets would be even more expensive. While critics raised questions about assumptions and predictions in the report, it made clear that without a substantial increase in funding for research and development of cultured-meat technology and infrastructure well beyond the over $3 billion from private equity and corporate investments in cultured-meat start-ups since 2013, this industry will not be able to make a meaningful shift in consumption practices by 2030.

Over the last five years, though, the nonprofit organization the Good Food Institute (GFI) has championed investment in cultured-meat technology as an essential strategy in ending industrial animal agriculture, driven by the assumption that the vast majority of consumers are unwilling to give up animal products and that the only effective way to change the negative impacts of their dietary practices is to replace those products with less harmful but equally desirable alternatives, like cultured meat. As GFI director and cofounder Bruce Friedrich put it, "What I've come to understand is that the vast majority of people are not going to radically change their diet on the basis of really anything other than price, taste, and convenience" (EA Global 2018). Assuming this is true, for the sake of argument, while also noting that many activists disagree and that evidence supporting this claim is far from conclusive, a crucial question arises: What do we do if we can't offer them cheap, tasty, convenient alternatives? If dietary intransigence is taken for granted, and a market-based, consumption-oriented strategy of product-substitution is prioritized as the most (or only) effective means of ending animal farming, what happens if the necessary innovations to realize that strategy never materialize? If we're going to channel all our resources into a deus ex machina techno-fix to the many harms of industrial animal agriculture, then we must be absolutely sure that technology can deliver on its promise. And based on all available evidence, we simply have no such guarantee with cultured-meat technology. Informed by four years of ethnographic research on cellular agriculture as well as personal experience working in the cellular agriculture nonprofit world, including nine months as a senior regulatory specialist at GFI, I argue in this chapter that the prioritization of market solutions over all others by channeling funding and resources into the development of the cultured-meat industry undermines equally important or even potentially more effective responses to this dilemma.

For the last several years, cultured meat has often been positioned in many—though not all—Effective Altruist circles as a grand solution to the problem of animal agriculture and its disastrous impacts on animal well-being, human health, and the environment. Even without everyone in the Effective Altruist community supporting this position, it has largely reconfigured the financial and strategic landscape of vegan dietary activism, channeling significant funding streams away from vegan outreach and other strategies and into advocacy for and investment in venture capitalist tech start-ups seeking to replace conventional animal agriculture with cellular agriculture, a strategy strongly endorsed and encouraged by the Effective Altruist organization Animal Charity Evaluators (ACE) through its support for GFI. ACE rates animal charities for effectiveness in order to guide donations to the ones it deems most effective. According to the principles listed on its website, the organization is committed to promoting welfare: "All other morally relevant factors being equal, the best action is the one that is expected to result in the highest net welfare" (Animal Charity Evaluators 2021b). And it claims to base its determination of best actions on "empirical evidence and logical reasoning" (Animal Charity Evaluators 2021b). ACE estimates that it has influenced donations of over $10 million to its ranked charities in 2020 (and over $24 million from 2014 to 2019) (Animal Charity Evaluators 2021a). GFI was ranked by ACE as a "Top Charity"—its highest designation—five times from 2016 to 2020. As a result, ACE estimates that it directly or indirectly influenced $3,192,965.87 in donations to GFI in 2020 (Animal Charity Evaluators 2021a).

Since its founding, ACE has had a significant impact on the strategies of the animal protection movement. It is common knowledge across organizations in the movement that a "Top" or even "Standout" ranking by ACE can have a significantly beneficial impact on fundraising, and this has spurred many conversations across organizations about whether and how to shift mission foci to fare better in ACE assessments. But ACE's support of GFI's advocacy for tech start-ups in the nascent cultured-meat industry presents a cautionary case for the dangers of a market-based approach to activism, as well as the dangers of allowing one perspective on activism to dominate the funding structure of an entire movement.

In 2018, the same year ACE awarded GFI "Top Charity" status for the third year in a row, the Intergovernmental Panel on Climate Change (IPCC) released its sobering special report on the impending catastrophic impacts of global warming above 1.5°C on the planet, emphasizing that the dire necessity of keeping global warming below the 1.5°C threshold "would require rapid and far-reaching transitions in energy, land, urban and infrastructure (including transport and buildings), and industrial systems" (Animal Charity Evaluators 2021a). Among the necessary transitions in land use was a significant reduction in pastureland used for animal farming. A more recent report by the IPCC released in the summer of 2021 has moved up the timeline for reaching 1.5°C based on current emissions, predicting that we could reach this threshold by 2034 if we do not drastically cut emissions before then (McGrath 2021).

With the global livestock sector estimated to contribute at least 14.5 percent of all anthropogenic greenhouse gas emissions, including 44 percent of anthropogenic methane emissions and 53 percent of anthropogenic nitrous oxide emissions of total emissions in the agricultural sector—two of the most potent drivers of global warming—it is imperative that a drastic reduction in farmed animals is part of any strategy for reducing emissions over the next few years. And yet even a separate, more optimistic techno-economic analysis commissioned and touted by GFI does not predict the kind of rapid technological advancement that would be needed to solve the animal agriculture problem in the necessary time frame to avoid the impending catastrophes of a post-1.5°C future. According to the GFI-commissioned analysis produced by the research consulting firm CE Delft—which GFI states "is the only publicly available techno-economic analysis we are aware of that uses actual data submitted by companies producing cultivated meat and its inputs, shared under NDA directly with the CE Delft team" (Fassler 2021)—the hypothetical mega-facilities required to produce cost-competitive cultured-meat products by 2030 would produce 10,000 metric tons (22 million pounds) of cultured meat per year. But as Fassler explains:

> For context, that volume would represent more than 10 percent of the entire domestic market for plant-based meat alternatives (currently about 200 million pounds per year in the US, according to industry advocates). And yet 22 million pounds of cultured protein, held up against the output of the conventional meat industry, barely registers. It's only about .0002, or one-fiftieth of one percent, of the 100 billion pounds of meat produced in the US each year. JBS's Greeley, Colorado beef-packing plant, which can process more than 5,000 head of cattle a day, can produce that amount of market-ready meat in a single week. . . . [A]t a projected cost of $450 million, GFI's facility might not come any cheaper than a large conventional slaughterhouse. With hundreds of production bioreactors installed, the scope of high-grade equipment would be staggering. According to one estimate, the entire biopharmaceutical industry today boasts roughly 6,300

> cubic meters in bioreactor volume. . . . The single, hypothetical facility described by GFI would require nearly a third of that, just to make a sliver of the nation's meat. (Fassler 2021)

Put simply, even if the CE Delft study was correct that price parity with conventionally produced meat could be achieved by 2030, and even if all the necessary innovations were achieved to make that hypothetical possibility a reality, the amount of cost-competitive meat being cultured by the end of the decade would not be anywhere near enough to supplant conventional meat products as rapidly as is necessary to cut down agricultural emissions in time, especially not through a strategy based entirely on market substitution.

To be clear, this is not intended as a critique of the potential benefits of cultured-meat innovations. As GFI readily points out, animal agriculture also poses significant threats to biodiversity, human health, food scarcity and inequality, and, most significantly, animal well-being, given the tens of billions of land animals and over a trillion aquatic animals abused and killed every year for human consumption. Although I share some of the other concerns raised by critics of cultured meat (Clean Meat Hoax, n.d.a), I think the overwhelming magnitude of the many harms caused by animal agriculture outweigh the potential harms of cultured meat. And I agree with GFI's position that both analyses underscore the argument for investing public funds in the advancement of meat-culturing technology so that it can at least help reduce the size of the conventional animal agriculture industry (starting with, for example, the tens of billions of dollars currently used to subsidize conventional animal agriculture) (Bomkamp et al. 2022), as other advocates of cultured meat have also argued. But by making it clear that the billions of dollars in private funding already invested in cultured-meat start-ups are insufficient to develop the industry quickly enough, these reports also suggest that channeling funding streams that could be supporting other activist strategies targeted at ending animal agriculture into cultured-meat advocacy is actively impeding progress, highlighting the clear dangers in casting venture capital as our best hope for a systemic solution.

Given the dire necessity of reducing global greenhouse gas emissions to zero by the end of the decade to stave off severe climate-related impacts, and the impossibility of any future cultured-meat industry replacing conventional animal agriculture to any significant degree within that time frame, the strategy of focusing on investment in this technology as the main solution to the problem of animal agriculture has amounted to a disastrous hijacking of both financial and activist resources to make a small group of venture capitalists richer in the short term—indeed, one might be hard-pressed to distinguish this strategy from other manifestations of disaster capitalism (Klein 2007). At the same time, it makes a self-fulfilling prophecy out of the claim that activism can never convert people away from omnivory by dangling an empty promise before consumers that they can have their meat and eat it too. We may have lost precious years of more effective activism on this over-hyped cell rush, and perhaps the ultimate lesson to be taken from this debacle is that (to paraphrase Audre Lorde) a capital-based activism strategy will never dismantle the capitalist system of animal exploitation that is rapidly destroying our planet.

The cultured-meat case also has implications more broadly for Effective Altruism and its prescriptive agenda for maximizing the positive social and environmental impact of financial resources. The Effective Altruist model of charitable investment reinforces the same capitalist system that produced the current mega-crisis of mutually intensifying ecological and social disasters in the first place, making one wonder if it essentially functions, whether by design or mere epiphenomenon, as a sort of activism Ponzi scheme, funneling wealth and resources into market- and consumption-oriented "solutions" that actually serve to sustain the political-economic system that drives the very crises it seeks to solve. Given that one of the fundamental contradictions of capitalism is its insatiable drive toward infinite growth within a natural system of very finite resources, there are many reasons to be very skeptical of a plan designed to ameliorate the many injustices and inequities of our capitalist system while relying on the structures of that system for its success. As Dinesh Wadiwel argues, "The tactical challenge for animal advocates today is not what products we should buy, or which entrepreneurs we should pin our hopes to, but how we can build a democratic movement that can radically transform societies. By definition, such a movement is not going to be driven by venture capitalists" (Clean Meat Hoax, n.d.b). Friedrich has said that GFI's goal is to take ethical considerations off the table (Illing 2016), but when it comes to the existential threats animal agriculture poses to all beings, ethics is the whole meal. Retreating from ethics will not lead us to salvation in capitalism. Animal agriculture is a world historical atrocity that should have ended long ago, and now its intensifying contribution to climate change has made that moral imperative even stronger.

The promises of cultured meat have proven to be illusory, assuring benefits it can't deliver, at least not in time. Perhaps the obsessive desire to have our meat and eat it too as reflected in the cultured-meat replacement strategy is a sign that we have transitioned from the Climate Denial stage of eco-grief to the Climate Bargaining stage, but this misguided meat triumphalism only serves to delay the necessary recognition of the pressing need for the radical and immediate transformation of our food system. We are not just at the precipice of climate disaster, we are Wile E. Coyote spinning our legs in midair while we dangle over the abyss. It is long past time to transition to Climate Acceptance, which means collectively coming to terms with the fact that we must do everything we can to end animal agriculture now, long before cultured-meat technology will be capable of replacing it.

References

Adams, Carol J. (2018). *Burger*. New York: Bloomsbury.

Animal Charity Evaluators. (2021a). "Giving Metrics Report." Walnut, CA: Animal Charity Evaluators, August. https://animalcharityevaluators.org/about/impact/giving-metrics/.

Animal Charity Evaluators. (2021b). "The Philosophical Foundation of Our Work." Walnut, CA: Animal Charity Evaluators, May. https://animalcharityevaluators.org/about/background/our-philosophy/.

Bomkamp, Claire, Liz Specht, and Elliot Swartz. (2022). "Preliminary Review of Technical Assumptions within the Humbird Analysis." Washington, DC: Good Food Institute. https://gfi.org/cultivated/preliminary-review-of-humbird-report/.

Clean Meat Hoax. (n.d.a). "The Capitalist Free Market Has Always Betrayed Animals—and It's Doing It Again." https://www.cleanmeat-hoax.com/capitalism-isnt-going-to-save-the-animals.html.

Clean Meat Hoax. (n.d.b). "Leading Voices within the Animal Advocacy Movement *Speak Out* against Clean Meat." https://www.cleanmeat-hoax.com/animal-advocates-speak-out.html.

Crosser, Nate, Caroline Bushnell, Elizabeth Derbes, Bruce Friedrich, Jen Lamy, Nicole Manu, and Elliot Swartz. (2019). *2019 State of the Industry Report: Cultivated Meat*. Washington, DC: Good Food Institute.

EA Global. (2018). "Bruce Friedrich: From Agitator to Innovator." *Effective Altruism Forum*, June 8. https://forum.effectivealtruism.org/posts/sDRhddmEJYczdWEEg/bruce-friedrich-from-agitator-to-innovator.

Fassler, Joe. (2021). "Lab-Grown Meat Is Supposed to Be Inevitable. The Science Tells a Different Story." *The Counter*, September 22. https://thecounter.org/lab-grown-cultivated-meat-cost-at-scale/.

Humbird, David. (2020). "Scale-Up Economics for Cultured Meat: Techno-Economic Analysis and Due Diligence." Prepared for Open Philanthropy, San Francisco, California. Revision 3: December 29. engrXiv (Engineering Archive). https://engrxiv.org/preprint/view/1438.

Illing, Sean. (2016). "Ethical Arguments Won't End Factory Farming. Technology Might." *Vox*, October 11. https://www.vox.com/conversations/2016/10/11/13225532/bruce-friedrich-good-food-institute-meat-factory-farming-vegetarianism.

Klein, Naomi. (2007). *The Shock Doctrine: The Rise of Disaster Capitalism*. New York: Henry Holt.

McCormick, Erin. (2021). "Eat Just Is Racing to Put 'No-Kill Meat' on Your Plate. Is It Too Good to Be True?" *Guardian*, June 16. https://www.theguardian.com/food/2021/jun/16/eat-just-no-kill-meat-chicken-josh-tetrick.

McGrath, Matt. (2021). "Climate Change: IPCC Report Is 'Code Red for Humanity.'" BBC News, August 9. https://www.bbc.com/news/science-environment-58130705.

Stephens, Neil, and Martin Ruivenkamp. (2016). "Promise and Ontological Ambiguity in the In Vitro Meat Imagescape: From Laboratory Myotubes to the Cultured Burger." *Science as Culture* 25 (3): 327–355.

Wurgaft, Benjamin Aldes. (2019). *Meat Planet: Artificial Flesh and the Future of Food*. Berkeley: University of California Press.

11

How "Alternative Proteins" Create a Private Solution to a Public Problem

Michele Simon

I have spent my 25+year career in the food movement, and for most of that time, the animal rights movement included an educational model for promoting veganism to address the entrenched problems caused by factory farming. In recent years, some animal rights activists have morphed into venture capitalists, marketing experts, and "food tech" entrepreneurs. Backed by millions of dollars from donors and investors alike, these activists have pushed aside all other solutions in favor of their approach that emphasizes the development and promotion of "alternative proteins."

This "free market" wing of the vegan movement has isolated itself by promoting a private capital solution to the myriad problems caused by factory farming, thus moving these problems out of the public policy arena. At the center of this theory of change is a relatively new organization, the Good Food Institute (GFI).

GFI is an organization with deep ties to Effective Altruism: cofounded by a leading promulgator of Effective Altruism in the animal advocacy movement (Nick Cooney), led by an EA proponent (Bruce Friedrich), endorsed by the EA-based Animal Charity Evaluators (ACE), and supported by funders influenced by EA principles. GFI ensures its chief spokespeople, including Friedrich,

Michele Simon, *How "Alternative Proteins" Create a Private Solution to a Public Problem* In: *The Good It Promises, The Harm It Does*. Edited by: Carol J. Adams, Alice Crary, and Lori Gruen, Oxford University Press.

DOI: 10.1093/oso/9780197655696.003.0011

speak at EA events.[1] Friedrich himself has provided an autobiographical statement at an EA event tracing his evolution to adopting EA principles (Friedrich 2018). EA funders recommend funding GFI. RC Forward (n.d.)—the Canadian aggregate giving website—emphasizes evidence-based funding to effective organizations and notes that "GFI was born out of the Effective Altruism movement." (RC Forward, n.d.).Animal Welfare Funds (n.d.) identifies GFI as a charity to which donations can be made directly (see also EA Funds, n.d.). Open Philanthropy Project (OPP), another major donor committed to the principles of Effective Altruism, is a major donor to the Good Food Institute, donating $6.5 million in 2021 alone (Open Philanthropy 2022). The Effective Altruism Forum website carries an update from ACE about its top charities, including GFI. For 2021, however, ACE removed GFI from its list of "recommended charities" (Spurgeon 2021).

The Good Food Institute's agenda is to end factory farming by working to "accelerate alternative protein innovation." GFI asserts that "by making meat from plants and cultivating meat from cells, we can modernize meat production" (Good Food Institute 2022b). One can find this language about *alternative proteins* on the pages of its supporters as well: under a heading "Supporting research on and advocacy for alternative proteins" the Animal Welfare Fund (n.d.) reports that "finding culinary alternatives to meat is an important step toward reducing the suffering of animals raised for food," and they link to the web page of the Good Food Institute.

How the Phrase "Alternative Proteins" is Harmful

The phrase "alternative proteins" does not originate with the animal welfare world. The phrase came from the business world to

[1] He has been a featured speaker numerous times at the annual EA Global events for 2016, 2017, and 2019 as well (see Friedrich 2016, 2017a, 2017b, 2017c, 2018, 2019; see also Weston 2020 and Parr 2020).

describe a variety of alternatives to meat as a source of protein, which could include plants but also insects (Bashi et al. 2019). The phrase has become part of the vernacular in the past few years, as a catch-all to include both plant-based and technology-created alternatives to meat from animals. GFI heavily promotes "alternative proteins." Yet the phrase is not used by those working in the food movement: advocates, authors, organizations, and community groups that have been at the forefront of working toward a better food system for many decades no longer refer to alternative proteins.

The food writer Alicia Kennedy (2020) dives into the history of food to make the point that "meat alternatives" are nothing new, imploring us to remember "that plant-based protein has existed since long before the term 'plant-based.'" She is referring to centuries' old traditional foods like tofu and tempeh, but she could have included falafels, seitan, and food traditions offering rice and beans, or rice and pulses. By adopting the new term "alternative proteins," GFI and its associates ignore this long history and play into the hands of the meat lobby, which has always emphasized "protein." But protein is not a food; it's a macronutrient. We eat foods that contain nutrients.

A quick primer: Food consists of three macronutrients: carbohydrates, fats, and protein. We need all three to thrive; one is not more or less important than the other. From either a nutrition or food systems perspective, a focus on one nutrient makes no sense. By narrowing the conversation so that it is about nutrients instead of food, one can ignore how food is made and who controls the means of production. This reduces whole animals even more than the meat industry. Animals become meat, meat becomes protein, and animals become protein delivery systems.

Plants also contain protein, but through a concerted public relations campaign that included disseminating free "nutritional" material to elementary schools, the meat industry convinced people to believe that protein comes only from animals, so meat must be essential to the diet. Not only does "alternative protein" perpetuate this meat-industry-propagated nutrition misinformation, but focusing on protein sells plant-based sources of protein short: whole foods such as beans come with health-promoting fiber (never found in animal products), as well as important phytonutrients.

Adopting and promoting the use of the term "protein" reveals a simplistic understanding of food as a source of nutrition and betrays a more holistic view of both how food and the food system operate. In addition, the term "alternative protein" deliberately blurs the line between foods made with ingredients grown in the ground and those that are technology-driven—entirely new categories of food. Why is this important? Because from a food systems perspective, where food comes from and how it is grown matters. Who is in control of the food also matters.

The "alternative protein" model is only about displacing farmed animals "by any means necessary," ignoring work by the food movement. For example, one of the reasons for advocating for a plant-based diet is that growing a diversity of plants can enrich the soil in ways that growing monocrops (such as soy and corn for animal feed) does not (Fuhrer 2021). The reasons for caring about soil health are myriad, but when it comes to humans, soil health is what helps give food its nutrients (Brevik et al. 2017). On the flip side, when soil is contaminated, it has detrimental impacts on human health. Humans need soil to be healthy and thrive.

Promoting technology as a solution further separates how we eat from agriculture, when for decades the food movement has been trying to get the public to understand and appreciate the deep connections to the food on our plate and where it comes from.

What Happened to Caring about Health?

As GFI advocates for a food system that deliberately creates replicas of animal foods, it does so without attending to the potential negative consequences to human health. The original, women-centered, plant-based foods movement emphasized cooking whole foods to promote optimum health. It also focused on the simplicity of real food versus processed food, grown sustainably in ways that can solve many societal problems at once. Promoting only highly processed meat alternatives and technology-driven replicas of meat ignores the public health consequences of the Standard American Diet. Almost every major public health organization has acknowledged that a diet based on whole, plant-based foods is superior to one based on animal products, junk food, and other highly processed foods (Aramark and the American Heart Association 2019).

While working on the 2015 US Dietary Guidelines for Americans, as part of a larger campaign devoted to "eat less meat," the advocates I worked with were especially focused on the science behind reducing "red meat" to decrease harm to human health, because that's what multiple studies have shown (Harvard Medical School 2012). In addition, from an environmental standpoint, "red meat" production (raising cattle) is a major contributor to greenhouse gas emissions (Magill 2016).

For the first time, the 2015 US Dietary Guidelines Committee was willing to consider environmental sustainability, so we had a unique opportunity to talk about the problems of conventional beef production, from both an environmental and a health perspective. Despite this obvious strategic advantage, Bruce Friedrich (prior to the launch of GFI) called to tell me to stop calling for "less red meat," because he feared that would only result in consumers shifting to eating chicken, which would "harm more animals," since more chickens are killed for food then cows. (This reflected the evolving position of EA proponents to focus on those foods that they claim will save the greatest number of animals.)

It was surprising that Friedrich urged me to ignore the nutritional studies that show that eating too much red meat is especially harmful to health, and that he was asking a long-time public health advocate to do so. I declined. But I realized this meant that a coalition of advocates for "less meat" could not count on some animal groups that had adopted this EA approach. We had enough on our hands dealing with the meat lobby (which was ultimately successful) but now we had infighting too.

Working with "Big Meat" Won't Work

EA proponents work with "Big Meat," regardless of these companies' notoriously unethical business practices. Just four massive meat packing companies control over 80 percent of the US beef supply. These companies are Tyson, Cargill, JBS, and National Beef (Ostlind 2011). Smithfield Foods is the largest pork producer, while Tyson is the largest chicken company (Souza 2020). Of these companies, all except National Beef also sell plant-based meats, something that the Good Food Institute and many others in the EA world celebrate. From their perspective, companies that jump on the plant-based meat bandwagon would allegedly be making a "monumental shift" away from factory-farmed meat, becoming "protein companies" instead (Balk 2021).

In a podcast interview on the EA program *80,000 Hours*, Lewis Bollard, the program officer for the Open Philanthropy Project's Farmed Animal Protection grants, lists as "progress" the fact that major food corporations such as Nestle and Tyson are getting into the plant-based alternatives game. He is especially happy about the Impossible Whopper® at Burger King, given it's in several countries, not just the US (Harris and Wilbin 2021).

In another example, GFI's Zac Weston made this announcement at EA Global 2020:

> One other exciting development we've seen on the retail side is that the world's largest food and meat companies have begun launching their own lines of plant-based and blended plant and

> animal protein products—companies that are known more for their animal meat products than for anything else. *These include Tyson, Perdue, Hormel,* and large CPG [consumer packaged goods] companies like *Nestle and Unilever,* which haven't previously had animal meat businesses. (Weston 2020)

Why is the "Effective Altruist" wing of the vegan movement celebrating these well-known unethical and even law-breaking meat giants? JBS is especially notorious. In 2020, the company's owners were fined $280 million by the federal government for bribery (Lane 2020). Celebrating Big Meat ignores the countless workers who have long suffered and even died for these unethical companies.

The argument for celebrating these corporations seems to be that meat giants will somehow turn the company vegan, either by acquiring a plant-based brand or by making vegan food themselves, or that these products will somehow "balance out" their meat offerings. But none of these groups (GFI, HSUS, OPP), have offered any evidence that when conventional meat companies sell plant-based alternatives, animals are saved. The companies themselves certainly are not reducing their animal production.

The reason the market is dominated by animal products is because of the economic benefits that the meat, egg, and dairy industries have enjoyed. These benefits are the results of political power at the federal, state, and local levels that have brought about economic concessions and valuable subsidies. The EA approach does not consider the massive imbalance of political power that exists.

In fact, besides the government subsidies to animal agriculture, we have plenty of evidence that displacement of animal meat will not happen. All we need to do is look at the natural foods sector more broadly to interrogate the EA hypothesis that the more conventional food companies jump on the "alt protein" bandwagon, the better. For decades now, natural food brands have been bought up by conventional companies. In the early days of large food companies acquiring natural and organic brands, some observers made similar predictions of a transformation in the conventional companies: that the acquired company's lofty ideals would have a positive upward influence on their parent company. After decades of examples to the contrary, no one in natural foods is making that argument now. If anything, some have expressed regret (Thomas 2017).

When any food company expands its portfolio, either with its own new line or through acquisition (or investment), the company does so assuming it will not cannibalize its own profits. How do we know this? They tell us so. Back when Tyson released its original "Raised and Rooted" line, which consisted of a "blended burger" and a mostly plant-based chicken nugget, they said in a 2019 news release (emphasis added): "For us, this is about 'and'—not 'or.' *We remain firmly committed to our growing traditional meat business* and expect to be a market leader in alternative protein, which is experiencing double-digit growth and could someday be a billion-dollar business for our company" (Tyson Foods 2019). Translation: It's about adding to Tyson's bottom line, not displacing their animal sales.

Are Meat Alternatives "Saving" Animals?

What really matters is whether consumers are swapping out animal meat burgers with plant-based versions, regardless of who makes them, Tyson or Beyond Meat. The presumption that this is happening, and will happen, is the raison d'être of an organization like GFI, and almost everyone in the plant-based foods movement seems to be assuming this is the case. But is it?

In dollars, 2020 plant-based meat retail sales were $1.4 billion. Impressive, until you realize that total beef sales alone topped a whopping $30 billion—up $5.7 billion from 2019 (Millspaugh 2020). In other words, *just the increase from 2019 to 2020 in beef sales was more than four times the total sales of all plant-based meats at retail.* Moreover, many vegans and vegetarians are purchasing these vegan burgers, too. While it's true this group represents a small part of the population, it's still significant. For these consumers, the only food they are displacing is other vegetarian options. And, in fact, that could also be true for nonvegetarian consumers as well. Not that they are changing out beef for Beyond Beef, but one vegetarian option for another.

Much has been made of the "flexitarian" consumer as the main driver of the growth of plant-based foods. These are consumers who are swapping out meat occasionally for plant-based options. They help explain the mainstreaming and growth of the category; at least one survey estimates this segment as high as 36 percent of the population (*PRNewswire* 2020). But we still do not know if even this population is displacing other vegetarian options. We are simply assuming that because they sometimes eat animals, they must be displacing animal meat with plant-based food. No data exists to support this assumption. Rather than claiming that self-described flexitarians are contributing to sales growth, we still need to know much more detail about these consumers' eating habits before we can celebrate.

Even Tyson seems to favor the displacement of other veg options, for obvious reasons: Tyson does not want to negatively impact its own meat sales. In May 2021, the meat giant re-released its "Raised and Rooted" line with 100-percent plant-based products, after a failed "blended" burger and egg-laden chicken nugget. "People are swapping out other meals, like carb-based or vegetable meals, and actually replacing them with higher protein," Tyson explained to *Business Insider* (Bitter 2021). This means that Tyson's target customer is not the meat eater but rather someone *eating other veg options* and replacing a healthier "carb-based or vegetable" meal with a highly processed option instead.

Restaurants often put plant-based options on the menu not to displace their meat options, but rather to be "on trend" and avoid the dreaded "veto vote." This occurs when a group of diners is deciding where to eat, and someone is vegetarian. If your restaurant cannot accommodate that eater, you lose the entire party. The "veto vote" was explained to Bloomberg News by the CEO of the burger chain "BurgerFI": "When a group of diners with varying tastes is choosing a restaurant, the availability of a vegetarian option can be the deciding factor" (Patton and Shanker 2021).

Let's say a family of five decides to go to Burger King. The teenage daughter is vegan, so she gets the Impossible Whopper®. The other four family members order regular meat burgers. It's entirely possible in this scenario that the Impossible Whopper® being on the menu causes more animals to be eaten, not fewer. Why? Because there aren't many other options for the meat eaters, who would maybe consume less meat somewhere else—say a pasta dish or a salad if they were at a different restaurant. At Burger King, it's either eat the vegan burger or eat meat.

There is evidence that the hype surrounding the introduction of plant-based meats into large fast-food chains has not been sustained by consumers. According to Bloomberg (Patton and Shanker 2021):

- In 2021, Dunkin' removed Beyond Meat's breakfast sausage from thousands of locations.
- KFC, which ran trials of Beyond Meat's chicken nuggets, has yet to turn them into a regular menu item as of October 2021.
- At Little Caesars a trial of Impossible Foods' sausage did not prove popular enough to keep on the menu.

Even the much-touted introduction of the Impossible Whopper® at Burger King seems to be losing steam. Burger King started out with a huge media blitz in 2019 to promote the plant-based option, but then significantly cut back its marketing spend in 2020. Customer awareness on social media plummeted, and the largest Burger King franchisee in the United States reported that sales of the Impossible Whopper had fallen by about half since its introduction in August 2019.

We Need a Political Movement to Save Farmed Animals

Organizations like GFI, and its EA supporters, claim to care about food but have not yet collaborated with even one other organization in the food movement. Unlike EA-based groups, the food movement talks about inequity and social justice. It works with many community-based groups that have been fighting against factory farms in their backyards. EA, by continuing to support groups like GFI with their focus on "alternative protein" isolates the vegan movement from other social justice concerns—even more than it always was. (Though ACE did not recommend GFI in the latest year available at the time of this writing, it was not because of its focus on alternative proteins but rather its workplace culture.)

In 2020, and again in 2021, Senator Cory Booker introduced a powerful bill that, unlike the promotion of "alternative proteins," could reduce the harm from factory farms. Called the "The Farm System Reform Act," the proposed law would, among other things, crack down on the monopolistic practices of meatpackers and place a moratorium on large factory farms (Booker 2021a). The bill has a broad base of support, but as of July 2021, very few vegan organizations have signed on (Booker 2021b). Notably, GFI has not.

Senator Booker, himself a proud vegan, enjoys a coveted seat on the Senate Agriculture Committee. Other committee members hail from "meat states" like Colorado, Iowa, Kansas, and Nebraska, so Senator Booker needs all the help he can get. That the EA world has not jumped in to support this bill speaks volumes about disconnectedness from the real world of political change.

EA's current focus on markets to save animals is doomed to failure because it does nothing to address the political and economic engine of the meat and dairy industries. The reason the market is dominated by animal products is because of the economic benefits that the meat, egg, and dairy industries have enjoyed for decades. These benefits are the results of political power at the federal, state, and local levels that have brought about economic concessions and valuable subsidies. The EA approach does not consider the massive imbalance of political power. This may be because of who controls most of the well-funded EA donations and recipient organizations: a small band of white men who are removed from the lived experiences and day -to -day realities that much of the rest of the food movement recognizes.

Instead of the promotion of "alternative proteins," we need a more inclusive approach, to create a political movement that brings in a wide range of people and organizations.

References

Animal Charity Evaluators. (2017). "Conversation with Bruce Friedrich and Clare Bland of the Good Food Institute." Walnut, CA: Animal Charity Evaluators, August 9. https://animalcharityevaluators.org/charity-reviews/charity-conversations/2017-conversation-with-bruce-friedrich-and-clare-bland-of-gfi/.

Animal Charity Evaluators. (2021). "Recommended Charity Fund: Six-Month Update." Effective Altruism Forum, August 2. https://forum.effectivealtruism.org/posts/mkrHnEPEYq3dN27qe/recommended-charity-fund-six-month-update-1.

Animal Welfare Fund. (n.d.). "Basic Info." https://funds.effectivealtruism.org/funds/animal-welfare#about.

Aramark and the American Heart Association. (2019). "The Power of Plant-Based Eating." New York: American Heart Association. https://www.heart.org/-/media/healthy-living-files/healthy-for-life/power-of-plantbased-eating-eng.pdf?la=en.

Balk, Josh. (2021). "Can an Animal Protection Lens Create an Equitable and Sustainable Food System?" *Eat for the Planet with Nil Zacharias*, August 23. https://eftp.co/146-josh-balk.

Bashi, Zafer, Ryan McCullough, Liane Ong, and Miguel Ramirez. (2019). "Alternative Proteins: The Race for Market Share Is On." McKinsey & Company, August 16. https://www.mckinsey.com/industries/agriculture/our-insights/alternative-proteins-the-race-for-market-share-is-on.

Bitter, Alex. (2021). "Tyson Foods's First Foray into Alternative Meats Included Half-Meat, Half-Plant Burgers. An Executive Explains Why the Newest Products under Its Raised & Rooted Brand Are 100% Plant-Based." *Business Insider*, May 3. https://www.businessinsider.com/how-tyson-is-expanding-its-raised-and-rooted-plant-based-lineup-2021-4.

Booker, Cory. (2021a). "Booker Reintroduces Bill to Reform Farm System with Expanded Support from Farm, Labor, Environment, Public Health, Faith Based and Animal Welfare Groups." Cory Booker, July 15. https://www.booker.senate.gov/news/press/booker-reintroduces-bill-to-reform-farm-system-with-expanded-support-from-farm-labor-environment-public-health-faith-based-and-animal-welfare-groups.

Booker, Cory. (2021b). "Farm System Reform Act." Cory Booker, July 13. https://www.booker.senate.gov/imo/media/doc/farm_system_reform_act1.pdf.

Brevik, E. C., L. C. Burgess, A. Cerdà, and J. J. Steffan. (2017). "The Effect of Soil on Human Health: An Overview." *PMC*, July 17. https://www.ncbi.nlm.nih.gov/pmc/articles/PMC5800787/.

EA Funds. "The Good Food Institute (GFI)." https://funds.effectivealtruism.org/partners/good-food-institute.

Friedrich, Bruce. (2016). "Rethinking Meat and the End of Factory Farming." EA Global Conference, San Francisco. Centre for Effective Altruism YouTube Channel. https://www.youtube.com/c/EffectiveAltruismVideoshttps://forum.effectivealtruism.org/posts/LePnHrQRNvhjibHRJ/claire-zabel-lewis-bollard-isha-datar-bruce-friedrich-tobias.

Friedrich, Bruce. (2017a). "Bruce Friedrich & Paul Shapiro: Fireside Chat." *Effective Altruism Forum* (blog), August 11. https://forum.effectivealtruism.org/posts/vq98sQBzjCZhzAq2u/bruce-friedrich-and-paul-shapiro-fireside-chat-2017.

Friedrich, Bruce. (2017b). "Bruce Friedrich: Can Food Technology and Markets Get Us to Animal Liberation? Interviewed by Brian Katreman." EA Global: Boston. *Effective Altruism Forum* (blog), June 2. Youtube Effective Altuism Channel. https://www.youtube.com/watch?v=WByIMdjjZ3g&list=PLwp9xeoX5p8Pi7rm-vJnaJ4AQdkYJOfYL&index=18tohttps://forum.effectivealtruism.org/posts/6FoCyz3yy63MLZMwu/bruce-friedrich-can-food-technology-and-markets-get-us-to.

Friedrich, Bruce. (2017c). "EAs in Entrepreneurship." *Effective Altruism Forum (blog)*, August 11. https://forum.effectivealtruism.org/posts/mvkKjYWWKZuK6ZBXM/joan-gass-bruce-friedrich-svetha-janumpalli-spencer.

Friedrich, Bruce. (2018). "From Agitator to Innovator." Oxford: Centre for Effective Altruism. https://www.effectivealtruism.org/articles/ea-global-2018-agitator-to-innovator/.

Friedrich, Bruce. (2020). "Creating a New Agricultural Revolution." *Effective Altruism Forum* (blog), January 22. https://forum.effectivealtruism.org/posts/qFEcGbwzogFSuX4wv/bruce-friedrich-creating-a-new-agricultural-revolution.

Fuhrer, Jay. (2021). "Soil Health: Principle 3 of 5—Plant Diversity." Natural Resources Conservation Service North Dakota. https://www.nrcs.usda.gov/wps/portal/nrcs/detail/nd/soils/health/?cid=nrcseprd1300918.

Good Food Institute. (2019). "Good Food Institute Welcomes Tyson Foods to the Plant-Based Party." Washington, DC: Good Food Institute, June 13. https://gfi.org/press/good-food-institute-welcomes-tyson-foods-to-the-plant-protein-party/.

Good Food Institute. (2022a). "About GFI." Washington, DC: Good Food Institute. https://gfi.org/about/.

Good Food Institute. (2022b). "Modernizing Meat Production." Washington, DC: Good Food Institute. https://gfi.org/.Open Philanthropy. (2022).

Hals, Tom, and Tom Polansek. (2020). "Meatpackers Deny Workers Benefits for COVID-19 Deaths, Illnesses." Reuters, September 29. https://www.reuters.com/article/health-coronavirus-jbs-colorado/meatpackers-deny-workers-benefits-for-covid-19-deaths-illnesses-idUSKBN26K334.

Harris, Keiran, and Robert Wilbin. (2021). "Lewis Bollard on Big Wins against Factory Farming and How They Happened." *80,000 Hours*, February 15. https://80000hours.org/podcast/episodes/lewis-bollard-big-wins-against-factory-farming/.

Harvard Medical School. (2012). "Cutting Red Meat—For a Longer Life." Cambridge, MA: Harvard Health Publishing, June 1. https://www.health.harvard.edu/staying-healthy/cutting-red-meat-for-a-longer-life.

Kennedy, Alicia. (2020). "Plant-Based Meat Alternatives Have Existed for Centuries." *Tenderly*, March 11. https://tenderly.medium.com/plant-based-meat-alternatives-have-existed-for-centuries-4c96735e3306.

Lane, Sylvan. (2020). "Owners of Meatpacker JBS to Pay $280M Fine over Foreign Bribery Charges." The Hill, October 14. https://thehill.com/policy/finance/521070-owners-of-meatpacker-jbs-to-pay-280m-fine-over-foreign-bribery-charges.

Magill, Bobby. (2016). "Studies Show Link between Red Meat and Climate Change." Climate Central, April 20. https://www.climatecentral.org/news/studies-link-red-meat-and-climate-change-20264.

Millspaugh, Rev. John. (2020). "Will Plant-Based Food Technology Save Animals?" Farm Forward, September 30. https://www.farmforward.com/#!/blog/will-plant-based-food-technology-save-animals/farm-forward.

Open Philanthropy. (2022). "Grants Database." https://www.openphilanthropy.org/giving/grants.

Ostlind, Emilene. (2011). "The Big Four Meatpackers." *High Country News*, March 21. https://www.hcn.org/issues/43.5/cattlemen-struggle-against-giant-meatpackers-and-economic-squeezes/the-big-four-meatpackers-1.

Parr, Richard. (2020). "Taking Good Food Global." *Effective Altruism Forum* (blog), July 20. https://forum.effectivealtruism.org/posts/YSwkYDB2jtQ6xBj2f/richard-parr-taking-good-food-global.

Patton, Leslie, and Deena Shanker. (2021). "Faux Meat Falters at the Drive-Thru." Bloomberg News, September 24. https://www.bloomberg.com/news/articles/2021-09-24/which-fast-food-has-fake-meat-not-many-serve-beyond-meat-impossible-foods.

PRNewswire. (2020). "Flexitarian on the Rise in U.S., Reports Packaged Facts." *PRNewswire*, October 29, 2020. https://www.prnewswire.com/news-releases/flexitarianism-on-the-rise-in-us-reports-packaged-facts-301154622.html.

ProVeg International. (n.d.). "We Are ProVeg." https://proveg.com/uk/about/.

RC Forward. (n.d.). "The Good Food Institute." https://rcforward.org/charity/gfi/.

Riordan, Casey. (2020). "Beliefs about Chickens & Fish and Their Relationship to Animal-Positive Behaviors." *Effective Altruism Forum*, November 11. https://forum.effectivealtruism.org/posts/tDo3WvGp5xofTfD2d/beliefs-about-chickens-and-fish-and-their-relationship-to.

Schlosser, Eric. (2020). "America's Slaughterhouses Aren't Just Killing Animals." *Atlantic*, May 12. https://www.theatlantic.com/ideas/archive/2020/05/essentials-meatpeacking-coronavirus/611437/.

Souza, Kim. (2020). "Tyson Foods the Largest U.S. Chicken Processor in 2019; George's Ranked 9th." *TB&P*, August 26. https://talkbusiness.net/2020/08/tyson-foods-the-largest-u-s-chicken-processor-in-2019-georges-ranked-9th/.

Spurgeon, Jamie. (2021). "Changes to Recommendation Status of The Albert Schweitzer Foundation and the Good Food Institute." Walnut, CA: Animal Charity Evaluators. https://animalcharityevaluators.org/blog/changes-to-recommendation-status-of-the-albert-schweitzer-foundation-and-the-good-food-institute/.

Thomas, Daniel. (2017). "The Man Who Built a Drinks Empire . . . Twice." BBC, October 2. https://www.bbc.com/news/business-41390704

Tyson Foods. (2019). "Tyson Foods Unveils Alternative Protein Products and New Raised & Rooted® Brand." Tyson Foods, June 13. https://www.tysonfoods.com/news/news-releases/2019/6/tyson-foods-unveils-alternative-protein-products-and-new-raised-rootedr.

Weston, Zak. (2020). "Growing Meat—A Market-Based Approach to Building an Ethical Food System." *Effective Altruism Forum*, July 14. https://forum.effectivealtruism.org/posts/ZxH5dRZDhk3GmNwiD/zak-weston-growing-meat-a-market-based-approach-to-building.

XPRIZE. (2021). "Tomorrow's Proteins." https://www.xprize.org/prizes/feedthenextbillion.

Yearby, Ruqaiijah. (2021). "Meatpacking Plants Have Been Deadly COVID-19 Hot Spots—But Policies That Encourage Workers to Show Up Sick Are Legal." *The Conversation*, February 26. https://theconversation.com/meatpacking-plants-have-been-deadly-covid-19-hot-spots-but-policies-that-encourage-workers-to-show-up-sick-are-legal-152572.

12

The Power of Love to Transform Animal Lives

The Deception of Animal Quantification

Krista Hiddema

On October 7, 2018, a groundbreaking event at the Ontario Veterinary College Hospital (OVC), Guelph, Canada, took place. The occasion was a ribbon-cutting ceremony to unveil a new, state-of-the art, diagnostic, interventional, and intraoperative imaging scanner. The scanner has a 1.2 meter (3.94 feet) variable geometry tilting gantry, with the ability to scan the head and neck of a standing horse with 3D resolution. Purchases with a price-tag of US$650,000 are a bit unusual for veterinary hospitals, even for a cutting-edge institution that is home to some of the world's best large animal veterinarians, but the real reason for celebration, and why the purchase of the scanner has become an iconic success story in the global animal advocacy movement (AAM), has to do with the scanner's first client, a pig named Esther.[1]

I first met Esther, and her dads Steve and Derek, in 2013. At that point, Esther was only a few months old. Despite my almost lifelong work advocating for farmed animal protection, I'd never met a pig who lived in a house—particularly not one who, regardless of

[1] See "Best day ever, The Esther Scanner is officially available for public use," Esther The Wonder Pig Facebook Page, https://www.facebook.com/watch/?v=696208210751302.

Krista Hiddema, *The Power of Love to Transform Animal Lives* In: *The Good It Promises, The Harm It Does.* Edited by: Carol J. Adams, Alice Crary, and Lori Gruen, Oxford University Press.
 DOI: 10.1093/oso/9780197655696.003.0012

what Steve was told at the time, was not a mini-pig, because mini-pigs simply don't exist. Instead, Esther was bred to be a commercial pig, and despite her modest weight of only about fifty pounds at the time, she was going to keep growing and growing and growing.

When I met Esther that day, she was, and still is, a big, beautiful, funny, smart, wonderful pig. Esther, even in those early days, was clearly loved by her dads. She had captured their hearts, and she was, for all intents and purposes, their daughter, and a deeply treasured member of their family.

Steve, being a typical proud dad, and thinking that his daughter was the most beautiful girl in the world, wanted to share her with his friends and family. So, he started posting pictures of Esther on his Facebook account. Little did he know that a few short years later, Esther's popularity across multiple social media platforms would grow to a monthly reach of between twelve and fourteen million, with Esther's Kitchen,[2] a second social media account sharing "Esther-approved" recipes, enjoying another one and a half million. Not to mention the fact that Esther's story became the subject of two *New York Times* bestselling books, *Esther the Wonder Pig—Changing the World One Heart at a Time* and *Happily Ever Esther: Two Men, a Wonder Pig, and Their Life-Changing Mission to Give Animals a Home*. Esther has also authored two children's books, *The True Adventures of Esther the Wonder Pig* and *Esther's Christmas Coat*.

Esther was well loved at home and by people all over the world who had followed her story on social media and who had read her books. Esther sparked the hearts of millions of people, most of whom had never even met a pig, certainly not one who lived as an indoor family member. By this time, Esther and her dads had moved to a sanctuary that now bears her name, the Happily Ever Esther Farm Sanctuary. Esther was no longer restricted to a small

[2] See Esther's Kitchen, Facebook Community, https://www.facebook.com/EstherApproved/.

backyard in a residential neighborhood to play in. At the sanctuary, she had virtually unfettered access to nearly fifty acres of land. Esther was a very active young woman who loved going on long walks at all hours of the day and night. Then, one day, everything changed. The deep bonds and love remained ever strong, but Esther, who was so full of life and vigor, fell ill. What had been a Happy Ever Esther story changed into a journey of uncertainty, fear, and grief.

Steve started noticing a change in Esther starting in the fall of 2017. She had become uncharacteristically uninterested in long walks, and on some days she wasn't interested in walking at all. Steve knew, just like we all know when those who are closest to us act out of character, that something was wrong. Then, on one fateful October day, Esther suddenly began to struggle for breath, she started to tremble, and began to turn blue.

Steve and Derek were terrified. They immediately rushed Esther to the OVC in Guelph, Ontario. Despite the status of this hospital and those within it, the reality was that Esther could not be properly diagnosed because she was too large to fit into the diagnostic equipment they had, and no other suitable solution could be found anywhere else in Canada. The equipment that was needed to diagnose Esther simply did not exist in the whole of the country.

Those of us who were closest to Esther and who loved her so very much were distraught, and we needed to find a solution. Esther's international followers were also devastated. We explored sending Esther to Cornell Veterinary Hospital in New York, but it presented a laundry list of logistical and safety challenges, primarily due to the hazards of transportation. It is well known that one of the most stressful and potentially dangerous times in the life of a pig, and all other animals that are used for food, is during transport. And, on top of that, going across the border into the United States would have meant that a mandated extensive quarantine requirement would be imposed when she came home. As a pig, Esther is legally classified as a food animal by the Canadian Food Inspection Agency, and there was absolutely no way that we would ever put Esther in quarantine. The very idea of putting her into a small solitary pen for several months was simply unfathomable.

We all reached out to anyone and everyone we knew, looking for a solution, no different than anyone would do for any loved one in distress. Then, one day during this awful and difficult time, Steve called me and suggested that we buy the necessary diagnostic machine. At first I thought he was joking, but as we talked more it started to make sense.

We talked about the fact that this situation was about more than just Esther, this lack of diagnostic equipment meant that no large animal in Canada could be diagnosed and treated as effectively as they deserved to be. This really became a matter of doing what was right. Not just for Esther, *but for all Esthers*—for all large mammals who deserve proper medical care.

While we each may know and interact with a large number of people at work, school, and in our various communities, locally, abroad, or at work, there are some people in our lives whose every breath and very well-being are so intrinsically tied to our own that when they become ill or their lives are threatened in any way, every aspect of our own lives changes. When the situation is life or death, then no matter what the outcome, our own lives are indelibly altered. This is what happened to millions of people worldwide when news of Esther's crisis came out.

Steve mobilized immediately and after intensive research identified The Pegaso™, an imaging instrument that is big enough to accommodate Esther's size—weighing in at around 700 pounds at that time. All we had to do was just buy it and get it to Guelph. Easy, right? Yes, yes it was, and this is the crux of Esther's story. With the help of all of those who love her all over the world and the generosity of nearly 12,000 people from fifty-eight countries, the funds were raised, and the scanner was purchased, shipped, and installed. In just three months, *three months*, Esther transformed from being a sick pig to a worldwide cause supported by millions of people. An absolutely staggering accomplishment!

We, including me, who became a founding board member and the president of the board of directors for the sanctuary for almost six years, signed a contract with the manufacturer of The Pegaso™ on December 31, 2017, New Year's Eve, just before midnight. It was in the nick of time, since the price of the scanner was going up significantly the very next day. At the same time, we were negotiating with University of Guelph administrators to build the space needed to house the imaging instrument. The CT scanner was shipped to Guelph, which involved a rainbow of details, including obtaining all of the necessary permits from the Canadian government, a custom-made radiation-proof steel door for the room, and arranging for hospital staff to be trained on how to use the scanner.

It was a success. Esther got the life-saving diagnosis that she needed. She was diagnosed with breast cancer. She was treated immediately, and today, three year later, is thriving with her family and is back to taking walks on the fifty acres that she calls home. Her followers have continued to grow by leaps and bounds, and they keep an attentive eye on Esther's progress—as do I, not only because of this amazing journey I have been blessed to travel, but because Esther and I share something else. We are both breast cancer survivors.

Now, while I am certainly oversimplifying the back-end process of buying the largest CT scanner in the world, I am not oversimplifying the outpouring of love and support from all over the world. If you were to do a simple google search using the words "The Esther Scanner," you would see that it yields over thirteen million hits—13,900,000 to be exact, as of this writing. With the addition of this scanner, the world of veterinary medicine in Canada has been forever improved. All because of the love for one pig.

Esther and her now countless other "family members"—together with her social media followers—have accomplished something extraordinary. They have shown the world the power of love,

love as the transformative catalyst for making profound and far-reaching cultural change in how humans regard animals—and each other. Esther has brought humans together as well. Yet, despite this success, some of those considered to be the most respected leaders in the AAM are critical, maintaining it is not love or respect or far-reaching generosity, but numbers, that count in the abacus of morality.

Not long after the ribbon-cutting ceremony, I was sent a video that was posted on October 4, 2019, by Peter Singer, a professor of bioethics and author of the 1975 then groundbreaking book *Animal Liberation*. The video was posted on a paged called iamvegan.tv. In the video, Singer criticized the purchase of The Esther Scanner, calling it "not effective" and "not good value for the money."[3] Singer's exact words were:

> An example of altruism that I think is not really as effective as it could have been, would be the raising of $650,000 to provide a large animal scanner. So that Esther, a pig who was the companion animal for one person, could be scanned to see where she was having tumors. I think breast cancer.
>
> I appreciate that people were touched by the plight of Esther and of Esther's owner. But to spend $650,000 on getting a scanner for one pig, which may not even help that pig to live longer, I think there are better things that you could do with that money. You could help many, many animals also pigs, each one of them just as much a worthwhile individual animal as Esther was. You could, for example, support organizations that are trying to help people to understand what the lives of pigs in factory farms are like, and therefore, hopefully to persuade them no longer to buy those products. So that the number of pigs who have to suffer on factory farms, pigs who don't have a good life like Esther is

[3] See "Peter Singer: Sauver le maximum d'animaux," iamvegan.tv Facebook Page, October 4, 2019, https://www.facebook.com/watch/?v=166297644277336.

having, will be reduced. And I think that would be a more worthwhile use of that kind of money.

People who gave money to help her were altruistic. They were giving money to help another being, another sentient being, and that's altruistically motivated. But Effective Altruists say, "We shouldn't just be motivated by the thought that, here's somebody I want to help. We should be motivated also by reasoning," which says, "I want to do good in the world, but is this the best way of doing good in the world? Is this the way to get the best value for the money I'm spending?"

This is something that we think about very naturally when it comes to buying something for ourself. If you want to buy a new camera, you won't just impulsively go and buy the first camera you see. You will do some research as to which is the best camera, which gives me the best value for money that provides the features I need, and doesn't cost 10 times as much.

We should think the same about altruism. This may be something that in itself is good, but maybe I could help 10 times as many animals or a hundred times as many animals or a thousand times as many animals quite possibly for the same amount of money that is here being spent on one animal. And that's not getting good value for the money you're donating.

Despite Singer's almost idol-like stature for some in the AAM, I felt that I needed to respond. My response to Singer, which I posted on October 8, 2018, was as follows:

Peter,

It is with a heavy heart that I am compelled to write this letter to you, a person whom decades ago inspired so much of my own activism. A person who has inspired so many of us, and has been a true leader in ushering our movement into the mainstream.

This letter is in connection with what I can only assume is an ill-informed position regarding the recent purchase of The Esther

Scanner ("Scanner"), and as such, I will provide you with a degree of enlightenment.

Yesterday marked the ribbon cutting ceremony of The Esther Scanner at the Ontario Veterinary Hospital in Guelph, Ontario. A small group of individuals were on hand to celebrate the largest CT scanner in the world now being available to not only large animals, but also small animals in Canada.

Here is just a short list of what The Esther Scanner has done and will do:

1. We enjoyed media attention for a full year, beginning with Esther's illness, the realization that diagnostic equipment was not available, the fundraiser, the purchase of the Scanner, her breast cancer diagnosis, and her cancer-free outcome. The media attention was international. It is impossible to quantify the value of this volume of media coverage, nor is it possible to quantify the number of dinner table discussions that took place as a result.
2. Close to 12,000 people from 58 countries gave to our fundraiser—from Bulgaria to Japan to Seychelles. I'm not sure if you realize Peter, but when people give their hard-earned money to help animals they are giving far more than money, they are giving a part of themselves. Each of these gifts undoubtedly spawned countless discussions about the compassion for all life.
3. Our supporters have such compassionate hearts that even when we had met our fundraising goal—they continued to give. We have now established The Esther Shares program where we have the privilege of helping other sanctuaries with the medical bills of their residents.
4. The Scanner will provide life-saving diagnostic treatment and allow for a level of surgical precision not previously available to all animals in Canada. The Scanner will be operational for at least ten years if not longer, and the number of lives that it will

be instrumental in saving cannot be known until the Scanner is no longer in use.

5. The Scanner will allow veterinary students to be trained in advanced diagnostics using cutting-edge technology.
6. Research that is now possible with the Scanner will provide information about aging farmed animals that has never been amassed before. The information will be stored in a first-of-its-kind large animal database, and be available to all large animal veterinarians in the same way as has been done exclusively for traditional companion animals in the past.
7. The Scanner has already been earmarked for the most advanced research study on dogs with colorectal cancer in the world. This study will also have applicability for treating colorectal cancer in humans.
8. Discussion is underway for the possibility of the Scanner being used for human bariatric patients in the future.
9. And, we know that through our message of "kindness is magic," tens if not hundreds of thousands of people have decided to leave animals off their plate.
10. We, through all of our social media pages and platforms have shared our message of compassion for all life with in excess of 2 million people every single day, and the number keeps growing!

Peter, I challenge you to share with all of us what possible better use there is for this money. As a former vice president of one of the largest animal protection organizations in the world, I can tell you that some of the math that has been used to quantify what they are able to do with each dollar is simply false, and the welfare commitments that are being used to calculate these numbers simply have not occurred—they are no more than a "hoped for" future state with no mechanism to even determine if they are happening. And, we also know that many of these commitments could cause more harm to animals, not less.

The Effective Altruist obsession with quantification not only leads to development of junk-math, but it is fundamentally misogynistic. It completely fails to consider feminist principles of care and empathy. Instead, our work is real, it is tangible, it is helping real animals every day, it is showing that every single life is important. And this message is inspiring people all over the world. We are building an army—Esther's Army—of people all over the world who value life, every single life, and who are changing their own lives by finding compassion in themselves for Esther, and hence, for all animals, and for themselves.

Peter, if you would like to learn more about our work, and learn more about the value of The Esther Scanner, please feel free to contact me. It would be my pleasure to have a discussion from one academic to another.

Krista Hiddema

President, Happily Ever Esther Farm Sanctuary[4]

Singer did not respond.

Sadly, Singer's position regarding The Esther Scanner is shared by many influencers and donors in the AAM, who tend to denigrate the value of love, care, and individual animal relationships in our advocacy efforts. While many have sought to quantify and calculate advocacy, the calculations tend not to translate well for breathing, feeling, compassionate human beings, and many of the attempts at creating quantifiable equations are simply inadequate.[5]

[4] See Krista Hiddema Facebook Page, "My response to Peter Singer's comment about The Esther Scanner," October 8, 2018, https://www.facebook.com/Krista.Hiddema/posts/872409616297565.

[5] Mathematical estimates attempting to quantify animal welfare initiatives by certain animal advocacy groups have traditionally relied on forced commitments by animal protein producers and other procurers of animal products with extremely limited knowledge of the number of animals utilized. Estimates are based on proxies such as the number of restaurant locations and are often inaccurate, differing between groups. The cited commitments are always future dated, sometimes as far as ten years in the future,

The very idea that we should calculate, and be able to anticipate, the consequences of every advocacy decision, a fundamental tenant of Effective Altruism (EA), is not practical or reasonable. EA thinking, as promoted by Singer and others, while perhaps realistic for Commander Data and Spock from *Star Trek*, is not how most people make decisions. It is also not reasonable to suggest that a third-party research organization, using EA philosophies and principles, is able to engage in calculations, and subsequently make "effective" advocacy recommendations for donors. These groups cannot serve as Data or Spock on our behalf because the very notion that the lives of animals and the value of animal advocacy can be quantified at all is a flawed baseline.

EA, predicated on the principle of utility, which includes being reasonably certain of the consequences of our actions for the greatest number of those effected, would mean that the film *Blackfish*[6] should not have been made, as it was produced to highlight the horrendous conditions of one killer orca whale, Tilikum. Yet this work, inspired by the desire to help one animal, had the sweeping effect of almost eradicating SeaWorld and other similar aquatic circuses. EA-based activism would have argued against People for the Ethical Treatment of Animals' (PETA) campaign to free seventeen Silver Spring monkeys in 1981, which arguably launched the modern-day animal rights movement. It would mean that animal activists today should not waste their time fighting to free the approximately two dozen elephants who are currently used in circuses in the United States. It would mean that animal activists should not work to put an end to greyhound racing or the use of horse-drawn carriages in large urban cities. It would have meant that we would not have purchased The Esther Scanner and would not be contributing to life-changing research for prostate cancer

with no oversight or ability to track outcomes. The value of welfare initiatives for the animals is also subjective.

[6] https://www.blackfishmovie.com.

in human men that is currently being done out of Grand River Hospital in London, Ontario, a benefit that I was unaware of when I wrote the response to Singer above. Research that I have been told[7] would simply not be possible without The Esther Scanner.

What EA thinkers continually to fail to realize is that emotions are why people stop eating meat (Kunst and Hohle 2016), and why people stop going to SeaWorld, and, why people don't buy fur coats. Emotions. Not numbers. While reason and the rational do enter into decision-making, science and experience both demonstrate that emotions play an integral and vital role, and as such, the AAM should draw from both, not trade one for the other.

The hard truth is that the AAM has been hijacked by EA for too many years. EA is failing its clients, the animals. As one example, although EA funders such as the Open Philanthropy Project (OPP) gave $144,201,999.00 from February 2016 to June 2021[8] in support of EA-based animal advocacy such as cage-free initiatives, global per capita consumption of meat, dairy, and eggs increased over this same period of time.[9] These statistics are only one example that demonstrates that EA is not effective at achieving its purported goal of saving animals. While some thinkers argue that emotions can lead us astray, the reality is that the AAM seems to have become an emotionless movement, and this lack of emotion-centered work has worsened the situation for animals. And the real irony is that this worsening is quantitatively borne out, yet to my knowledge is not discussed, nor is there a questioning of what is and is not working. Instead, the "same old" advocacy continues to be given priority funding.

These EA funders have a disproportionate influence on the type of activism that is done within the AAM, because the reality is that

[7] Personal conversation with the head of radiology at the Ontario Veterinary Clinic, Guelph, Ontario. Used with permission.

[8] https://www.openphilanthropy.org/giving/grants.

[9] https://ourworldindata.org/grapher/per-capita-meat-consumption-by-type-kilograms-per-year?country=~OWID_WRL.

they hold the proverbial purse strings. While EA has been adopted by thousands of people and numerous organizations such as OPP, it fails to consider factors that are immeasurable, such as political change, justice, equality, urgency, and systematic change, as well as respect and dignity for each living being. The EA dominance in the AAM must change, and it must start with funders. The power of money must be harnessed to power love. Emotions and love are often the place where the spark of change begins. They are a springboard that connects us and inspires grass-roots advocacy, integrity, political action, and changes that people make every day in their everyday lives. Human history is littered with the tragedies caused by leaders who believed in numbers. We cannot continue to make this mistake for animals.

If we are to truly transform how animals are viewed and treated, it must start with compassion, respect, understanding, open-hearted listening, and humility. It must start with love. In the words of the feminist writer and social activist bell hooks: "Being part of a loving community does not mean we will not face conflicts, betrayals, negative outcomes from positive actions, or bad things happening to good people. Love allows us to confront these negative realities in a manner that is life-affirming and life-enhancing" (2000, 139).

References

hooks, bell. (2000). *All about Love*. New York: HarperCollins.

Kunst, J. R., and S. M. Hohle. (2016). "Meat Eaters by Dissociation: How We Present, Prepare and Talk about Meat Increases Willingness to Eat Meat by Reducing Empathy and Disgust." *Appetite* 105: 758–774.

13
Our Partners, The Animals
Reflections from a Farmed Animal Sanctuary

Kathy Stevens

I've just come from the pasture inhabited by Tucker and Amos, two elderly steers who've been with us since they were six months old. It is 97 degrees at Catskill Animal Sanctuary (CAS) today, and the air is so thick I feel it sitting on me. The boys, remarkably, seem relatively comfortable in their airy barn nestled amid a cluster of trees at the top of a hill. Me? I am *drenched* with sweat, and my chin and right cheek are burning and a bit raw, because I've allowed Amos to slather me in kisses. It's his go-to greeting.

Amos was rescued from an uncertain fate when Catskill Game Farm, a local zoo with a petting zoo component, closed for good in 2006. A coalition of animal advocacy organizations saved 207 of the 2,000 or so Game Farm residents. Judging by the trucks that filled the parking lot the day the animals were auctioned off, their cabs emblazoned with names like Safari International, Trophy Hunting Adventures, and Jersey Taxidermy, the rest had grisly endings. Amos and his best friend Jesse were among the lucky ones whose lives were spared, and Amos has been creating vegans ever since.

When the boys were little, we took unsuspecting guests into the pasture with them. They were *delighted* to have company and displayed their joy with goofy cow kicks as they ran towards us, then scratchy kisses planted on the hands, arms, cheeks of willing recipients. As they matured, those kisses continued. Amos and

Kathy Stevens, *Our Partners, The Animals* In: *The Good It Promises, The Harm It Does*. Edited by: Carol J. Adams, Alice Crary, and Lori Gruen; Oxford University Press.
DOI: 10.1093/oso/9780197655696.003.0013

Jesse were not only deeply affectionate with each other; Amos in particular craved *human* attention. He still does. We endure his kisses (think of a massive cat tongue) because he needs to give them. Amos is love on four legs.

Tucker, meanwhile, arrived one year after Amos. He, too, came from a petting zoo. It was the end of the season, and he, a four-month-old calf, was to be sold at auction, a common practice of seasonal zoos, since it's cheaper than feeding and housing animals over the winter. When spring arrives, voila! A new batch of animals appears, only to live a dreary, mundane life as roadside entertainment for a few months before being sent to slaughter—"auction," of course, is a euphemism. There is simply no demand for pet cows, pigs, or other farmed animals. Whether to be used as food or as entertainment, their species virtually always seals their fate.

So precious Tucker, a red and white Holstein, was another of the lucky ones. He gamboled down the trailer ramp, his massive doe eyes blinking. We placed him in a paddock next to my house for the requisite quarantine period, and I promptly fell in love with the 200-pound bovine puppy, who followed me around, ate my hair, and, naturally, offered slobbery, ouchy facials. At night, he "mooed" relentlessly: "*I'm lonely! Come play with me!*" he called. And so I would. Our bond is powerful.

Over the next thirteen years, Tucker lived with various bovine buddies as herds grew with each new rescue, shrank when a cow passed away, or were reconfigured when, say, a younger boy started to challenge a senior for "top steer" status. But most of his friendships were long-term, and when Tucker's friend Caleb died, Tucker's grief was so profound that we worried he was sick. He stopped eating. He separated himself from the rest of the herd. He accepted our affection but didn't return it. It was clear that *Tucker was mourning*, and it was excruciating to witness.

Amos, too, suffered a devastating loss when Jesse, his lifetime companion, passed away suddenly, presumably from a heart attack.

And so, the two massive steers, each well over 2,500 pounds, found themselves alone: Big-hearted, affectionate Amos, alone in his pasture. Gentle, emotional Tucker, alone as a free-ranger after we separated him from younger cows who started to pick on him. Imagine our delight when Tucker's travels repeatedly took him to Amos's pasture, where the two boys stood, separated by a fence, and began to groom each other, those tongues once again able to channel the love from their bovine hearts. Introducing them to each other—hornless Tucker, and Amos with massive, two-foot horns pointing skyward—was reassuringly uneventful. Months later, we smile as they wander their pasture, sleep side by side, and, of course, keep those tongues in good working order.

Catskill Animal Sanctuary has welcomed thousands of animals since we opened our doors in 2001: Rambo, the sheep who spent eleven years with us as an uncanny "watch sheep;" Peabody, a rooster who ran to us at the sound of his name, sat with human audiences at vegan cooking demos happily accepting samples of vegan grilled cheese, vegan egg salad, and more, often while nestled in a guest's lap; Jasmine—oh, St. Jasmine!—a former feral pig who generously accepted the role of stepmom to twelve rescued piglets who needed her . . . *relentlessly*. Thousands of discards, escapees from agribusiness or live markets, victims of animal hoarders. We know these animals as well as you know the dog who sleeps at the foot of your bed, or the cat who says "good morning" by sprawling over your face as you sleep. Each chicken is *remarkably* individual: the shy one, the insolent one, the one who just won't stop talking, the cuddler, the precocious one, and the not-the-sharpest-tool-in-the-shed. The same is true of the pigs and cows and ducks and turkeys and others lucky enough to find sanctuary: each is a nuanced individual who expresses their individuality in myriad ways. Joy. Impatience. Gratitude. Worry. Excitement. Fear. Anticipation. Contentment. Industries that profit from animals don't want us to see this truth, but that doesn't make it any less true.

Many folks who visit farm sanctuaries around the world expect something akin to a petting zoo. At Catskill, what they often get instead is what I've described above: chickens who fall asleep in their arms; turkeys who accompany them on tours, assertively expecting affection; pigs who come running at the sound of their names, flopping deliriously on their sides for belly rubs; and free-range sheep eagerly approaching them.

"Sit down with them," we encourage. "They want to look you in the eyes."

And when visitors sit, Scout or Zeke, Stewart or Nina come so close that guests can feel their breath. The sheep stare deeply into our guests' eyes in a way that often brings people to tears. Sometimes, they press themselves into our visitors, either forehead to forehead or forehead to chest. These are moments that put the lie to lifetimes of cultural conditioning—conditioning that results in some animals being seen as "pets," others as commodities.

They are the moments when visitors come undone.

"They are so soulful," says a woman.

"I feel their love," says a child.

"I had no idea that this is who they are," says a man, as tears stream down his cheeks. Over and over and over and over again at farm sanctuaries around the globe, animals tug powerfully at human hearts, compelling those good hearts to face their complicity in unspeakable suffering and irreparable planetary damage. Life-changing epiphanies. In other words, in a world in which animals are utilitarian only, and farmed animals lack any consideration whatsoever, sanctuaries are powerful vegan-makers, to use my friend Rachel McCrystal's term. And yet Effective Altruism ignores us, "proving" through charts and graphs, the use of "impact calculators," and "return on investment" (ROI), that other forms of farmed animal activism are wiser places for your charity dollars.

I agree *wholeheartedly* with EA's commitment to wise funding, and love the fact that farmed animal welfare is one of its recommended giving areas. But why the bias, why the myopia, why, most disturbingly, the persistent disinterest in evaluating the impact of sanctuaries? How can such a heady, mathematical approach to giving be embraced when it minimizes, misunderstands, and misrepresents—indeed virtually *dismisses*—the entire sanctuary movement, inarguably a leading contributor to veganism, and therefore a leading force for change for farm animals?

While I will leave it to the academics included in this book to speculate about the various "why's" underlying Effective Altruism's position, I offer a few additional thoughts.

First, a quick review of social change history tells us that social change is tough stuff, and that when it comes—in fits and starts, as it invariably does—it comes from a variety of approaches. And with our very survival at stake—our consumption of animal products driving both climate change and the rise of pandemics—the urgency of ushering in a vegan world can't be overstated.

However, to believe that a radical transformation to veganism can happen *without the help of the animals* is like believing that the LGBTQ movement could have made the inroads it has if none of the rest of us knew gay people. In fact, pick your social change movement: civil rights, women's rights, immigrant rights, labor rights. To imagine that these movements would have grown without the active involvement of the oppressed group or without the rest of us having those folks—women or people of color or immigrants or what have you—in our lives is, of course, *preposterous*. For many of us, we care about *what we know*. Our sense of justice is ignited when someone in our circle has been harmed. Providing "animal lovers" the ability to connect powerfully with the beings for whom we advocate is one of the greatest tools our movement has, a fact borne out by post-survey data from CAS showing that 93 percent of nonvegan visitors intend to reduce or eliminate animal products from their diets.

Interestingly, research consistently shows that health concerns, environmental concerns, and ethical concerns influence the transition to plant-based living roughly equally. By way of example: the "regulars" in our vegan cooking classes rarely visit the animals. Rather, they appreciate not only our chef's insanely delicious recipes, but also her knowledge of nutrition. They're "with us" to eat well and get (or stay) healthy. Most of my personal friends, on the other hand, have had those experiences I spoke of earlier: they've experienced Michael the turkey falling asleep in their laps. They've laid in the grass embracing a pig, listening to her grateful "mmmphs." The sanctuary experience "connects the dots" for people who identify as "animal lovers." So, since one of the most compelling reasons for adopting veganism is *the ethical one* (the desire not to contribute to the suffering of others), the more we provide people the opportunity to know those "others" (the more we center the animals at the heart of our movement), the stronger the resolve of those who are "in it for the animals" will be.

Can an initiative be scaled, and can it be scaled cost-effectively? These are questions Effective Altruism suggests we use to guide funding decisions. Here, on the surface, sanctuaries fall woefully short. A thousand sanctuaries could open tomorrow and make little measurable dent in farmed animal suffering. The need for rescue is simply too great, the need for space too limited, and, most importantly, as sanctuary people acknowledge, *we can't rescue our way out of the problem of institutionalized animal abuse.* There's a point of diminishing returns with individual rescue if (and only if) our sole goal is to end the farming of animals for food and other products. Each sanctuary needs but a handful of each "food animal" species as ambassadors: having thirty cows arguably makes no more difference than having three. But sanctuaries *do* scale—just not in the way that Effective Altruism assumes or appears to be able to measure.

Here are but a handful of *thousands* of actual examples from Catskill Animal Sanctuary:

- For one weekly volunteer, the experience with the animals morphed into a personal transition to veganism, the conversion of her family to veganism, and the launching of two vegan businesses. How many vegans has that one woman created?

- A child who visited CAS started an animal rights club at her school and convinced her principal to have an Animal Rights Day. The entire school attended, and vegan lunch was served in the cafeteria. That child's friends, in turn, attended *Camp Kindness*, where they cared for animals, cooked vegan lunches, and went back to their lives to influence countless others.
- A weekend at CAS for one family, during which they took a tour, volunteered with the animals, and enjoyed amazing vegan breakfasts prepared by our innkeeper, ended with the entire family of nine committed to going vegan. These nine family members returned to their workplaces, their places of worship, their friends. As they navigate their new lives, how many vegans will this family of nine create?

In short, in order to fathom a sanctuary's *true impact*, we have to look way beyond individual lives saved. If we were to use the Effective Altruism approach, we'd calculate the number of human lives transformed by the sanctuary experience, and then the exponential numbers of others transformed through their engagement with that single human being, and then somehow arrive at an ROI figure. I can't do that math, but EA sure could—*if* they were interested in understanding our impact. They have figured out how to do it by measuring the impact of leafleting. And, frankly, sanctuaries are better than leafleting at making more vegans. EA's obstinate refusal to engage with sanctuaries is irrational, and we have to ask, "Why?"

Effective Altruism's approach is to decenter, and hence to devalue, the animals themselves. How profoundly, how ironically speciesist! EA results in (a) less consideration of the animals as individuals deserving of their lives, (b) less funding to support those individual lives, and (c) fewer individual lives saved as a consequence. As we're marching toward our shared and glorious vision of a world free from suffering, is it truly okay to ignore the *mind-numbing suffering* of *those we could save* in order to produce more leaflets, launch more undercover investigations, or grow a grass-roots protest movement? Substitute puppies, kittens, or kids here, and see how this sits with you. Individual lives matter. Period. The end. With the world off its axis, our giving needn't be, probably *shouldn't be*, either/or. The push to scale clean meat. Street activism like The Save Movement and Direct Action Everywhere. Undercover investigations. Vegan mentoring programs. These and many other bold initiatives are *all* worth supporting. But could we please remember the beings at the center of *all* of our efforts? The ones who want their lives every bit as much as you and I want ours? The ones who experience every emotion we do? The ones who are *just like us* in the ways that matter? The ones who are our very best vegan-makers, not because that is their instrumental purpose, but because vegan-making is connected to the recognition of animals as individuals.

Effective Altruism is right about one thing: it is expensive to feed Amos and Tucker. But those boys meet thousands of visitors each season of their long lives. When people sit in the grass with these gentle giants, stroking their faces or necks, accepting ouchy kisses, then hearts open and epiphanies come: Oh, *so this is who they are.* In that same visit, guests learn from engaging guides about the horrors of the dairy industry, and about our diet's devastating impact on the environment. They sample vegan food at tastings, and in that moment, with their understanding deepened and their hearts wide open, they sign up, if they choose, to work with a vegan mentor, *for free.* Nor is Catskill alone in offering programming to complement those life-changing moments with animals. Rowdy Girl, Sweet Farm, Indraloka, Barn Sanctuary—these are just a few of many others offering programming that is truly groundbreaking. In fact, I don't know of another animal rights initiative that's so complete.

Sanctuaries will carry on with the animals as our partners. After all, we've got a vegan world to make and precious little time to make it. As we have for years, Catskill Animal Sanctuary invites Effective Altruism and its proponents—organizations like Animal Charity Evaluators—to study our impact in order to arrive at a *legitimate* ROI figure for those for whom such a measure has meaning. In the meantime, if you've been to a sanctuary, over and over again, bringing friends and family to be inspired by the chickens and sheep, turkeys and pigs, and all the rest who call CAS home, you don't need EA's endorsement, because you've felt our scratchy kiss of an impact. You told us: it changed your life for good.

14

The Wisdom Gained from Animals Who Self-Liberate

Rachel McCrystal

In August 2018, at an auction house in Hackettstown, New Jersey, over sixty goats, sheep, and piglets escaped through a fence that was pushed open overnight.

Auction houses are terrifying for farmed animals—full of sheep, goats, and baby cows who don't know each other and are crammed into tight spaces, and then touched and yelled at by humans that they also don't know. These auctions take place in rural farming communities all across the country and are where smaller farms send animals they've either bred for slaughter or those they can no longer use for breeding. So there is a combination of middle-aged and baby animals. Many are sick. Everyone is terrified. With rare exceptions, like petting zoos buying for their seasons, the auctions end with those animals being sent either to feed lots or directly to slaughterhouses.

There's nothing newsworthy about an auction house. But suddenly, the one in Hackettstown was in the news and all over social media. Dozens of animals were freed in the night by an unlikely hero. News coverage and local opinion were clear—Fred had freed them. Fred, a feral goat, had himself escaped from that very auction house a year earlier. He had been living in the woods for a year as a bit of a local celebrity; he was a smaller light-colored goat with a very fluffy coat that probably helped him survive the winter. People had taken photos of him in their yards and in the woods and posted

Rachel McCrystal, *The Wisdom Gained from Animals Who Self-Liberate* In: *The Good It Promises, The Harm It Does.* Edited by: Carol J. Adams, Alice Crary, and Lori Gruen, Oxford University Press.
 DOI: 10.1093/oso/9780197655696.003.0014

them all over social media. Now the community was sure he was back to save others.

The *New York Post* quoted the auction house manager as saying, "It was him [last night]. I think he's the culprit. He must have banged that fence and let them out last night. I'm almost positive. He must have put a lot of force into that" (Bains and Woods 2018).

Many of the animals—but not Fred—were captured and returned to be sent to the slaughterhouse (Kausch 2018a). The very next day, Fred was back at the auction house, presumably having returned again to free the captured animals. He was headbutting the holding fence that the auction house manager accused him of opening the night before. This time there was no mistaking that it was indeed Fred, and that he was attempting to free those who had been captured.

I am the executive director at Woodstock Farm Sanctuary, a farm sanctuary a few hours from the auction house. In our care we have many animal residents who have freed themselves—jumped off the back of transport trucks, run from auctions, or escaped directly from farms. Animal exploiters do not like the notoriety that comes with stories of self-liberating farmed animals, so as I read the story in the *New York Post*, I knew that Fred was going to be a target. We put out an announcement offering sanctuary to Fred and to those animals who were still out in the woods with him. In the announcement I said what we kept saying to each other at the Sanctuary as we anxiously waited to hear anything: "Stay free, Fred."

Other sanctuaries and activists reached out as well and tried to locate Fred—there was a good network in the area, including protesters who organized weekly vigils outside of the auction house. We were being informed through this whisper network that the owner of the auction house wanted Fred caught and preferably dead. And then the word was received that the rest of the freed animals from that first night had been caught and returned to the building where they were going to be sold. No one knew if Fred was there among them.

Our shelter director drove down to New Jersey with a trailer to see if he could convince someone to surrender Fred to us. An auction house worker told him that Fred wasn't there, but that they would let him know if Fred was caught. But that was obviously just a lie to get him to leave.

Weeks passed without an update. Then we were told that a female goat in heat had been put on a trailer and was used to lure Fred onto the trailer where he was then trapped. After a year of rebellion and freedom, he had been tricked (Kausch 2018b). The whisper network informed us that Fred may have been sold to a slaughterhouse conglomerate and was on his way to a "live-kill" market in the Bronx. Live-kill markets are legally operating small slaughterhouses where animals can be bought and killed onsite; there are over eighty of them in New York City. We again tried every avenue we could think of—first reaching out to the slaughterhouse owner with a story about wanting to buy a goat as a family pet. Then, through New York City connections, we connected with some Muslim men who were able and willing to go to the Halal slaughterhouse to ask about him and see if he was there. They were told he wasn't. We didn't know what happened to him or if he was alive or dead.

Meanwhile, as I stayed up at night worried that this brave goat had just been shot by the owner of the auction house, another local news story came out: "Fred the Goat Will Live Out His Life on a Farm" (Kausch 2018c). This was another obvious misdirection from the auction house, as no one would have purchased him as a breeding goat—he was good at escaping, not the right breed, and, at this point, older. Goats are cheap and farmers breed out defiant characteristics; they wouldn't intentionally breed a goat with the intelligence and will of Fred. I called the reporter who had been covering this story from the start and left her a few messages and sent her emails letting her know she was definitely being lied to, but she never responded.

Again, the whisper network reached out to us to tell us that that Fred was dead. Maybe just killed the same night he was captured with all of those he had liberated. Maybe soon after. Maybe after being tricked onto the trailer with the female goat. Maybe at the slaughterhouse. But killed anyway.

It was devastating to hear.

At that point, I would have drained my entire bank account to save his life. Yes, I could hypothetically take that money now and give it to animal agriculture awareness campaigns, which would spare the lives of some other goats. But sometimes ethics are abstract and sometimes they are what is right in front of you. Every individual deserves the dignity of liberation. If Fred was able to be saved and come to Woodstock Sanctuary, where it would cost tens of thousands of dollars to care for him over his life, I would have done it in a second.

But while Fred fought for his own liberty and that of others, I often worry that I am working in a movement that would tell me I was wasting money to fund that liberty through rescue and lifelong sanctuary. That it's a movement in fact financed by people who have no direct relationships with farmed animals, know nothing about them, and have no knowledge of them as individuals. Where when I try to make the case for liberation, I am told that a few animals at a few sanctuaries around the country as "representatives" or "symbols" would be adequate—as if we were discussing a question of representation, not the act of saving individual lives.

Those who exploit animals are scared of animal liberators. And by "animal liberators," I mean those nonhuman animals who struggle to free themselves and to save others. The monkeys who release others from labs, the elephants who trample fencing to free their friends, the goat who came back to a place to save others from death. The person or persons who caught Fred didn't want more attention brought to the animal trade happening in his nondescript corner of New Jersey where rural and strip mall meet.

Self-liberation is literally bred out of domesticated farmed animals, as it is part of their wildness. Those animals bred for slaughter like Cornish chickens or Yorkshire pigs tend to be the most docile of their species, having been forced to evolve for thousands of generations by breeding that encourages ease of handling by humans, lack of territoriality, and the ability to live in tight quarters with many other animals without fighting or self-harm. Animal agriculture is built on trying to squelch all freedom and rebellion. When a cow bound for the kill floor runs or a pig fights back when she's being moved from gestation crate to farrowing crate, those acts are flames of liberation that farmers know would burn down the entire system.

So I know why animal agriculture and those who profit from it don't celebrate freedom and rebellion. But why are those who say they are fighting for lives actually unwilling to fight for lives? Is it perhaps that they've never understood farmed animals as actual beings? I recall speaking with the leader and founder of a nonprofit that is solely funded by Effective Altruist dollars, whom I met at an animal rights conference a few years ago. I invited him to come to Woodstock Farm Sanctuary if he was ever in New York, and he said, "I'd like to—I've never been to a sanctuary." Had he ever met any farmed animals—in a barn, a slaughterhouse, an auction house? Yet he was very welcome in all the conference rooms and meeting rooms to make decisions about the lives of animals found in barns, slaughterhouses, auction houses—and sanctuaries. What this means is that the people responsible for making choices that will impact billions of farmed animals through advocacy and legislative work do not know the beings whose rights are named in the "animal rights movement."

I want an animal rights movement where Fred is the hero. Where Fred's bravery and act of liberation is told and celebrated. And where if we were able to save Fred from those who wished him harm, from those who knew his power, our funders and allies would see that his life would be worth it.

Those who profit off of animal agriculture know the power of individual farmed animals and their acts of rebellion. There is a reason why they are hidden from the public behind deceptive marketing campaigns, lobbying efforts, and locked gates. There is a reason why rebellion is bred out of domestic farmed animals. The owners of farming corporations large and small know that to hide and obfuscate individual animals is just as much a foundation to their business as physical exploitation and harm.

I failed to find Fred before he was killed. His story remains extremely painful for me to think about. But I try to remember that he was free; for a short time, he was truly free. And his freedom and his drive to liberate others was so powerful and threatening that he was killed for it.

Stay free, Fred.

References

Bains J., and Woods A. (2018). "Rogue Goat May Have Helped Dozens of Farm Animals Escape." *New York Post*, August 9. https://nypost.com/2018/08/09/rogue-goat-may-have-helped-dozens-of-farm-animals-escape/.

Kausch, K. (2018a). "Dozens of Sheep, Goats Break Free from Hackettstown Auction. *The Patch*, August 9. https://patch.com/new-jersey/longvalley/dozens-sheep-goats-break-free-hackettstown-auction.

Kausch, K. (2018b). "Fred the Goat Captured in Hackettstown." *The Patch*, August 29. https://patch.com/new-jersey/hackettstown/fred-goat-captured-hackettstown.

Kausch, K. (2018c). "Fred the Goat Will Live Out His Life on a Farm." *The Patch*, September 4. https://patch.com/new-jersey/hackettstown/fred-goat-will-live-out-his-life-farm.

15

Effective Altruism and the Reified Mind

John Sanbonmatsu

> The ideas of the ruling class are in every epoch the ruling ideas, i.e. the class which is the ruling *material* force of society, is at the same time its ruling *intellectual* force. . . . The ruling ideas are [thus] nothing more than the ideal expression of . . . the dominant material relationships grasped as ideas.
>
> —Marx and Engels, *The German Ideology*

One of the most striking things about the Effective Altruism (EA) movement is its complacent view of itself. Innocent of any social origins, so its advocates suppose, the doctrine is said to represent no interest or constituency beyond that of *reason*, and to compass no ambition larger than the general happiness or well-being of all sentient life on earth. Having thus arrogated to itself the twin estates of reason and happiness, Effective Altruism presents itself to the world as the humble bearer of an ultimate truth, a solution to the great problems of history and society. Confounding its many critics, EA thus cheerfully marches on, extending its imperial reach over global philanthropy and social movement discourse alike.

We know, however, that unequal social conditions produce an unequal circulation of ideas, enabling some intellectual positions to assume preeminence over others, not because of their truth value, but because of their degree of compatibility with ascendant structures of the dominant economic system. In the early modern

John Sanbonmatsu, *Effective Altruism and the Reified Mind* In: *The Good It Promises, The Harm It Does.* Edited by: Carol J. Adams, Alice Crary, and Lori Gruen, Oxford University Press.
 DOI: 10.1093/oso/9780197655696.003.0015

era, we find Descartes's conception of animals as machines modeled on early capitalist relations and mechanization, while in the late nineteenth century we find Charles Darwin projecting prevalent laissez-faire views of society as a natural competition between individuals onto relations between species. Today, similarly, we find Effective Altruism formally mirroring the objective structures of late capitalism. The fact that EA has won the support of powerful billionaires is but one indication of how smoothly its ideas fit the status quo. The movement has indeed become virtually indistinguishable from its financial network of wealthy supporters, who now include some of the richest, most powerful people on earth.[1]

Advocates of EA are nothing if not bullish about the virtues of the free market. "Effective altruists are usually not radicals or revolutionaries," explains Robert Wiblin, the director of research for 80,000 Hours and the former executive director of the Centre for Effective Altruism, because "sudden dramatic changes in society usually lead to worse outcomes than gradual evolutionary improvements." Wiblin (2015) admits that he "personally favor[s] maintaining and improving mostly market-driven economies," only because capitalism happens to be the most efficient mechanism for doing good. On this telling, EA has only an *accidental* relationship to capitalism. However, once we examine the matter closely, we find extensive homologies between capitalist institutions and norms, on the one hand, and the epistemic and normative structures of Effective Altruism, on the other.[2] EA can in fact be seen as a symptom of *reification*—the process under advanced capitalism by which thought and culture come to resemble the commodity form.

[1] The web of relations behind the Open Philanthropy Project is indicative: essentially a nonprofit slush fund, the OPP was created by Dustin Moskovitz and his wife, Cari Tuna, a former reporter for the *Wall Street Journal*. (Moskowitz, a cofounder of Facebook, is the youngest self-made billionaire in history, according to *Forbes*.) Open Philanthropy was in turn "incubated as a partnership between Cari and Dustin's foundation, Good Ventures, and GiveWell" (Open Philanthropy, n.d.). GiveWell's main funding, in turn, comes from the Global Health and Development Fund, which is managed by Elie Hassenfeld—a former hedge fund manager and the cofounder of GiveWell.

[2] My analysis broadly follows Max Weber's approach to the interdependency of economic and religious phenomena in *The Protestant Ethic and the Spirit of Capitalism*.

Reification and the Commodity

To understand reification in its simplest form, we might begin with the ancient legend of King Midas, to whom Dionysus gives the power of turning everything he touches into gold. Alas, as the king quickly learns, such a power is inimical to life: Midas cannot eat or drink, because his food turns to gold at his touch, and when he embraces his daughter, she too is transformed into lifeless gold. *Reification*—from the Latin *res*, for "thing"—operates in a similar way, turning living processes into "dead" things. But while Midas was a fictional king, *reification* is a real historical process in which capitalism progressively strips human culture and consciousness of their qualitative features.

Georg Lukács developed the theory of reification in *History and Class Consciousness* (1923; reprinted 1971). In his analysis of commodity fetishism, Marx had shown that while past civilizations produced goods for a variety of symbolic and cultural purposes, capitalism organizes human labor instead around the production of goods solely for their "exchange value," enabling a dominant class to accumulate profit. In this system, all produced goods are treated as abstractly "equivalent" to one another, purely as *quantities*. The labor of human beings, too, is treated abstractly—as a commodity to be bought and sold on a market. With mechanized production and the scientific management of labor, workers now get treated as mere interchangeable parts in a machinery of accumulation. Capital's need to coordinate the minute activities of workers fragments the laborer's activity, in both time and space. Industrialization and urbanization uprooted human beings from the land and from the communal rituals of agrarian life. Meanwhile, the supremacy of standardized time—the mechanical clock counting out hours, minutes, and seconds for coordinating labor—stripped them too of any organic connection to the rhythms of nature.

Lukács's insight was to see how this fragmented commodity process came more and more to obliterate the "human" dimensions of our lives, reducing society to a general scheme of calculability and "rationalization" (the imposition of formal bureaucratic controls over society). Because capitalism is a "unified economic structure," it correspondingly generates too a "unified structure of consciousness" (1971, 100). The *objective* needs of capital require "the commodity structure to penetrate society in all its aspects and to remold it in its own image" (85), causing "the structure of reification [to sink] more deeply, more fatefully and more definitively into the consciousness of man" (93). Reification is thus the means by "which every phenomenon—independently of its real and material distinctiveness" is "subjected to an exact calculus" (129). All domains of knowledge and experience are "subjected to an increasingly formal and standardized treatment in which there is an ever-increasing remoteness from the qualitative and material essence of the 'things' to which bureaucratic activity pertains" (99). In this way, reification comes "to cover the whole surface of manifest phenomena," including the sciences, economics, journalism, the legal system, philosophy (208). It even "invades the realm of ethics" where, "[f]ar from weakening the reified structure of consciousness," it "actually strengthens it" (99).[3]

Because reification is not a "thing," but rather a set of cultural tendencies complexly related to the economic and technological system, we can recognize its presence only through its symptomology. The following are typical of the phenomenon:

- Calculability, or quantitative measurement, held as the supreme basis of human understanding—i.e., "the demand that mathematical and rational categories should be applied to all phenomena" (Lukács 1971, 113).

[3] As with capitalist development as such, reification is an uneven process—it does not extend its influence over all sectors of culture at once, nor to equal local effect. Reification is more advanced in some regions of culture and consciousness more than others, and is likewise more strongly resisted in some places than others.

- Denigration of the qualitative aspects of the human personality, such as intuition, empathy, community, love, etc.
- A naive empiricism rooted in the fragmentation of knowledge, such that objects of cognition are viewed as discrete facts, without reference to complex social geographies.
- A method of analysis that renders complex social problems in a purely formalistic way, without deeper theoretical analysis.
- The machine, or machinic logic, treated as the emblem of true rationality.
- Ahistoricism and homogeneous temporality—time shorn of its qualitative, "merely human" dimensions.
- The modeling of life on the commodity form, such that individuals are represented as fungible, interchangeable units whose lives and deaths can be swapped out for one another—in much the same way that integers may be "swapped out" in a mathematical operation.
- A conception of human agency centered around "the individual, egoistic bourgeois isolated artificially by capitalism" (Lukács 1971, 135). Correspondingly, a voluntarist conception of social change that nonetheless affirms a purely aggregative account of persons in society.

It is symptomatic of reification that these highly distorted views of reason and social being are in turn *hidden from the reified mind itself.* The latter remains oblivious to its own social determinations—i.e., to the totality of social relations that together constitute the epistemic ground beneath its own feet. The problem is not one of simple ignorance, but rather of a pervasive bad faith that impels the reified mind to obscure the truth of its own complicity in power and domination.

All of these symptoms of reification, to varying degrees, are readily observed in the discourses of Effective Altruism.

Effective Altruism as Reified Thought

A widely circulated 2018 TED Talk by William MacAskill, the Oxford philosopher who has become the leading advocate of the EA movement, demonstrates several features of reification, including calculability, elimination of the qualitative dimensions of experience, ahistoricism, and the fungibility of life. In his talk, MacAskill stands before a giant animated graph representing the totality of human civilization through time. Along the X axis is a timeline of the species, beginning 200,000 years ago; along the Y axis is GDP per capita, measured in constant US dollars. "This is a graph," MacAskill explains, "that represents the economic history of human civilization." As MacAskill sets the timeline in motion, we see the centuries along the X axis swiftly disappear off the left side of the screen. Along the Y axis, however, nothing changes—economic growth is flatlined for 2,000 centuries. "There's not very much going on there, is there?" MacAskill quips. "For the vast majority of human history," he continues, "pretty much everyone lived on the equivalent of one dollar per day, and not much changed. But then something extraordinary happened: the Scientific and Industrial Revolutions. And the basically flat graph you just saw? Transforms into *this*." Suddenly, the line along the Y axis takes a 90-degree turn upward. "What this graph means," MacAskill explains, "is that, in terms of the power to change the world, we live in an unprecedented time in human history" (MacAskill 2018).

In reality, human civilization is so richly manifold, composed of such irreducibly diverse forms of embodied cultural experiences that it is not possible to generalize in comparative terms about life in past epochs. With a touch of his remote, however, MacAskill obliterates all traces of the qualitative dimensions of the human experiment. In place of everything that has given human life meaning and purpose, joy and pain, for countless generations—art, science, philosophy, religion, government, social struggle, tradition, rituals of communal life—MacAskill substitutes a single quantitative metric—*per capita GDP*. The four-dimensional nature of our manifold existence as a species is thus collapsed into the two-dimensional Cartesian grid of a PowerPoint slide.[4] Recall Lukács: "[E]very phenomenon—independently of its real and material distinctiveness" must be "subjected to an exact calculus" (1971, 129).[5]

Other advocates of EA, too, assume that the most "rational" approach to social problems and aggregate human suffering is to assume that they can be stripped of their qualitative features and represented as discrete mathematical units, as QALYS (quality-adjusted life years) or DALYS (disability-adjusted life years). Examining the relative utility value of becoming a physician in the developing world versus becoming one in the overdeveloped world, Benjamin Todd comments: "Using a standard conversion rate (used by the World Bank among other institutions) of 30 extra years of healthy life to one 'life saved,' 140 years of healthy life is equivalent to 5 lives saved." Some careers are therefore better than others at maximizing outcomes—and we can calculate the latter using probability: "For instance, a 90 percent chance of helping 100 people is roughly equivalent to a 100 percent chance of helping 90 people" (Todd 2017). Reification is a "universal mathematics" for "calculating the effects of actions and of rationally imposing modes of action" (Lukács 1971,109) in which human activity is not to "go beyond the correct calculation of the possible outcome of the sequence of events" (117). Effective Altruists continually revert to economistic and mathematical terms to represent social problems, weighing philanthropic "investments" against "diminishing returns." As Ayeya Cotra (2017), a senior researcher at Effective Altruism, says: "When we're trying to calculate importance, it's

[4] PowerPoint is itself a significant vehicle of reification—see Tufte 2003.

[5] Only in this way can the reified mind then "predict with ever greater precision all the results to be achieved" (88).

crucial to do the math . . . to figure out how many people a problem affects, to figure out how badly it affects them." Cotra's PowerPoint slide emphatically sums the matter up: "IMPORTANCE = SCALE x SEVERITY"—"ACTUALLY DO THE MATH."

As others have observed, the self-understanding of Effective Altruists as impartial, "evidence-based" vessels of reason mirrors the Weltanschauung of a technocratic managerial elite for whom all phenomena can in fact be reduced to a balance statement, with losses on one side and gains on the other. In both cases, "'control' of reality" is to be effected through "the objectively correct contemplation" of "the abstract combinations of . . . relations and proportions" of assumed fact (Lukács 1971, 129). Inevitably, this top-down worldview leads to the over-valorization of billionaires and financiers in EA discourse, and a corresponding under-valorization of grass-roots activists and radicals. To the extent that EA can be described as a social movement, it is in fact a movement not of struggling social workers, English teachers, or iron workers, but of wealthy (mostly white and male) capitalists, analytic moral philosophers at elite institutions, and, significantly, technologists.

Technologists are frequently cited in EA's devotional accounts of the white male entrepreneur as the savior of society.[6] In one EA presentation, Cotra compares indiscriminate philanthropy to the missed opportunity of venture capitalists to invest in Microsoft in its early years. Displaying a photograph of Bill Gates and other nerdy young men in the late-1970s, Cotra asks, "Would you have invested in them? Most people didn't, and now they're worth $290 billion. The key to being a good investor, and to being a good altruist, is to dig past first impressions and actually do the research so you're more likely to be the one who makes the bet that pays off" (Cotra 2017). That Microsoft is a huge corporate polluter that boasts of its billions of dollars in contracts with the Pentagon, as well as one of

[6] 80,000 Hours particularly recommends that idealists pursue careers in quantitative hedge-fund trading, management consulting, and technology start-ups.

the planet's leading super-spreaders of reification in daily life, including in public education, goes unremarked by the presenter.[7] A similarly worshipful attitude toward technology entrepreneurs can be seen in other sectors of EA—as in the lobbying efforts of the Good Food Institute to promote cellular or synthesized meats (Sanbonmatsu et al. 2020).

As Lukács observed, "machinic" processes are central to reification; Herbert Marcuse later described "technological rationality" as "reification in its most mature and effective form" (Marcuse 2002, 172). In this context, the belief of elites that they can control and predict behavior in civil society is but an extension of the fragmented, mechanized labor process itself—i.e., the "structural analogue to the behavior of the worker vis-á-vis the machine he serves and observes":

> The distinction between a worker faced with a particular machine, the entrepreneur faced with a given type of mechanical development, the technologist faced with the state of science and the profitability of its application to technology, is purely quantitative; it does not directly entail *any qualitative difference in the structure of consciousness.* (Lukács 1971, 98; original emphasis)

Technologists view the world as an aggregate of resources to be manipulated and rearranged at will, such that "the principle of rational mechanization and calculability must embrace every aspect of life" (Lukács 1971, 91). It is not surprising, then, that Effective Altruists should frequently lionize Alan Turing, the father of the computer, nor that many of them, including Cotra, have professional backgrounds in computer science. For if mathematics is the software of reification, computerization is its literal hardware—the technological medium through which reified logics have come

[7] The Bill and Melinda Gates Foundation has imposed a reified pedagogy, through computerization, on millions of public school students (Stecher, Holtzman, et al., 2018).

to penetrate every aspect of human consciousness and daily life, through video games and Fitbits to online shopping, pornography, and the manipulation of elections by companies like Cambridge Analytica. Few aspects of our experiences today escape mediation by computer algorithms. If reification is, as Lukács described it, a "dehumanized and dehumanizing" process in which "the personality can do no more than look on helplessly while its own existence is reduced to an isolated particle and fed into an alien system" (1971, 90, 92), then computerization is the ideal form of this instrumentality, the instantiation of a narrow conception of reason purified of "contamination" by the body or its feelings, such as love, desire, passion, empathy, suffering, etc.

An expression of the mathematical mind, computing is admired in EA as the paradigmatic model of consciousness itself, as such, to such a degree that its proponents seem to model their *own* subjectivity on the disembodied logic of the computer. "I don't know about you," confesses Cotra, "but I'm a bleeding heart. If I were to just make up numbers for how important each [philanthropic] cause was, everything would be an 11 on a scale from 1 to 10. But there's going to be a world of difference between two causes that both seem like urgent life and death situations." In the interests of "fairness," then, we must "ruthlessly prioritize among causes" (Cotra 2017). Other Effective Altruists, too, caution against "choosing with the heart" or "going with our gut" when trying to promote the good. The movement is consequently hostile toward sentiment in general and empathy in particular. (Paul Bloom's book, *Against Empathy: The Case for Rational Compassion*, is widely admired in Effective Altruism circles [Elmore 2016].) The "rational" altruist tells us to place our trust neither in moral intuition nor in elemental fellow-feeling, but rather in the high priests who keep the numbers—bankers, policy wonks, economists, elite academics, and, especially, AI researchers.

In the 1960s, Norbert Wiener (1968) and other computer scientists fantasized about achieving perfect cybernetic control over the totality of human life. Since then, technologists attached to the national security state and corporate capital have sought to remake society in the image of mathematical machines. From their vantage point, there is no problem that cannot in theory be solved using a form of instrumental reason alienated from nature, the body, and the social. Effective Altruists too have made artificial intelligence (AI) central to their technocratic vision of mastery over social problems, with 80,000 Hours noting that "the next few decades might see the development of powerful machine learning algorithms with the potential to transform society" (80,000 Hours). While Effective Altruists warn that AI poses an "existential threat" to our species, suggesting that the emergence of a "superintelligence" could threaten human autonomy, they nonetheless embrace AI as a way to make the world "better," counseling budding altruists to pursue careers in "top AI labs." Unfortunately, however, since EA is unable to comprehend the *social* basis of technology in the structure of domination, its advocates fail to recognize its role in concentrating state and corporate power. 80,000 Hours thus encourages idealists wanting to change the world to build careers within the apparatus of the US national security state, by joining the Office of the Secretary of State, the National Security Council, or DARPA, the Pentagon's cutting-edge research arm ("The Highest Impact," 80,000 Hours)—despite the fact that the US spends nearly a trillion dollars annually on war-making, indiscriminately bombs civilians, props up dictatorships, and imposes unequal terms of trade on Third World economies. Somehow, on its path to "doing good," EA has wound up promoting radical evil.

Irrationality and Crisis

Under reification, "quantity alone determines everything," and time itself "sheds its qualitative, variable, flowing nature, [and] . . .

freezes into an exactly delimited, quantifiable continuum filled with quantifiable 'things'" (Lukács 1971, 89–90). This formulation, amounting to what Walter Benjamin (2019) termed "empty, homogeneous time," corresponds more or less exactly to the temporality depicted in MacAskill's TED talk—his collapse of human species history into a timeline of per capita GDP. Not content to homogenize the past, however, MacAskill in the same talk projects "empty, homogeneous time" onto the future, too. EA's proponents are in fact never more eloquent or ecstatic than when speaking of humans *who do not yet exist*, whose lives and interests they nonetheless imbue with greater moral importance than the *merely existing* humans and nonhuman animals of the present. By colonizing other planets, MacAskill thus maintains, *Homo sapiens* might live for "billions" more years, while EA advocate Toby Ord, in his bestselling book *The Precipice*, similarly invites the reader to imagine the "millions of generations" of future humans yet to come—provided only that we first dispatch the "existential threats" facing our species. Given the imminent collapse of the earth's ecosystem, such views—which characterize existence only in terms of *quantities* of experience—are not so much optimistic as dissociative.

This homogeneous rendering of time finds its complement in the occlusion of historical fact—as when MacAskill credits the growth of GDP to "the Scientific and Industrial Revolutions," rather than to the birth of capitalism. That MacAskill fails even to mention capitalism—the chief structuring principle of human economic and social life for the last five hundred years—is hardly an accident: only by mystifying the social origins of economic growth can he sell his cheerful vision of transhistorical progress. For to admit where all this miraculous wealth came from—viz., the violent appropriation of the resources, lives, and labor of countless millions of humans and nonhumans—would otherwise require him to confront such horrors as the Atlantic slave trade, the genocide of Indigenous peoples in the Americas, Australia, and New Zealand, the destruction of the great forests of Europe, and the extermination of billions of land and sea animals to satisfy Europe's insatiable markets for fur, fish, meat, and whale oil.

It is ironic, in this connection, that EA should pride itself on being "evidence-based" when its naive rejection of historicism and critical theory renders it *anti-empirical* in orientation. Ostensibly, the "principle of rationalization" enables the knower to "to predict with ever greater precision all the results to be achieved" (Lukács 1971, 88). In reality, however, a chasm opens up between the form and content of knowledge—i.e., between the conceptual apparatus of the "knower" and the actual content of social life. Trapped within a reified system with which it "[harmonizes] its own structure" of thought (95), the reified mind is only able to "grasp what it itself has created" (121–122). It "surrenders to the immediate facts," and in so doing "repels recognition of the factors behind the facts, and thus repels recognition of the facts, and of their historical content" (Marcuse 2002, 101). Effective Altruism's empirical inadequacy is for this reason incurable, since the "facts" that it posits are shorn of their wider sociohistorical context and significance. Because reification leads "to the destruction of every image of the whole" (Lukács 1971, 103)—occlusion of the totality of social relations—the Effective Altruist is chronically "unable to grasp the meaning of the overall process as it really is," the " 'organic' unity of phenomena" (182, 188). This renders EA incapable of perceiving the patterned forces in society that lead to harm.

Though MacAskill, Peter Singer, and other Effective Altruists make much of the "good" that the rich effect in giving away portions of their fortunes in "effective" ways, the philanthropy of the rich recedes into insignificance alongside the global destruction wrought by concentrated wealth. Since the signing of the Paris Agreement on climate change in 2016, for example, "banks have facilitated almost $4 trillion of financing for fossil fuel companies, including $459 billion worth of bonds and loans for oil, gas and coal companies" in 2021 alone (Gelles 2021), a figure that is an order of magnitude greater than all US philanthropic giving in the same period. Some of the same corporate leaders praised by Effective Altruists for having committed themselves to a net-zero carbon future have meanwhile resisted policy changes that could threaten corporate bottom lines. At the COP26 UN Climate Change Conference in Glasgow in 2021, for example, Jamie Dimon, the CEO of JP Morgan Chase, who has championed climate reform, pushed back against the demands of radical activists at the conference, warning that it was important for banks "to keep funding conventional energy production." "You're not going to get rid of oil and gas consumption tomorrow," he told reporters (Gelles 2021). Financiers at the summit furthermore blamed the divestment movement for energy shortages and soaring energy prices, with Laurence D. Fink of BlackRock—a leading corporate figure in "conscious capitalism" (Currie 2020)—warning that transitioning too quickly away from oil would hurt emerging economies.

The reason Effective Altruists are unable to "connect the dots" between the capitalist system and its manifest consequences is that their "philosophic critique finds itself blocked by the reality from which it dissociates itself" (Marcuse 2002, 139). Doomed to mistake its own "rational and formalistic mode of cognition" for "the only possible way of apprehending reality" (Lukács 1971, 104–105, 121), EA remains helpless before the complex mediations of culture, society, and economy, unaware "that the world lying beyond its confines, and in particular . . . its own underlying reality lies, methodologically and in principle, beyond its grasp" (104). If society really did consist merely of quantifiable facts, then EA's faith in dispassionate reason and calculation might be justified. Alas, society does not resemble the rational scheme that effective altruists attribute to it, leaving the latter blind to the "irrationality of the total process" (Lukács 1971, 102). Within EA's cramped intellectual rooms, there is no space for Marx or Freud, or for feminism, critical race theory, or any other historicist framework that would enable it to comprehend the social origins of, say, authoritarian populism, male violence against women, or the destruction of animals and nature. Such phenomena simply "do not compute" within EA's own mathematicized schema, leaving the "reified mind . . . unable to perceive a pattern in this 'chaos'" (Lukács 1971, 105). As a consequence, the movement can take aim only at the *secondary effects of the primary phenomena*. In his TED talk, MacAskill thus misidentifies the biggest problems today as global health, factory farming, and existential threats (chiefly, nuclear war, meteor strikes, and AI "singularities"). However, the global poor suffer from adverse health outcomes because of *capitalist social relations* (i.e., from a coercive division of labor rooted in exploitation and domination); the suffering of animals stems not from "factory farming," but from long-standing patterns of human, patriarchal domination, on the one hand, and capitalist accumulation, on the other; and though we may have good reason to worry about accidental nuclear war and stray asteroids, we face more urgent concerns today—including, and above all, the mass extinction crisis. (The latter, though by far the worst catastrophe to befall terrestrial life in 66 million years, goes strangely unmentioned by MacAskill, both in his TED talk and in *Doing Good Better*, his bestselling book.)

An inability to comprehend "the phenomenon of crisis" (Lukács 1971, 105) is thus itself one of the symptoms of the reified mind. If Effective Altruists have failed to recognize the true scale of the catastrophe, or to grasp its origins, it is because today's global crisis—the destruction of the ecological order and the breakdown of the economic, social, and political structures that have long organized human life—is rooted in fundamentally irrational social structures, institutions, and norms of which Effective Altruists can form no definite idea. As a consequence, Effective Altruists will no doubt continue to see hopeful signs of incremental, quantitative progress in specific areas of policy—e.g., in extreme poverty or malaria reduction—right up to the moment when the entire system collapses, leaving billions to starve to death and all animal life obliterated.

Subverting Praxis and Mystifying Social Change

The evidence suggests that EA comprehends reality only in its outermost form—in the realm of appearances or immediacy (i.e., not in its fundamental character). As such, it is unable to envision a society meaningfully different than the one we now have, and so ends up affirming a conservative politics that takes existing social arrangements for granted. (As Robert Wiblin [2015] says, "We don't want to burn the existing system to the ground," only "to make enduring improvements to national and international systems to ensure [that] the future is better than the past.") Such "operational rationality," as Marcuse termed it, seeks to improve the mechanisms of repression and control, without, however, questioning their "timeless" character. Since the "reified world appears . . . as the only possible world, the only conceptually accessible, comprehensible world vouchsafed to us humans" (Lukács 1971, 110), reality shrinks to mere "facticity," assuming the appearance of a fixed social order with "the patina of an eternal law of nature or a cultural value enduring for all time" (157). Forms of collective action and dissent that cannot be quantified are meanwhile viewed either as irrelevant or as a threat to rational planning.

The inability of Effective Altruists to picture a meaningfully different world helps explain their contempt for grass-roots activism, radicalism, and small-scale nonprofits. If existing institutions and norms are basically the right ones, and societal problems are a matter simply of reallocating resources, then attempts to disrupt or unsettle the status quo are rightly to be viewed skeptically. However, few of EA's own descriptions of moral life, human behavior, or history correspond to the observable features of reality.

This is especially true of the doctrine's representation of the history and phenomenology of collective action, which it falsifies. EA's claim that change occurs as the aggregate result of the rational, "evidence-based" choices of dispassionate individuals fails to comport with the history of social change, which is effected not so much through incremental adjustments as by impassioned social struggles with the force to shatter an existing status quo. Consider the following cases:

- To win voting rights, British women march in the streets, go on hunger strikes, and firebomb the homes of government officials.
- When a police squad stages a routine raid on a gay nightclub in lower Manhattan, the club's patrons respond by violently rioting (to the surprise of themselves as much as to the officers).
- To strike a blow against racial segregation, a coalition of Black Christian churches organizes a boycott of buses in Montgomery, Alabama.
- Women hold consciousness-raising groups in their homes, to share their common experiences of oppression by men.
- A Tunisian man sets himself on fire to protest the lack of democracy in his country, sparking a pro-democracy movement of millions that sweeps across the Middle East.
- An autistic teenage girl in Sweden stops attending high school so that she can hold a sign on the steps of the parliament—to demand government action on climate change.

Effective Altruists cannot easily account for these or other signal events in the history of social movements because their mechanistic, fragmented conception of the world leaves them without a proper account of human agency and will. They are unable to offer a meaningful description of the affective experiences of human beings involved in struggles to overcome structures and institutions of power and injustice. EA's notion that human agency should be purged of passionate feelings, including empathy—a recurring theme in utilitarian thought—furthermore mirrors a wider masculinist culture that eschews compassion and valorizes domination.[8] As phenomenologists and feminist care ethicists have shown, however, empathy plays an indispensable role in constituting our moral objects (Donovan 2011, 77–94), and is even a "precondition" for moral performance (Vetlesen 2014). Arguably, it is our very capacity to "feel" our way into the experiences of others that makes moral life possible. Edith Stein went so far as to claim that empathy is the ground of *intersubjectivity* itself (Hamington 2018).

That Effective Altruists nevertheless persist in denying these basic facts of moral and social cognition is itself a symptom of their reified worldview. They assume the dissociated stance of the "experimenter" or "pure observer" (Lukács 1971, 131), the knower who stands over or apart from "the known." As both Hegel and Marx noted, however, objective structures are realized or brought into being *subjectively* (i.e., though the passion, will, emotion, determination, etc., of flesh and blood human beings). Such a *dialectical* conception is foreign to EA, which conceives of society as a fixed system of "facts." Under the mantle of a supposed pragmatism, the Effective Altruist looks at the way things "really are," then adjusts his or her expectations and goals to suit the existing reality. The trouble is, when we set out believing and acting as though the world *already is what it is*—rather than something that can become *other than it is*—we foreclose on historical possibilities that might otherwise reveal themselves to us. "Only the man who wills something strongly," Antonio Gramsci observed, "can identify the elements which are necessary to the realization of his will," because "strong passions are necessary to sharpen the intellect and make intuition

[8] The repugnance of Effective Altruists for such "feminine" sentiments as compassion mirrors the movement's undertow of misogyny. Stijn Bruers, a leading Effective Altruist in Belgium, thus denies that women are systematically disadvantaged by men, saying that "the feminist movement's reaction against men's rights issues is irrational, with feminists misrepresenting a lot of men's rights activists as rape apologists." Bruers states that he "no longer believes in something like a patriarchal system that systematically privileges men and suppresses women" (Bruers 2017).

more penetrating" (1971, 171). Reality assumes determinate form only when we exercise our emotions, passions, intellect, and will as an organic unity, in concert with other perceiving, thinking, feeling beings.

There is nothing wrong with wanting to help minimize the suffering of others, nor with wanting to use one's limited time and resources wisely. These are sensible and admirable sentiments. (If nothing else, the success of Effective Altruism challenges us to confront more honestly the dearth of strategic thinking on the left, and the need for movements to develop more carefully worked through, long-term plans for social struggle.) However, while consequentialist theory is of use in moral philosophy, it is inadequate and even harmful as a guide to social and political emancipation. The consequentialism of both Bentham and J. S. Mill hewed closely to the common sense of the bourgeois class of the early manufacturing period—a "free market" in thought as in international trade; the isolated, monadic individual as the basis of social life; the reduction of moral life (in Bentham's version of the "hedonic calculus") to quantitative measures; the supremacy of formal over substantive conceptions of freedom. Today we find these same *asocial* assumptions embedded in EA discourse as well. MacAskill's morally repugnant call for an *increase* in the number of sweatshops in the Third World (2016, 128–132) is merely the artifact of a utilitarian ideology incapable of recognizing *exploitation* as a moral or social problem.[9]

Contrary to the claims of its advocates, then, EA is neither "impartial" nor politically neutral. As reified thought, EA is "anti-critical and anti-dialectical," serving to "absorb" into its own conceptual universe "the transcendent, negative, and oppositional elements of Reason" (Marcuse 2002, 100–101). Marcuse observed

[9] Mistaking the effect for the cause, MacAskill depicts sweatshops as the consequence of extreme poverty, rather than of a world capitalist system whose economic laws generate a perpetual need for cheap labor.

that the more we resist unfreedom, the more the dominant system appropriates our instinctual longings for emancipation and turns them against us, channeling our longings into cultural forms that serve only to strengthen the overall structure of repression. EA is but the latest entry in this dismal losing game. Trapped in the web of its own conceptual antinomies—reason vs. feeling, pragmatism vs. "idealism," quantity vs. quality—EA is unable to identify the root of our problems or to suggest plausible means for overcoming them. One need not doubt the good intentions of individual Effective Altruists to conclude that their approach ironically preserves the very institutions that cause humans and nonhumans the most suffering. Effective Altruism is not merely unhelpful; it undermines human collective yearning for what Lukács termed an "authentic humanity, the true essence of man liberated from the false, mechanizing forms of society."

References

Benjamin, Walter. (2019). "Theses on the Philosophy of History." In *Illuminations: Essays and Reflections*. New York: Mariner, 196–209.

Bruers, S. (2017). "It's Time to Take the Red Pill and Change Your Mind." In *Stijn Bruers, the rational ethicist* (blog), September 2. https://stijnbruers.wordpress.com/2017/09/02/its-time-to-take-the-red-pill-and-change-your-mind/.

Clean Meat Hoax. (n.d.). https://www.cleanmeat-hoax.com/.

Cotra, A. (2017). "Introduction to Effective Altruism." Address at the Effective Altruism Global X conference (EAGx Berkeley 2016); transcribed July 14, 2017. https://forum.effectivealtruism.org/posts/5EqJozsDdHcF7dpPL/introduction-to-effective-altruism-ajeya-cotra.

Currie, L. (2020). "The Rise and Rise of Conscious Capitalism." In *Meet the Leader* (blog), January 19. https://www.meettheleader.com/blogs-1/blog-the-rise-and-rise-of-conscious-capitalism.

Donovan, J. (2011). "Sympathy and Interspecies Care: Toward a Unified Theory of Eco- and Animal Liberation" In *Critical Theory and Animal Liberation*, edited by John Sanbonmatsu. Lanham, MD: Rowman & Littlefield, 277–294.

80,000 Hours. https://80000hours.org/career-reviews/ai-safety-researcher/.

Elmore, H. (2016). "We Are in Triage in Every Second of Every Day" Praises Paul Bloom's "Against Empathy: The Case for Rational Compassion." *Effective Altruism Forum*, August 6. https://forum.effectivealtruism.org/s/YCa8BRQoxKbmf5CJb/p/vQpk3cxdAe5RX9xzo).

Gelles, D. (2021). "With Climate Pledges, Some Wall Street Titans Warn of Rising Prices." *New York Times*, November 4. https://www.nytimes.com/2021/11/04/business/cop26-wall-street-pledges-fossil-fuels.html.

Gramsci, A. (1971). *Selections from the Prison Notebooks*. Edited by Quentin Hoare and Geoffrey Nowell Smith. New York: International Publishers.

Hamington, M. (2004). *Embodied Care: Jane Addams, Maurice Merleau-Ponty, and Feminist Ethics*. Urbana: University of Illinois Press.

Lukács, G. (1971). *History and Class Consciousness*. Cambridge, MA: MIT Press.

Marcuse, H. (2002). *One-Dimensional Man*. 2nd ed. New York: Routledge.

MacAskill, W. (2018). "What Are the Most Important Moral Problems of Our Time?" TED Talk, April 2018. https://www.ted.com/talks/will_macaskill_what_are_the_most_important_moral_problems_of_our_time?language=en#t-14221.

MacAskill, W. (2016). *Doing Good Better*. New York: Penguin.

Marx, K., and F. Engels. (1970). *The German Ideology*. Edited by C. J. Arthur. New York: International Publishers.

Open Philanthropy. (n.d.). "Press Kit." https://www.openphilanthropy.org/about/press-kit.

Stecher, B. M., D. J. Holtzman, et al. (2018). *Improving Teaching Effectiveness: Final Report: The Intensive Partnerships for Effective Teaching Through 2015-16*. Santa Monica, CA: RAND Corporation. https://www.rand.org/pubs/research_reports/RR2242.html.

Todd, B. (2017). "Can One Person Make a Difference?" 80,000 Hours, April 2017. https://80000hours.org/career-guide/can-one-person-make-a-difference/.

Tufte, E. (2003). *The Cognitive Style of PowerPoint*. Cheshire, CT: Graphics Press.

Vetlesen, A. (2014). *Perception, Empathy, and Judgment: An Inquiry into the Preconditions of Moral Performance*. University Park: Pennsylvania State University Press.

Wiblin, R. (2016). "Effective Altruists Love Systemic Change." 80,000 Hours, July 9. https://80000hours.org/2015/07/effective-altruists-love-systemic-change/.

Wiener, N. (1968). *The Human Use of Human Beings: Cybernetics and Society*. London: Sphere Books.

16

Against "Effective Altruism"

Alice Crary

Effective Altruism (EA) is a program for rationalizing charitable giving, positioning individuals to do the "most good" per expenditure of money or time. It was first formulated—by two Oxford philosophers just over a decade ago—as an application of the moral theory of consequentialism, and from the outset one of its distinctions within the philanthropic world was expansion of the class of charity recipients to include nonhuman animals. EA has been the target of a fair bit of grumbling, and even some mockery, from activists and critics on the left, who associate consequentialism with depoliticizing tendencies of welfarism. But EA has mostly gotten a pass, with many detractors concluding that, however misguided, its efforts to get bankers, tech entrepreneurs, and the like to give away their money cost-effectively does no serious harm.

This stance is no longer tenable. The growth of EA has been explosive, with some affiliated organizations, such as Open Philanthropy, now recommending grants amounting to hundreds of millions of dollars annually. Partly building on congenial trends in development economics, and in tandem with movements like "impact investing," EA has become a force capable of leaving its imprint on whole fields of public engagement. This is in evidence in the domain of animal advocacy, to which EA has brought substantial new attention and funding. One result of the windfall is that EA-guided ratings groups serve as kingmakers, raising up pro-animal organizations deemed "effective" by EA and denigrating

Alice Crary, *Against "Effective Altruism"* In: *The Good It Promises, The Harm It Does.* Edited by: Carol J. Adams, Alice Crary, and Lori Gruen, Oxford University Press. © Oxford University Press 2023. DOI: 10.1093/oso/9780197655696.003.0016 and partly defunding many organizations deemed "ineffective," while pressuring others to artificially shift their missions in order to conform to operative metrics of "effectiveness" and secure funding. This has led to objections from animal advocates (often muted due to fear of alienating EA-admiring funders). Yet champions of EA, whether or not they are concerned with the cause of animals, for the most part adopt the attitude that they have no serious critics and that skeptics ought to be content with their ongoing attempts to fine-tune their practice.

Yet there are formidable critical resources both inside and outside the philosophical tradition in which EA originates. In light of the undisputed impact of EA, and its success in attracting idealistic young people, it is important to forcefully make the case that it owes its success primarily not to the (questionable) value of its moral theory but to its compatibility with political and economic institutions responsible for some of the very harms it addresses. The sincere dedication of many individual adherents notwithstanding, EA is a straightforward example of moral corruption.

Anatomy of EA

Consequentialist ideas inform the way EA is implemented by many EA-affiliated groups focusing largely on human outreach, such as Development Media International, GiveWell, and Giving What We Can. Such ideas also inform EA's implementation by groups focusing largely on animals, such as Animal Charity Evaluators and Faunalytics, and by groups like Open Philanthropy that address both humans and nonhuman animals. Consequentialism is a rather big tent, accommodating a variety of EAs. Some advocates argue that it is not necessary for Effective Altruists to be consequentialists (Vinding 2018). Others go further, claiming that EA is "independent of any theoretical commitments" (McMahan 2016, 93). This last claim is false, reflecting ignorance of competing ethical traditions from which criticism of EA arises. But it is fair to set aside the question of whether one can be an Effective Altruist without being a consequentialist. The consequentialist stances that have figured in the articulation and institutional actualization of EA presuppose a distinctive philosophical worldview, and it is possible to move from criticism of this worldview to a thoroughgoing attack on EA's most destructive aspects. The resulting nonconsequentialist outlook makes it possible to expose EA-style talk of doing the "most good" as confused, delegitimizing evaluations of charitable organizations that presuppose such talk's coherence, and thus rendering moot the question of whether such evaluations are invariably consequentialist.

A short survey of consequentialist ideas may be helpful for those not familiar with the tradition. Consequentialism is the view that moral rightness is a matter of the production of the best consequences or best state of affairs. What is "best" is what has the most value. So consequentialist stances need to include theories of value. Within this scheme, consequentialists can be very open about what things are assessed as right or wrong (Parfit 1984, 25). They can talk about the rightness not only of actions but of anything with consequences, including desires, beliefs, dispositions, and sets of actions. While consequentialists can also be fairly open about what counts as values, their epistemological assumptions constrain what values can be like.

Effective Altruists often demonstrate consequentialist commitments by locating themselves within consequentialism's spaces of alternatives. During EA's brief history, self-avowed Effective Altruists have tended to take as the objects of moral assessment particular actions, while also taking as their core value the sort of well-being capturable by the metrics of welfare economics. One instrument that some have recommended for assessing actions in terms of well-being is the quality-adjusted life year, or QALY, an economic metric for health programs, which integrates measures of the value of extending individuals' lives with measures of the quality of life over the relevant period, with one QALY standing for one year of life in perfect health. Some Effective Altruists use QALYs to determine which of a set of actions (say, intervening medically to prevent "ten people from suffering from AIDs [versus intervening to prevent] one hundred people from suffering from severe arthritis") produces more well-being and does more good (MacAskill 2015, 34). The assessments often involve further steps, such as randomized controlled trials to get reliable accounts of interventions' consequences, calculations of interventions' marginal utilities, and counterfactual considerations of the value of outcomes that would be produced by different interventions individuals are positioned to make.

There is a further respect in which Effective Altruists fly consequentialist colors. Consequentialists sometimes gloss their take on the moral enterprise by saying that moral reflection is undertaken from the "point of view of the universe," accenting that they conceive such reflection as disengaged and dispassionate (Singer 2015, 84–85).[1] This abstract moral epistemology is one of the marks of a moral radicalism that, although sometimes criticized for the extent of its demands, gets celebrated by consequentialists. The morally radical suggestion is that our ability to act so as to produce value anywhere places the same moral demands on us as our ability to produce value in our immediate circumstances. A famous case from the prominent philosopher and EA advocate Peter Singer takes well-being as a value and suggests that our ability to act so as to address suffering in any spot on earth places the same moral demands on us as does our ability to address the suffering of an unaccompanied toddler drowning in a shallow pond next to the road on which we're walking (Singer 1972, 231).

This radical twist on consequentialism's abstract moral epistemology underlies two of Effective Altruists' signature gestures. First, Effective Altruists inherit it when they exhort us to be guided

[1] The original source of the gesture is Sidgwick.

by their recommendations in a way that treats as irrelevant the question of who is helped, without following our passions or favoring projects to which we have particular attachments (See Singer 2015, chapter 8; and MacAskill 2015, 41 and chapter 9). Second, Effective Altruists presuppose a radical take on an abstract moral epistemology in urging us to do the "most good." Their abstract approach excludes any virtue-oriented view on which the rightness of actions is appropriately engaged responsiveness to circumstances, and this makes it seem more natural to account for rightness by looking to the value of actions' consequences. Consequentialists may hold that there are multiple kinds of valuable things, and that there has never been "a consensus among [them] about the relative weights of any sets of values" (Hiller 2017, 270). But it is the idea that rightness is a matter of the value of quantifiable consequences, allowing for difficulties of juggling different classes of values, that makes it seem coherent to speak of single judgments about how to do the most good.

EA's god's eye image of moral reflection constrains how we can conceive of ethical thought and practice, leaving no room for views intolerant of the idea that moral reflection proceeds from the point of view of the universe (e.g., Lazari-Radeck and Singer 2014). Thereby excluded are views, such as some Kantian constructivisms, that combine accounts of moral reflection as essentially perspectival with understandings of theoretical reflection as maximally abstract (Korsgaard 2018, 9, 95). Also excluded are views that combine accounts of moral reflection as essentially engaged with understandings of theoretical reflection on which such reflection is likewise conceived as situated and non-abstract. Under the latter heading are various outlooks, some associated with strands of virtue theory, that represent values as woven into the world's fabric, so that particular sensitivities are required to recognize them.

Many Effective Altruists fail to register these exclusions as exclusions. Consider the views associated with virtue theory. EA's Oxford-trained founders work in a philosophical tradition, indebted to classic empiricism, shaped by the assumption that subjective endowments have an essential tendency to obstruct our access to the world. Thinkers in this tradition often take it for granted that any genuine aspects of the world are abstractly accessible. Acquaintance with local history suggests this posture is questionable. Twentieth-century Oxonian philosophy featured high-profile debates about whether subjective propensities internally inform our ability to bring the world into focus. Among the most outspoken participants were members of a set of women philosophers at Oxford during and after World War II—including G. E. M. Anscombe, Philippa Foot, and Iris Murdoch—who distanced themselves from the idea that subjective endowments invariably tend to block our view of things. These philosophers made room for views on which evaluative concepts trace out genuine forms of regularity that are only non-neutrally available.[2] To sideline this part of Anglophone philosophy is to overlook its most notable resources for criticizing consequentialism and consequentialism's EA-oriented offshoots.

EA's guiding ideas should be considered alongside the work of groups that implement them. Focusing on animal advocacy, we might take a snapshot of the activity of a prominent EA-affiliated animal charity assessor, Animal Charity Evaluators. Nine pro-animal organizations received either Animal Charity Evaluators'

[2] For discussion of the work of these philosophers, see Clare Mac Cumhaill and Rachael Wiseman, *Metaphysical Animals: How Four Women Brought Philosophy Back to Life* (Dublin: Penguin Random House, 2022). See also G. E. M. Anscombe, "On Brute Facts," *Analysis* 18, no. 3 (1958): 69–72; Philippa Foot, "Moral Arguments," *Mind* 268 (1958): 502–513; Iris Murdoch, "Vision and Choice in Morality," in *Existentialists and Mystics: Writings on Philosophy and Literature*, ed. Peter Conradi (New York: Penguin Books, 1997), 76–98. For the tradition's continuation, see Annette Baier, "What Do Women Want in a Moral Theory," *Noûs* 19, no. 1 (1985): 53–63; *Cora Diamond*, *The Realistic Spirit: Wittgenstein, Philosophy, and the Mind* (Cambridge, MA: MIT Press, 1991), and "'We Are Perpetually Moralists': Iris Murdoch, Fact and Value," in *Iris Murdoch and the Search for Human Goodness*, ed. Maria Antonaccio and William Schweiker (Chicago: University of Chicago Press, 1996), 79–109; Philippa Foot, *Natural Goodness* (Oxford: Oxford University Press, 2001); John McDowell, *Mind, Value and Reality* (Cambridge, MA: Harvard University Press, 1998), chaps. 3, 6, 7, and 10; David Wiggins, *Needs, Values, Truth*, 3rd ed. (Oxford: Oxford University Press, 2002), chap. 5.

highest ("top") or second-highest ("stand out") rating for 2019. Of these at least eight focus on farmed animals. (The one possible exception, Faunalytics, itself uses principles of EA to rate animal charities.) Animal Charity Evaluators' website explains that, for every dog or cat "euthanized" in a shelter worldwide, 3,400 farm animals are killed, yet spending on organizations that address animals in industrial agriculture is a small fraction of pro-animal giving. Of the eight recommended organizations that deal with farmed animals, six—or 75 percent—are primarily concerned with welfare improvements within industrial animal agriculture (the Albert Schweitzer Foundation, Animal International, the Humane League, Compassion in World Farming, The Federation of Indian Animal Protection Organisations, Sinergia Animal), with the other two (the Good Food Institute and Sociedade Vegetariana Brasileira) focused more on structural transformation. Animal Charity Evaluators' website explains that it has more confidence in assessments of the short-term impact of welfarist interventions than in those of the long-term impact of efforts at systems change.

The Institutional Critique

The most fully elaborated criticism of EA, developed largely by economists and political theorists, is sometimes referred to as the *institutional critique* (see, e.g., Berkey 2018). This critique attacks Effective Altruists for operating with a damagingly narrow interpretation of the class of things that are assessable as right or wrong. It targets Effective Altruists' tendency to focus on single actions and their proximate consequences and, more specifically, on simple interventions that reduce suffering in the short term. Advocates of the institutional critique are, on the whole, concerned to decry the neglect, on the part of EA, of coordinated sets of actions directed at changing social structures that reliably cause suffering. EA's metrics are best suited to detect the short-term impact of particular actions, so its tendency to discount the impact of coordinated actions can be seen as reflecting "measurability bias." A leitmotif of the institutional critique of EA is that this bias is politically dangerous because it obscures the structural, political roots of global misery, thereby contributing to its reproduction by weakening existing political mechanisms for positive social change.[3]

The institutional critique of EA can be brought to bear on Animal Charity Evaluators' 2019 ratings. Animal Charity Evaluators' favoring of welfare improvements in the conditions of farmed animals can be taken to reflect forms of ("measurement") bias in its metrics, which are best suited to detect the outcomes of simpler efforts with clear short-term impacts. This orientation speaks for striving to change the methods of meat companies in ways that leave unquestioned the larger political context in which the companies operate. The result is that, despite its sincere pro-animal stance, Animal Charity Evaluators is at risk of strengthening an industrial agricultural system that reproduces horrific animal suffering on a massive scale.

A number of Effective Altruists have responded to the institutional critique. Responses generally allow that some EA programs have placed undue stress on quantitative tools for capturing short-term effects of individual actions, and that, in thus overemphasizing "the importance of relying on quantifiable evidence of the kind that [randomized control trials] can provide" (Berkey 2018, 160), they demonstrate measurability bias (Sebo and Singer 2018, 34–35). The responses also mostly claim that, properly understood, EA calls on us to evaluate anything with relevant consequences, including

[3] See especially Emily Clough, "Effective Altruism's Political Blindspot," *Boston Review*, July 14, 2015, http://bostonreview.net/world/emily-clough-effective-altruism-ngos; Angus Deaton, "The Logic of Effective Altruism," *Boston Review*, July 1, 2015, http://bostonreview.net/forum/logic-effective-altruism/angus-deaton-response-effective-altruism. For critiques of humanitarian trends in development work that in some ways anticipate the institutional critique of EA, see, e.g., Mark Duffield, *Global Governance and the New Wars: The Merging of Development and Security* (New York: Zed Books, 2001); Didier Fassin, *Humanitarian Reason: A Moral History of the Present* (Berkeley: University of California Press, 2010).

collective efforts to produce institutional change. This is the stance of two advocates who argue that EA obliges us to take seriously the role that coordinated actions and other tactics can play "within and across social movements," where this involves being open to consulting fields such as "history and social, political and economic theory" for instruments to measure their effects (Sebo and Singer 2018, 40–41).

While replies to the institutional critique bring out that there is room to include collective actions among EA's objects of assessment, and to introduce new tools for capturing effects of such actions, they leave unexamined questions about whether it is confused to insist on causal effects as the standard for evaluating collective attempts to change the normative structure of society. The general idea is that EA can treat the institutional critique as an internal critique that calls for more faithfully realizing, not abandoning, its core tenets.[4]

Although this rejoinder to the institutional critique is to some extent valid, it would be wrong to conclude that Effective Altruists can simply treat the institutional critique as a merely internal one. The institutional critique can and should be given a philosophical twist that transforms it into a direct challenge to EA's main philosophical tenets.

The Philosophical Critique

The *philosophical critique* is an apt moniker for a cluster of attacks on EA that target the god's eye moral epistemology that makes it seem possible to arrive at single judgments about how to do the most good. These attacks charge that it is morally and philosophically problematic to construe moral reflection as abstract. This

[4] For talk of an internal critique, see Sebo and Singer 2018, 40; for similar responses on behalf of EA, see Berkey 2018; McMahan 2016.

charge is often built on a line of argument that Bernard Williams developed in publications in the 1970s and 1980s, about how efforts in ethics to look at our lives from a god's eye or Archimedean point obliges us to abstract from even our most valued relationships and practices and accordingly represent a threat to our integrity.[5] Effective Altruists who respond to the philosophical critique take Williams to be urging us to protect our integrity even at the cost of doing the wrong thing.[6] They regard this solicitude toward the self as misplaced and self-indulgent, and, because they assume that philosophical critics of EA operate with the same understanding of Williams, they dismiss these critics' gestures as without philosophical interest.

The stance of these Effective Altruists is understandable. The interpretation of Williams they favor is widely received, and it is difficult to find a philosophical critique of EA that is elaborated precisely enough to make clear that this take on it is inaccurate. At the same time, this is a major missed opportunity for critical reflection. It is not difficult to develop philosophical critics' worries about a god's eye morality so that they rise to the level of a devastating objection. All that is required is to combine worries about point-of-viewless moral reflection with views about values, like those championed by the group of mid-twentieth-century women philosophers at Oxford, on which concepts of values determine patterns that only show up under the pressure of an appropriately engaged gaze.[7] The

[5] Bernard Williams, "A Critique of Utilitarianism," in *Utilitarianism: For and Against*, ed. J. J. C. Smart and Bernard Williams (Cambridge: Cambridge University Press, 1973), 77–150; "Utilitarianism and Moral Self-Indulgence," in *Moral Luck: Philosophical Papers 1973–1980* (Cambridge: Cambridge University Press, 1981), 40–53; *Ethics and the Limits of Philosophy* (London: Routledge, 1985), chaps. 2 and 8. For references to Williams in philosophical critiques of EA, see, e.g., Nakul Krishna, "Add Your Own Egg: Philosophy as a Humanistic Discipline," *Point Magazine*, January 13, 2016, https://thepointmag.com/examined-life/add-your-own-egg; and Amia Srinivasan, "Stop the Robot Apocalypse," *London Review of Books* 37, no. 18 (September 24, 2015).

[6] See Berkey 2018, 169n67 and related text; McMahan 2016; Singer 2015, 48–49, 85, 102.

[7] For evidence that these thinkers were an important source for Williams's attacks on point-of-viewlessness, see Williams, *Ethics and the Limits of Philosophy*, 141n7.

point of the philosophical critique is not that EA's abstract moral epistemology imposes integrity-threatening moral demands. The more telling charge is that an Archimedean view deprives us of the resources we need to recognize what matters morally, encouraging us to read into it features of whatever moral position we happen to favor.[8]

It might seem that Effective Altruists are justified in dismissing the charge. The target is EA's point-of-viewless moral epistemology, and this moral epistemology is at home within a larger philosophical outlook, itself a pivot of contemporary analytic philosophy, on which abstraction is a regulative ideal for all thought about the empirical world. Why should Effective Altruists take seriously an attack on a philosophical worldview that many of their colleagues take as an unquestioned starting point?

The late twentieth and early twenty-first centuries witnessed significant philosophical assaults on abstract conceptions of reason, and there is a notable philosophical corpus in which the merits of these assaults get debated.[9] Although it is by no means obvious that those who favor abstract views have better arguments, and although their interlocutors raise fundamental questions about these views' tenability, abstract construals of reason have for more than half a century played an organizing role in the discipline of philosophy, structuring research programs in numerous subfields (Crary 2019, 47–61). This suggests that the construals' staying power is at least partly a function of ideological factors independent of their

[8] See Lisa Herzog, "Can 'Effective Altruism' Really Change the World?," *Open Democracy*, February 22, 2016, https://www.opendemocracy.net/en/transformation/can-effective-altruism-really-change-world/; and Srinivasan, "Stop the Robot Apocalypse," on how EA demands the wrong things.

[9] Within the analytic tradition, Wittgenstein and Austin offer two of the most significant twentieth-century attacks on abstract conceptions of reason, and their efforts have been taken up and elaborated by philosophers such as Stanley Cavell, Cora Diamond, John McDowell, and Hilary Putnam. Wittgensteinian ideas have also resonated in debates about how to conceive of reason within history and philosophy of science. For one high-profile strike, from here, against conceiving reason abstractly, see Lorraine Daston and Peter Galison, *Objectivity* (New York: Zone Books, 2007).

philosophical credentials. That—the fact that these conceptions of reason are manifestly open to contestation—is one reason why Effective Altruists should attend to a philosophical critique that depends for its force on rejecting abstract images of reason. A second reason for Effective Altruists to attend to the philosophical critique has to do with the seriousness of the moral charge it levels against them. It alleges nothing less than that their image of the moral enterprise is bankrupt and that moral assessments grounded in this image lack authority.

The philosophical critique brings into question Effective Altruists' very notion of doing the "most good" or having the "greatest impact." Effective Altruists invite us to regard the rightness of a social intervention as a function of its consequences, with the outcome involving the best states of affairs counting as doing the most good. This strategy appears morally confused when considered in terms of the ethical stance of the philosophical critique. To adopt this stance is to see the weave of the world as endowed with values that reveal themselves only to a developed sensibility. To see things this way is to make room for an intuitively appealing conception of actions as right insofar as they exhibit just sensitivity to the worldly circumstances in question. This is consistent with allowing that right actions can have the end of promoting others' happiness or flourishing. Here acting rightly includes acting, when circumstances call for it, in ways that aim at the well-being of others, and, with reference to this benevolent pursuit of others' well-being, it makes sense to talk—in a manner that may seem to echo Effective Altruists—about good states of affairs. But it is important that, as the philosopher Philippa Foot once put it, "we have found this end within morality, forming part of it, not standing outside it as a good state of affairs by which moral action in general is to be judged" (1985, 205). Here right action also includes acting, when circumstantially appropriate, in ways that aim at ends—e.g., giving people what they are owed—that can conflict with the end of benevolence. Apt responsiveness to circumstances sometimes requires acting with an eye to others' well-being and sometimes with an eye to other ends. In cases in which it is not right to attend to others' well-being, it is incorrect to say that, because we haven't thus attended, we achieve a morally worse result. Things only seem this way if we allow our understanding to be shaped by a confused understanding of morality. What we should say is that the result we wind up with is morally best. That is what it comes to to say that, within the context of the philosophical critique, there is no room for EA-style talk of the "most good."[10]

This critique alleges that EA's claim to be doing the most good founders on a misunderstanding of the nature of morality and that the enterprise needs to be either radically reconceived or abandoned altogether. It confronts EA with challenges that it cannot meet with mere internal adjustments.

The Composite Critique

The philosophical critique charges that EA's god's eye moral epistemology disqualifies it from authoritatively trafficking in values, and it thus casts new light on the institutional critique's charge that EA fails to do justice to sets of actions aimed at progressive social change. The resulting composite critique presupposes, in line with the philosophical critique, that values are essentially woven into the texture of the social world and that EA's Archimedean take on moral reflection deprives it of resources needed to describe—irreducibly normative—social circumstances. The upshot of this new line of criticism is an update of the institutional critique, charging that EA cannot give accurate evaluations of sets of actions because it forfeits the capacities necessary for all social assessment. This means that the tendency of EA-affiliated organizations to wrongly prioritize

[10] For a satirical version of this argument, see Annette Baier, "A Modest Proposal," *Report from the Center for Philosophy and Public Policy* 6, no. 1 (1986), 4, 26.

evaluation of the proximate effects of particular actions is not a fixable methodological flaw. The organizations focus on these evaluations because it is only here that their image of the moral enterprise seems plausible. It is often right to act in ways that aim to improve the welfare of others. But recognizing the instances in which this is (or isn't) right requires capacities for engaged social thought that EA disavows. Further, when it comes to evaluating actions coordinated with an eye to social transformation, EA's image of the moral enterprise is patently implausible. Such actions are efforts to restructure the normative organization of society, and their relevant "effects," far from obeying merely causal laws, are at home in the unpredictable realm of politics. Attempts to evaluate these efforts in EA's terms are manifestly confused.

This composite critique finds extensive support in philosophical reflection about the social sciences. At the critique's heart is an image of the social world as irretrievably normative, such that understanding it requires non-neutral resources. A classic argument for this image within social philosophy centers on a conception of actions as conceptually articulated and constitutively normative. Granted that social concepts are categories for actions (or for character traits, practices, and institutions that can themselves only adequately be understood in reference to actions), it follows that these concepts need to be understood as tracing out patterns in an irreducibly normative ground—patterns that only reveal themselves to an evaluatively non-neutral gaze (Winch 2008, 98–99).[11] Further arguments for conceiving social understanding as thus normative can be found in numerous discussions about methods and authority of the social sciences. This includes anti-positivist debates in sociology,[12] disputes in anthropology about the need for

[11] For commentary, see, e.g., Linda Zerilli, *A Democratic Theory of Judgment* (Chicago: University of Chicago Press, 2016), chap. 8.

[12] See, e.g., Theodor Adorno, et al., *The Positivist Dispute in German Sociology*, ed. Glyn Adey and David Frisby (London: Heinemann, 1977).

ethnographic methods alongside quantitative ones,[13] and calls by Frankfurt School theorists to retain an ineluctably normative notion of social analysis.[14] These interrelated literatures supply additional backing for the verdict that EA, with its abstract methods, bars itself from dealing responsibly in social assessments.

Yet further support can be found in contemporary discourses of liberation. Anguish at the violence of being forced to live within "false universals" is a rallying cry echoing through numerous strands of twentieth- and twenty-first-century emancipatory thought. What inspires the cry is the experience of being subjected to forms of social life that appear to conform to laudable social ideals (e.g., equality, freedom, and nonviolence) only when looked at from elite perspectives that are wrongly presented as neutral and universal. Expressions of this experience often go hand in hand with claims about how the route to a just understanding of a set of unjust social circumstances must involve not a new supposedly neutral stance, but a stance shaped by an appreciation of the suffering of the marginalized. Such claims recur in a wide array of overlapping—feminist, anti-racist, decolonial, anti-ableist—liberating theories,[15] and, against the backdrop of this theoretical corpus, EA's insistence on an abstract approach to evaluation assumes the aspect of a refusal to listen to demands for justice.

In practice, the composite critique suggests that, within any domain in which they operate, charities guided by EA ratings will in general direct funds toward simple interventions capturable with

[13] See, e.g., Veena Das, *Life and Words: Violence and the Descent into the Ordinary* (Berkeley: University of California Press, 2007) , and *Textures of the Ordinary: Doing Anthropology after Wittgenstein* (New York: Fordham University Press, 2020).

[14] See, e.g., Axel Honneth, *Freedom's Right: The Social Foundations of Democratic Theory* (New York: Columbia University Press, 2014).

[15] For general discussions, see, e.g., Charles Mills, "Alternative Epistemologies," in *Blackness Visible: Essays on Philosophy and Race* (Ithaca, NY: Cornell University Press, 1998), 21–39; and "Ideology," in *The Routledge Handbook of Epistemic Injustice*, ed. Gaile Pohlhaus Jr., et al. (London: Routledge, 2020), 100–112. See also my article "The Methodological Is Political: What's the Matter with "Analytic Feminism,"" *Radical Philosophy* 2, no. 2 (2018).

metrics such as income levels or health outcomes, and in a manner relatively insensitive to whether these interventions contribute to perpetuating the institutions that reliably produce the ills they address, while also disparaging as less "effective" systematic attempts to change these institutions. This is what typically happens with EA-oriented organizations that rate animal charities. In addition to emphasizing welfare improvements in the treatment of animals caught up in industrial "farms," these organizations tend to depreciate pro-animal organizations that are dedicated to transforming social attitudes toward animals and whose achievements aren't demonstrable in EA's terms. This includes vegan organizations in predominantly Black and brown neighborhoods in the United States that seek to address people not through easily quantifiable methods like leafleting but through outreach to churches and regular participation in local markets and fairs. It includes many long-standing activist groups in the Global South working to contest the spread of factory farms; many sanctuaries for domestic animals; and, more generally, a vast array of grass-roots pro-animal organizations and movements that, even when working in solidarity with larger networks, arrive at their methods in ways that are context-sensitive and bottom-up.

EA as Moral Corruption

EA is a movement based on a flawed conception of morality that encounters opposition not only from ethics, political theory, and philosophy of the social sciences, but also from many critical theorists, organizers, and activists who are committed to causes, such as animal protectionism, that Effective Altruists support. This raises the question of the source of its appeal. Effective Altruists couch their moral assessments quantitatively in terms of doing the most good, trafficking in tropes of economic efficiency that align them with the institutions of neoliberal capitalism. It's no secret that EA urges its adherents to work within these institutions. Singer is openly dismissive of critiques of global capitalism in its current form,[16] and, along with MacAskill and many other proponents of EA, he encourages the practice of "earning to give"; that is, taking high-paying jobs in business and finance in order to be able to give more.[17] Singer goes so far as to laud the billionaire philanthropists Bill Gates and Warren Buffett as "the greatest Effective Altruists in human history."[18] EA owes its success as a philosophical-philanthropic movement largely to its eagerness and ability to work within existing political-economic systems.

This source of EA's success is also its most grievous shortcoming. Effective Altruists present their philanthropic program as the expression of an uncontextualized moral theory, in a manner that reflects no awareness of the significance of their situatedness within capitalist forms of life. How it happens that EA has at its disposal an audience of people with excess wealth is not a question that they take up. Within discussions of EA, it is difficult to find a hint of the plausible and well-grounded view—defended in the writings of many theorists of care, ecofeminists, ecological Marxists, and other theorists of social reproduction—that the disproportionate material advantages of the wealthy in the Global North depend

[16] See, e.g., Singer 2015, 49–50.

[17] Singer 2015, 39–40; MacAskill 2015, 76–77, and chapter 9.

[18] Singer 2015, 50. Singer returns to these topics in a very recent interview, describing as merely "realistic" the belief that we will continue to have billionaires and opining that "it's much better to have billionaires like Bill and Melinda Gates or Warren Buffett who give away most of their fortune thoughtfully and in ways that are highly effective" ("Peter Singer is Committed to Controversial Ideas," an interview with Daniel A. Gross, *The New Yorker*, April 2021). In this interview, Singer traces sources of many of his philosophical ideas, including his commitment to EA, to his sense of the lack of "impact" of the ideas of an anti-capitalist Marxist group called Radical Philosophy that was at Oxford when he was a student there. Some of this group's members went on to found the eponymous journal in which this chapter was originally published (see Chris Arthur et al., "Reports," *Radical Philosophy* 1, no. 1 [1972], 30–32). It struck me as fitting to use the journal to observe that Singer owes his undeniable "impact" substantially to his accommodating attitude toward neoliberal capitalism, and that, far from vindicating his youthful impatience with radical philosophy, that "impact" has been in large part a damaging one.

on continuously treating as "free resources" not only animals and other aspects of the nonhuman natural environment, but also the reproductive labor of women and the subsistence and care work of marginalized people the world over.[19] It is equally hard to find mention of the now extensive literature on how practices of "internalizing" these things into capitalist markets displace without halting or slowing the devastation of nature and the oppression of vulnerable humans.[20] Critical outlooks in which these ideas are at home have played no discernible role in discussions of EA, where there is rarely any suggestion of a tie between the forms of misery we are enjoined to alleviate and the structures of global capitalism. What is foregrounded instead is a paternalistic narrative about how the relatively wealthy should serve as benefactors of relatively poor and precarious humans and animals, and thus "do good."

Granted this tendency toward ahistorical theorizing, it is unsurprising that enthusiasts of EA tend to regard reliance on ideals of economic efficiency as in itself unproblematic. Among other things, they betray no worry that the reach of these discourses into domains in which EA operates will displace political discourses shaped by values not capturable in terms of the logic of exchange. This insouciance about depoliticization—another expression for EA's lack of any meaningful response to the institutional critique—is the counterpart of an inability to recognize how the instrumentalization of public space can produce outcomes, rational only from the standpoint of capital, that reliably generate the forms of suffering EA aims to stamp out.[21]

[19] For some central treatments of these themes, see John Bellamy Foster, *Marx's Ecology: Materialism and Nature* (New York: Monthly Review Press, 2000); Joan Martinez-Alier, *The Environmentalism of the Poor: A Study of Ecological Conflicts and Valuation* (Cheltenham, UK: Edward Elgar, 2002); Maria Mies and Veronika Bennholdt-Thomsen, *The Subsistence Perspective: Beyond the Globalized Economy* (London: Zed Books, 2000); and Ariel Salleh, *Ecofeminism as Politics: Nature, Marx and the Postmodern* (London: Zed Books, 1997).

[20] For a helpful overview, see Johanna Oksala, "Feminism, Capitalism, and Ecology," *Hypatia* 33, no. 2 (2018): 216–234, esp. 223–229.

[21] See Rupert Read, "Must Do Better," *Radical Philosophy* 2, no. 1 (2018).

This weakness is devastating when it comes to EA's capacity to make a positive contribution to animal protectionism. Effective Altruists' pro-animal efforts are to a large extent devoted to attending to suffering visited upon animals in factory farms. But their characteristic theoretical stance prevents them from registering the significance of the fact that these "farms" are capitalist phenomena. Alongside the unspeakable torments that factory farms visit on animals—bioengineered for the growth rates of their edible tissues, raised on unnatural diets, crammed mercilessly together with conspecifics, and slaughtered on assembly lines where they are all too often dismembered while still conscious—there are terrible costs to humans. The environmental impact of confined animal feeding operations is severe. They are sources of air and water pollution that disproportionately harms members of the already socially vulnerable human populations living in proximity to them; they produce approximately 15 percent of global greenhouse gas emissions; and the need they generate for grazing land is a major factor in deforestation worldwide, which itself produces not only around a fifth of global greenhouse gas emissions but also significant soil erosion and related polluting run-off. Industrial animal agriculture also poses serious threats to public health. It is a breeding ground for zoonoses, and, because it relies on the mass prophylactic use of antibiotics to mitigate its own disease-causing conditions, it adds to the prevalence of deadly infections of antibiotic-resistant bacteria such as salmonella. Industrial slaughterhouses are well-documented sites of systematic violations of the rights of "kill floor" workers, a group that, in the United States, has since the 1990s been in large part made up of Latin American immigrant and African American men, and whose poor conditions, economic precariousness, and vulnerability to abuse was exposed during the COVID-19 pandemic in which many industrial abattoirs continued to operate even while those working in them suffered disproportionate rates of illness and death. Industrial animal agriculture is a raging social pathology, intelligible only in terms of the protection and growth of meat companies' profits.

To note that Effective Altruists aren't guided, in their forays into animal protectionism, by insight into the capitalist origins of the "third agricultural revolution" that gave us confined animal feeding operations and industrial abattoirs is not to say that their interventions on behalf of farmed animals are bound to misfire.[22] There is no reason to doubt that the welfare adjustments to the treatment of farmed animals that are favored by EA-affiliated groups can lessen the pain of many such animals. It is even possible that in calling for these adjustments, Effective Altruists will hasten the demise of the industrial system that torments and kills billions of creatures annually. But it is also possible that the interventions of Effective Altruists will, because they affirm this system's underlying principles, contribute to its perpetuation, perhaps even precipitating the arrival of a further, more horrific "agricultural revolution." What is certain is that Effective Altruists' theoretical commitments lead them to approach animal protectionism without proper reference to political and economic forces that sustain factory farms. Anyone seeking substantial steps toward shutting down these "farms" would be well advised to exchange EA for efforts informed by an understanding of these forces. Only such interventions have a shot at being more than accidentally effective.

Drawing on a flawed understanding of the moral enterprise, EA directs its followers to respond to human and animal suffering in a manner that deflects attention away from how an image of humans as *homo economicus* contributes to the reliable reproduction of such suffering. At the same time, EA as a movement benefits from its embrace of those who "earn to give," accumulating wealth in the

[22] For discussion of this "third agricultural revolution," see John Bellamy Foster, "Marx's Theory of Metabolic Rift: Classical Foundations for Environmental Sociology," *American Journal of Sociology* 105, no. 2 (1999): 366–405.

economic arena that it leaves critically untouched. It is a textbook case of moral corruption.[23]

EA has not been wholly unresponsive to criticism. In addition to responding—unsatisfactorily—to the institutional critique, Effective Altruists have attempted to respond to the charge that EA has "been a rather homogeneous movement of middle-class white men" (Srinivasan 2015), by placing new stress on inclusiveness. Two prominent Effective Altruists have urged effective animal altruists to "consider how the history and demographics of the animal rights and Effective Altruist movements might be limiting their perspective" (Sebo and Singer 2018), and a number of EA-associated groups have made diversity a central institutional ideal. Animal Charity Evaluators, for instance, now includes diversity among the issues it considers both in its own staffing and in that of animal organizations it assesses, and Oxford EA has made a big push for diversity. These moves toward inclusiveness are typically presented as intended not just to bring in participants with different social identities, but to make room for their perspectives and ideas as well. As initially attractive as such gestures are, there is every reason to be skeptical about their significance. They come unaccompanied by any acknowledgment of how the framework of EA constrains available moral and political outlooks. That framing excludes views of social thought as engaged and irretrievably perspectival—views

[23] For an account of the relevant—classic—idea of moral corruption, see the writings of Stephen M. Gardiner, especially *A Perfect Moral Storm: the Ethical Tragedy of Climate Change* (Oxford: Oxford University Press, 2011), chap. 9. Gardiner describes "corruption that targets our ways of talking and thinking, and so prevents us from even seeing the problem in the right way" (301). To speak of such corruption is not to "vilify any particular individuals" (6), but to highlight forms of moral evasion to which we are especially susceptible—and to which we can succumb in "good faith" (307)—when we face circumstances of great urgency traceable to practices or institutions in which we participate, and when a clear-sighted and responsible response would impose substantial demands. There is a particular danger in cases like these of sliding into reliance on distorting claims and methods that are themselves a "manifestation of the underlying problem" (Stephen M. Gardiner, "Geoengineering: Ethical Questions for Deliberate Climate Manipulators," in *Oxford Handbook of Environmental Ethics*, ed. Stephen M. Gardiner and Allen Thompson [Oxford: Oxford University Press, 2017], 501–514, 511). EA is a perfect fit for this familiar notion of moral corruption.

associated with central strands of feminist theory, critical disability studies, critical race theory, and decolonial theory. Despite its signaling toward diversity of ideas, EA as it stands cannot make room for individuals who discover in these traditions the things they believe most need to be said. For EA to accommodate their voices, it would have to allow that their moral and political beliefs are in conflict with its guiding principles, and that these principles themselves need to be given up. To allow for this would be to reject EA in its current form as fatally flawed—finally a step toward doing a bit of good.[24]

References

Berkey, Brian. (2018). "The Institutional Critique of Effective Altruism." *Utilitas* 30 (2): 143–171.

Crary, Alice. (2019). "Objectivity." In *Wittgenstein on Philosophy, Objectivity, and Meaning*, edited by James Conant and Sebastian Sunday, 47–61. Cambridge: Cambridge University Press.

Foot, Philippa. (1985). "Utilitarianism and the Virtues." *Mind* 94: 374.

Hiller, Avram. (2017). "Consequentialism in Environmental Ethics." In *Oxford Handbook of Environmental Ethics*, edited by Stephen Gardiner and Allen Thomas, 199–210. Oxford: Oxford University Press.

Korsgaard, Christine. (2018). *Fellow Creatures: Our Obligations to the Other Animals*. Oxford: Oxford University Press.

MacAskill, William. (2015). *Doing Good Better: Effective Altruism and How You Can Make a Difference*. New York: Gotham Books.

[24] This article was prompted by conversations with directors of animal advocacy organizations and other animal advocates, at a February 2020 Miami meeting of the Brooks Institute for Animal Law and Policy, at which many described damaging effects of EA on their work. Accounts of EA-driven disparagement and funding loss convinced me of the need for a thoroughgoing philosophical and political critique of EA. I am grateful for helpful feedback I received at workshops at Oxford Public Philosophy, the Freie Universit, the University of East Anglia, and Abo Akademi. I have benefited from helpful discussions of these topics over the last several years with Jay Bernstein, Cora Diamond, Lori Gruen, Timothy Pachirat, and Amia Srinivasan. I owe thanks to Carol Adams, Victoria Browne, Robin Celikates, Joel de Lara, Diamond, Aaron Gross, Lori Gruen, Nathaniel Hupert, and Timothy Pachirat for insightful comments on an earlier draft.

McMahan, Jeff. (2016). "Philosophical Critique of Effective Altruism." *Philosopher's Magazine* 73 (2).

Parfit, Derek. (1984). *Reasons and Persons*. Oxford: Oxford University Press.

Sebo, Jeff, and Peter Singer. (2018). "Activism." In *Critical Terms for Animal Studies*, edited by Lori Gruen, 33–46. Chicago: University of Chicago Press.

Singer, Peter. (1972). "Famine, Affluence, and Morality." *Philosophy & Public Affairs* 1 (3): 229–243.

Singer, Peter. (2015). *The Most Good You Can Do: How Effective Altruism Is Changing Ideas about Living Ethically*. New Haven, CT: Yale University Press.

Singer, Peter, and Katarzyna de Lazari-Radek. (2014). *The Point of View of the Universe: Sidgwick and Contemporary Ethics*. Oxford: Oxford University Press.

Srinivasan, Amia. (2015). "Stop the Robot Apocalypse." London Review of Books 37 (18). https://www.lrb.co.uk/the-paper/v37/n18/amia-srinivasan/stop-the-robot-apocalypse.

Vinding, Magnus. (2018). *Effective Altruism: How Can We Best Help Others*. Durham, NC: Neuroethics Foundation.

Winch, Peter. (2008). *The Idea of a Social Science and Its Relation to Philosophy*. London: Routledge.

17

The Change We Need

Lori Gruen

> After over forty years of working in the environmental movement and in international development, I have come to the conclusion that our largest problems—from climate change to inequality and poverty—are deeply rooted in the fundamentals of our political-economic system. Working within that system to achieve incremental changes, however valuable, will never be enough. The current system is simply not programmed to secure the well-being of people, place, and planet. . . . If we are to escape the crises now unfolding all around us, we must create a new system.
>
> —Gus Speth, "Getting to the Next System"[1]

Social justice activists and scholars alike have a seemingly endless list of problems to address. The daunting work to achieve even minimally positive outcomes for the huge number of humans and animals who are struggling against marginalization, violence, war,

[1] James Gustave "Gus" Speth is the cofounder of Natural Resource Defense Council, the founder and president of the World Resource Institute, former administrator of the UN Development Programme and chair of the UN Development Group, former dean of the Yale School of Forestry and Environmental Studies, and is currently a professor of law at Vermont Law School and senior fellow at Demos, the Democracy Collaborative. I include this information here because I am inspired by the fact that someone who worked so deeply *within* the system trying to make meaningful change has determined that this isn't, after all, the right way to go.

Lori Gruen, *The Change We Need* In: *The Good It Promises, The Harm It Does*. Edited by: Carol J. Adams, Alice Crary, and Lori Gruen, Oxford University Press. © Oxford University Press 2023.
DOI: 10.1093/oso/9780197655696.003.0017

hunger, lack of healthcare, the impacts of climate change, and more can seem overwhelming. Effective Altruists (EA) have responded to global problems by working to minimize immediate suffering. Some activists who identify with EA, and many of those who don't, are working to try to make unjust systems less harmful and exclusionary. Other activists and scholars argue that these systems are working precisely the way they are designed to work—they can't be fixed because they aren't actually broken—and we need radical social change. In this chapter I will first discuss the contours of the debate between improving existing social arrangements and transforming them. I will then introduce "non-reformist reforms" as a helpful way of gauging whether or not certain campaigns will ultimately help us as we work to create a genuinely just, caring, and meaningful world.

Revolution vs. Reform

Those involved in various movements for social change are familiar with debates, often quite raucous ones, about strategies. One of the central points of contention in many movements for social justice is whether it is possible to make meaningful social change incrementally, by reforming a problematic system, or whether we need to overturn that system altogether. Socialist disagreements about strategy at the turn of the twentieth century perhaps best illustrates this debate. The clash between Rosa Luxemburg and Eduard Bernstein about whether democratic socialism and capitalism are compatible was at the core of many discussions among social theorists and activists. Bernstein argued that reform was plausible. Luxemburg, in her book *Reform or Revolution* (1899), argued that Bernstein was out of touch with the conditions of workers and that, importantly, his strategy was antithetical to socialism and must be rejected. This debate was theoretically rich while grounded in the experiences of workers, and it raised profound questions about whether reforming an unjust, alienating system was possible, or whether revolution was needed. Many of the strategic questions that were central at the height of socialist organizing continue to animate many radical movements for social change.

In the civil rights struggle in the United States, for example, debates over strategies are often linked to the different styles and messages coming from leaders like Martin Luther King Jr. and Malcolm X. King famously advocated for nonviolence, working to bring policy and practice in line with the founding ideals of the United States. Malcolm X, in contrast, at least early in his public life, viewed those founding ideals as rooted in white supremacy that must be overthrown "by any means necessary." Scholars have since analyzed the contrast and found that at certain points it wasn't as conflictual as it often appeared. Indeed, as James Baldwin (1972) wrote, "[b]y the time each met his death, there was practically no difference between them."[2] Despite this apparent rapprochement, the core of the debate between revolution and reform still reverberates in combatting anti-Black racism. Afropessimists, for example, unlike those seeking liberal reforms for racial inclusion, see anti-Blackness as a permanent state, remnants of the unending status of Black people as slaves. Frank Wilderson III, one of the leading proponents of Afropessimism, argues that the structural category of the "nonperson" is necessary in society and thus the only way to overcome anti-Blackness is to end the world, essentially arguing that Black people will only be free after revolution when something fundamentally different can emerge (Wilderson 2020, see also Wilderson 2010). In a similar, but slightly less pessimistic, vein, the radical Black feminist position, powerfully articulated in the 1977 Combahee River Collective Statement, echoes of which can be heard in many Black Lives Matter protests, argues that ending the low status of Black women requires a thorough reworking of structures of racism, patriarchy, capitalism, and other

[2] Both Martin Luther King and Malcom X died just before their fortieth birthdays.

oppressive systems that require the subordination of Black women to function. Although many Black women have a "strongly-felt need for some level of possibility," reform and assimilation will not do. Freedom for all requires the destruction of the current systems that deny possibility to so many.

The dynamic tensions between revolution and reform also play out in the animal advocacy movement. Many in the animal movement are focused on ending suffering and promoting well-being. But there are activists who believe that the pursuit of reforms is inconsistent with the goal of ending the use of animals, and that we ought to, as a matter of strategy, fight against all animal use. Indeed, some of these activists refer to themselves as "abolitionists."[3] The debates between these different positions often become quite heated. Abolitionist Gary Francione, for example, who wants to rid the world of the use of animals for any reason writes:

> [O]ur recognition that no human should be the property of others required that we *abolish* slavery and not merely *regulate* it to be more "humane," our recognition that animals have this one basic right [not to be property] would mean that we could no longer justify our institutional exploitation of animals for food, clothing, amusement, or experiments. (Francione 2000, xxix)

Effective Altruist Peter Singer has argued "it's absurd" to suggest that because we currently use animals as things that we shouldn't try to minimize their suffering, noting "you might as well have said in the debate about slavery that we shouldn't have had laws to prevent

[3] See Claire Jean Kim's "Abolition" chapter in *Critical Terms for Animal Studies*, edited by Lori Gruen, for a critique of this usage. She argues that the appropriation of the term "relentlessly displaces the issue of black oppression, deflecting attention from the specificity of the slave's status then and mystifying the question of the black person's status now. According to animal abolition's narrative of racial temporality, black people at some point (variously, Emancipation, Reconstruction, the civil rights movement) moved demonstrably from slavery to freedom, from the outside in, from abjection to inclusion" (Kim 2018, 18).

masters beating their slaves because as long as they are slaves they are just things and you might as well beat them as much as you like" (quoted in Leider 2006). Though both Francione and Singer have problematic understandings of the structure of human slavery, the core of the debate here is clear. For abolitionists/revolutionaries, we must not violate animals today in the hopes of freeing them tomorrow. For the reformers, who believe that the ultimate goal of liberation is currently out of reach, allowing billions of animals to suffer horribly and die while waiting for an end to all animal suffering allows for too much needless suffering.

One popular animal reform campaign—cage-free farming—illustrates how these different strategies lead to different assessments of the problems nonhuman animals face. Factory farming is a system of mass violence, designed to most efficiently turn living beings into commodities to eat. The suffering involved in this system, for animals as well as many workers, is extreme.[4] Animals are genetically modified before they are born to grow quickly, and they are kept in conditions of intense confinement. They are often unable to stand up, lie down, turn around, or fully extend their limbs. Cage-free campaigns have been organized for chickens raised for meat, for pigs, and for egg-laying hens. It has been estimated that animal organizations spent between $54 million and $120 million from 2005 to 2018 in campaigns to encourage corporations to go cage-free (Simcikas 2019).

Here I'll just focus on the hens. The battery system of egg production is particularly exploitative and painful for hens. They are kept in small cages with six to eight other birds, none of them can stretch a wing; they are surrounded by tens of thousands of other hens also in small cages; and all the cages are stacked in rows in large, ammonia soaked, dark sheds. According to Animal Charity Evaluators (ACE), the Effective Altruist organization that recommends the "most effective" animal charities for concerned people to donate

[4] See, for example, Crary and Gruen 2022 and Pachirat 2011.

to, there are 7.47 billion egg-laying hens in the world, with an estimated 60 percent or more in battery cages. In the United States, about 70 percent of egg-laying hens live in battery cages.[5]

In response to the awful reality these hens are forced to endure, many animal advocacy organizations are working to get egg producers to switch to "cage-free" systems that gets hens out of cages, but still keep thousands of them crammed in large, dark sheds. The hens are still de-beaked—the painful process that involves using a hot blade to cut through the complex horn, bone, and sensitive tissue of the hen's beak. This amputation can lead to deformities that prevent hens from eating, drinking, or preening normally. And industrial egg production, whether using battery cages or not, still kills millions of male chicks when they are hatched. Cage-free hens, like their battery-caged sisters, are sent to slaughter after just about a year of life. Sometimes cage-free hens can go outside of the shed, but the exits are very small and the sheds so crowded that the only hens that could get out would be those closest to the doors, and because hens like to be with other hens, very few of those who have the opportunity to go outside do so.

The move from the battery cage system of egg production to the cage-free system represents an improvement in the welfare of the hens, albeit a rather small improvement. But so many hens suffer horribly that improving the conditions even minimally amounts to a vast overall improvement in the amount of suffering, given that people are still eating eggs. This aggregate reduction of suffering matters to reformers, and to the hens not confined to battery cages too. One Effective Altruist researcher estimates that "for every dollar spent on cage-free and broiler corporate campaigns, 9 to 120 chicken years are affected." He is impressed by the "big difference" that can be made for "just one dollar," and says "I would

[5] https://animalcharityevaluators.org/research/research-briefs/what-is-the-effect-of-cage-free-corporate-outreach-on-egg-laying-hens-welfare/.

strongly consider donating money to activities related to corporate campaigns. I don't know of any other altruistic intervention that has this much impact per dollar spent at reasonable robustness of the evidence" (Simcikas 2019). ACE is impressed too and writes that one of their multiyear top-ranked charities, The Humane League's (THL), "main historical achievements are focused on securing cage-free commitments for egg-laying hens . . . THL reported that they have a 60 percent implementation rate of their corporate commitments and have impacted 10 hen-years per dollar received."[6]

For abolitionists/revolutionaries, cage-free systems of egg production work to prolong the violation of the rights and dignity of these animals while making people feel better about their use and abuse of other living creatures. The emphasis on improved welfare may also lead some people to conflate "cage-free" with "cruelty-free." These small improvements may in fact encourage complacency and hinder efforts toward genuine liberation. Some abolitionists argue that creating more humane conditions while still using animals is essentially an endorsement of consuming animals, and they fear that the number of animals used will increase rather than decrease as a result. This fear isn't off base—while awareness of animal suffering has increased over time, so has the number of animals who suffer in the food system. Of course, the very idea of "corporate campaigns" raises suspicions, as collusion with capitalism will not support animals or the humans that are exploited so that a very few can profit.

Effective Altruists fit squarely into the reformist camp. Will MacAskill, in defining Effective Altruism, emphasizes that their approach is "welfarist" and boasts that "in 2016 alone, the effective altruism community was responsible for . . . sparing 360 million

[6] https://animalcharityevaluators.org/charity-review/the-humane-league/#comprehensive-review.

hens from living in caged confinement." He goes on to articulate the Center for Effective Altruist's definition of EA as:

1. the use of evidence and careful reasoning to work out how to maximize the good with a given unit of resources, tentatively understanding "the good" in impartial welfarist terms, and
2. the use of the findings from (1) to try to improve the world. (2019, 14)

And improving the world here doesn't necessarily mean changing it, but rather impartially improving the amount of welfare it contains. EA's impartialism is particularly concerning in the current context of extreme racial, gender, and economic injustices. By assuming all things are more or less equal, which is one of the demands of impartialism, EAs ends up condoning a variety of institutions and practices that disempower, ignore, or violate the dignity of far too many. In a comment that clearly identifies EA's inability to acknowledge injustice as bad, MacAskill writes, "I think that it is unlikely in the foreseeable future that the [EA] community would focus on rectifying injustice in cases where they believed that there were other available actions which, though they would leave the injustice remaining, would do more good overall" (2019, 18).

Non-Reformist Reforms

Fortunately, debates like the ones I have been describing, between revolution and reform, or abolition and welfarism in the animal advocacy context, can be interrupted by exploring a "third way." Socialist theorist André Gorz introduced the idea of "non-reformist reforms" as a way to provide another option, beyond what often seem to be all-or-nothing strategies. He suggested that some reforms could make more immediate gains without compromising the larger goals of social movements for radical change.

In his *Strategy for Labor*, published in 1967, Gorz described "non-reformist reforms," sometimes calling them "structural reforms," as reforms that are clearly antithetical to the interests of capitalism, but don't lead to immediate social transformation. These sorts of reforms have the potential to empower grass-roots activism in the pursuit of more meaningful, liberatory ends and certainly don't promote the systems that are in need of change.

Amna Akbar (2020) has recently highlighted three characteristics of non-reformist reforms. First, non-reformist reforms "advance a radical critique and radical imagination," and in so doing provide frameworks "that will undermine the prevailing political, economic and social system from reproducing itself." Second, non-reformist reforms actively shift power from the center to the margins and work to empower those who have been overlooked. And third, non-reformist reforms create the possibility for deepening independent thinking, developing creative demands, and forming new grass-roots political networks.

Discussions of non-reformist reforms have been particularly lively in the prison abolition movement. In the shadow of mass incarceration, within our society organized by profound inequality, prison abolitionists are working to develop more just and meaningful policy that will help support community needs and build alternative, humane institutions. The non-reformist reforms many are working to enact allow for the development of policies and practices that minimize harms, while not contributing to or reinforcing carceral logics. Abolitionists are providing mutual aid; working to redirect city budgets to allocate funds in caring, healthful ways; providing support for those who are food-insecure, housing-insecure, and vulnerable to substance use; developing opportunities to support youth; creating community based harm-reduction programs; working on supporting victims of harm through restorative justice practices and holding those who caused harm accountable; as well as other practical efforts to build more caring, empowered communities. These activities, like certain prison education programs and organizations providing books and libraries to prisoners,[7] work to provide incarcerated people with the tools to reinvent themselves, but don't overtly support the prison industrial complex.[8]

Within the animal movement there has also been theory, action, and community-building that can be seen as non-reformist reforms, although they are often not explicitly identified as such. For example, after the publication of Justin Marceau's 2019 book *Beyond Cages*, various scholars and activists began challenging the carceral turn in animal law and animal protection that relies on state apparatus to surveil and punish animal cruelty. Animal protection tactics often targeted workers of color in factory farms, rather than challenging the systems that promote and tolerate mass violence. "Anti-carceral vegans" oppose this reliance on the criminal legal system and are instead calling for more structural, interlocking critiques of racism, capitalism, and animal oppression.[9]

The work that Brenda Sanders and the AfroVegan Society do in Baltimore,[10] and the work others do in Black neighborhoods in New York, Atlanta, and other cities to introduce healthy, plant-based foods to the community, might also be considered non-reformist

[7] See, for example, https://freedomreads.org/.

[8] Whether particular campaigns are non-reformist is open for discussion among activists involved, and sometimes it is difficult to determine. Consider, for example, the fact that Open Philanthropy, an Effective Altruist organization, spun off a criminal justice reform program called Just Impact at the end of 2021. Just Impact "offers exceptional value to donors through our ecosystems approach, focus on grassroots impact, high rate of return on investment, and willingness to make big bets on early-stage leaders and campaigns." They work on "sourcing the best opportunities, achieving the greatest impact, and fulfilling donor investment requirements." This all sounds like reformist reforms. But they also claim to be "devoted to ending mass incarceration and building autonomous political power of communities most impacted by incarceration. Our team has a track record of backing leaders close to the problem who are winning real change for people and communities most impacted by mass incarceration." These goals are more consistent with non-reformist reform strategies.

[9] See for example, McNeil 2022. See also some of the essays in Gruen and Marceau 2022.

[10] See chapter 1.

reforms. Too many people in low-income neighborhoods in the United States don't have access to fresh, healthy foods. One study in New York City found that bodegas outnumbered grocery stores 18 to 1, and one of the poorest neighborhoods in Brooklyn had 57 bodegas for every 1 grocery store (Jeffrey-Wilensky 2022). The lack of access to healthy food, often framed as living in a "food desert" or as being subject to "food apartheid," has deep ramifications for communities of color, making people vulnerable to premature death. Fortunately, there are people and organizations fighting against this threat. As the AfroVegan Society website notes, many people "have come to view veganism as both a viable solution to some of the challenges that currently face our communities as well as a vehicle for resisting the systems that are responsible for creating those challenges."

Providing caring multispecies communities for formerly farmed animals at sanctuaries is perhaps the most striking example of non-reformist reforms in the animal advocacy movement. These sanctuaries not only provide meaningful, safe spaces for the nonhuman residents in their care, but also help us reframe and reimagine our relationships with animals, which have traditionally been relations characterized by power and control. In reimagining our relations with animal others, who are only now starting to be considered in larger social justice work, we open our minds to the expansive textures of exploitation, and in so doing we can deepen our moral perception of the damages of oppressive social structures. In addition to being sites of empathetic interactions with others, sanctuaries are, as Elan Abrell notes, "models of alternative modes of interspecies engagement . . . countersites to the political-economic arenas of animal use" (2021, 192–193) that provide a clear vision of what living ethically with others might look like, a vision that can ultimately lead to transformative social change.

Charity vs. Solidarity

Transforming the social structures that harm so many is a fundamentally different project than reforming systems in order to make them less harmful or more efficient at doing "good." Reforming the current system by working to change institutions of use, and in the process potentially strengthening their existence, rather than working to abolish them, is at the heart of the debate between revolution and reform/abolition and welfarism. Non-reformist reforms provide a path toward transformative change, while also responding to immediate suffering, loss, grief, and other vulnerabilities.

Effective Altruists, as Alice Crary notes,[11] seem to view criticisms that they are reformist as a part of what they have dubbed the "institutional critique," and they argue this is a misconception about EA. MacAskill, for example, writes that, "[o]f all the criticisms of effective altruism, the most common is that effective altruism ignores systemic change." He counters by claiming that EA is open to this sort of change, "both in principle and practice," and distinguishes between a broader sense of systemic change that "involves a one-off investment in order to reap a long-lasting benefit" and narrower sense of systemic change that "refers to long-lasting *political* change" (MacAskill 2019, 23; his emphasis). This characterization alone reveals one of the many ways that EAs are speaking at cross-purposes with at least some of their critics. Consider just a few of the ways that MacAskill endorses EAs' efforts supporting "political change." He notes that one of the "structural" reasons that people are poor is that they aren't able to leave their countries to become more productive, so working to support greater freedom of movement across borders is thought to be an efficient way to

[11] See chapter 16.

address poverty. But this misses the actual structures that produce and maintain wealth inequality as well as intergenerational wealth gaps that can't be solved through immigration reform. Another allegedly "political" change involves recommending careers in "policy-oriented civil service and think tanks." And, of course, he notes work supporting corporate campaigns to go cage-free as well as promoting scientific research and NGOs developing lab-grown meat and plant-based meat substitutes. This entirely misses the point of transformation and represents such a vanishingly "narrow" conception of systemic change that it's hard to think that it is the critics who have the "misconception."

MacAskill acknowledges that there may be "systemic" changes that the EA community are neglecting and argues that if that is the case, it is presumably because work for some changes has an "astronomically low" chance of being successful. But this relies on the questionable conception of "success" baked into Effective Altruism. It is instructive here to return to the wise thoughts of Gus Speth: "[W]hat is now desperately needed is transformative change of the system itself. We are confronted with a multifaceted, systemic crisis born of the inability of our current system of political economy to restore and sustain human and natural communities. . . . If some of these ideas seem radical today, wait until tomorrow. It will be clear before long that system change is not starry-eyed but the only practical way forward" (2015, 12).

Meaningful, non-reformist reforms must be designed to ultimately transcend the liberal, racialized capitalist paradigm and empower people to work in solidarity to bring about transformation of social/political systems. Non-reformist reforms are transitional steps that can build awareness and commitment toward radical change. As Gorz noted, "it is necessary to present not only an overall alternative but also those 'intermediate objectives' which lead to it and foreshadow it in the present. . ." They "must be conceived as means, not as ends, as dynamic phases in a process of struggle, not as resting stages." They serve "to educate and unite" people and present a larger vision for change (quoted in Engler and Engler 2021).

Effective Altruism doesn't have the tools to do the necessary analysis of the system in order to help think about strategies for non-reformist reforms, as many of the essays in this volume have argued. Given that EAs are committed to working within the unworkable systems that exist, their conception of "the most good" itself is truncated. Those engaged in projects of mutual aid, in contrast, do have tools to identify strategic paths forward, allowing us to move beyond the limitations of imagination embedded in Effective Altruism. One prominent proponent of mutual aid, Dean Spade, cites anarchist activist Peter Gelderloos, who provides guidance for assessing tactics:

> Does it seize space in which new social relations can be enacted? Does it spread awareness of new ideas. . . . Does it "achieve any concrete gains in improving people's lives"? Gelderloos wants to assess how the tactic might allow people to practice new ways of being, such as practicing solidarity across movements, collectively meeting our own needs rather than relying on harmful institutions, making decisions by consensus rather than by following authority, or sharing things rather than hoarding and protecting private property. (quoted in Spade 2020,133)

Nonprofit grant organizations like ACE don't engage in this sort of thinking and tend to reproduce top-down, antidemocratic relationships that further marginalize some of the most committed activists and their work.

In contrast to the reformist charity work done by Effective Altruists, solidarity is increasingly being promoted in seemingly unlikely spaces in the grant-making ecosystem. In a recent discussion about grant-makers in the art world, Nati Linares and Caroline Woolard (2021b) note that those with wealth can engage in systems-change work that addresses root causes rather than symptoms of cultural inequity as part of "an emergent movement in the United States that is known globally as the Solidarity Economy," which promotes "sustainable and equitable community-control of work, food, housing, and culture using a variety of organizational forms. The solidarity economy principles include cooperation, participatory democracy, intersectional equity, sustainability, and pluralism." They argue that artists and others "harmed by the current system of neoliberal and racial capitalism" are already creating community-controlled local projects that can be funded now, as more work is done to create and bolster the solidarity economy "as a path to valuing people and the planet over profits" (2021a).

Building solidarity with other animals, as I've mentioned, is happening now in the multispecies communities found at animal sanctuaries.[12] Their work engaging in non-reformists reforms serves as one model of what is possible. Creating spaces where new social relations are enacted, sanctuaries spread awareness of new ideas and new ways of knowing animals; and they help those who work at sanctuaries, those who visit sanctuaries, and those who follow sanctuaries virtually to imagine new ways of being in relationship. Of course, they are sites where animals themselves are valued for being who they are and who are able to live free from the demands of unjust systems that are unable to recognize the true value of their lives and experiences. There are also innovative, non-reformist reforms being enacted in various scholarly and activist communities working for animal justice, too, but more imaginative thinking and planning is warranted. The systems of exploitation that harm so many must end, and thinking in terms of non-reformist reforms while working to bring that system down may very well be the change we need.[13]

[12] See chapters 8, 12, and 13.

[13] Thanks to Elan Abrell, Carol Adams, and Alice Crary for comments on a draft of this chapter.

References

Abrell, Elan. (2021). *Saving Animals: Multispecies Ecologies of Rescue and Care.* Minneapolis: University of Minnesota Press.

Akbar, Amna A. (2020). "Demands for a Democratic Political Economy." *Harvard Law Review Forum* 134 (90): 90–118. https://harvardlawreview.org/2020/12/demands-for-a-democratic-political-economy/.

Baldwin, James. (1972). "Malcolm and Martin." *Esquire*, April 1, 1972: 94–97, 196–202.

Crary, Alice, and Lori Gruen. (2022). *Animal Crisis*. London: Polity Press.

Combahee River Collective. (1977). "Combahee River Collective Statement." https://combaheerivercollective.weebly.com/the-combahee-river-collective-statement.html.

Engler, Mark, and Paul Engler. (2021). "André Gorz's Non-Reformist Reforms Show How We Can Transform the World Today." *Jacobin*, July 22, 2021. https://www.jacobinmag.com/2021/07/andre-gorz-non-reformist-reforms-revolution-political-theory.

Francione, Gary. (2000). *Introduction to Animal Rights*. Philadelphia: Temple University Press.

Gorz, Andre. (1967). *Strategy for Labor.* Boston: Beacon Press.

Gruen, Lori, and Justin Marceau, eds. (2022). *Carceral Logics*. Cambridge: Cambridge University Press.

Jeffrey-Wilensky, Jaclyn. (2022). "Mayor Adams Wants to Fix Food Access. Here Are the Neighborhoods Lacking Supermarkets." *Gothamist*, March 22. https://gothamist.com/news/mayor-adams-wants-to-fix-food-access-here-are-the-neighborhoods-lacking-supermarkets.

Kim, Claire Jean. (2018). "Abolition." In *Critical Terms for Animal Studies*, edited by Lori Gruen. Chicago: University of Chicago Press, 15–32.

Leider, J. P. (2006). "Animal Rights Activist Peter Singer Explains his Views." *Minnesota Daily*, March 23. https://mndaily.com/236974/uncategorized/animal-rights-activist-peter-singer-explains-his-views/.

Linares, Nati, and Caroline Woolard. (2021a). "The Art Worlds We Want: Solidarity Art Economies." *Non-Profit Quarterly*, September 16. https://nonprofitquarterly.org/the-art-worlds-we-want-solidarity-art-economies/.

Linares, Nati, and Caroline Woolard. (2021b). "Solidarity Not Charity: A Rapid Report." Grantmakers in the Arts, March 2021. https://www.giarts.org/solidarity-not-charity.

Luxumburg, Rosa. (2006). *Reform or Revolution*. New York: Dover Books.

MacAskill, William. (2019). "The Definition of Effective Altruism." In *Effective Altruism: Philosophical Issues*, edited by Hilary Greeves and Theron Pummer. Oxford: Oxford University Press, 10–28.

Marceau, Justin. (2019). *Beyond Cages*. Cambridge: Cambridge University Press.

McNeil, Zane. (2022). *Vegan Entanglements*. Brooklyn, NY: Lantern.

Pachirat, Timothy. (2011). *Every 12 Seconds*. New Haven, CT: Yale University Press.

Simcikas, Saulius. (2019). "Corporate Campaigns Affect 9 to 120 Years of Chicken Life per dollar Spent." Effective Altruism Forum, July 8. https://forum.effectivealtruism.org/posts/L5EZjjXKdNgcm253H/corporate-campaigns-affect-9-to-120-years-of-chicken-life.

Spade, Dean. (2020). "Solidarity Not Charity: Mutual Aid for Mobilization and Survival." *Social Text* 38 (1(142)): 133.

Speth, James "Gus." (2015). *Getting to the Next System: Guideposts on the Way to a New Political Economy*. The Next System Project (NSP) Report 2. Shaker Heights, OK: Next System Project, October 14. https://thenextsystem.org/gettowhatsnext.

Wilderson, Frank. (2010). *Red, White, and Black*. Durham, NC: Duke University Press.

Wilderson, Frank. (2020). *Afropessimism*. New York: Liveright Books.

Coda

Future-Oriented Effective Altruism: What's Wrong with Longtermism?

Carol J. Adams, Alice Crary, and Lori Gruen

While this book was going through the copyediting process "longtermism," a particular application of Effective Altruism (EA) touched on in Chapters 6 and 15, captured the public's attention. Using the resources of EA, longtermism urges us to make the current generation's impact on future generations a moral priority (Ord 2021,; MacAskill 2022).

Concern for future generations is not new within ethics and social thought. There are long-standing moral and political traditions that stress our obligations to the not yet existing. Overlapping strands of feminist and antiracist thought have critically targeted social structures responsible for intergenerational setbacks with an eye toward repair for past injustices, while urging greater justice for succeeding generations. Environmentalists have placed particular emphasis on our duties to safeguard the earth and its ecosystems for those who come after us.

In some ways, longtermism takes up these earlier concerns. The main difference between earlier discussions of our obligations to future generations and the recent discussions is that in the earlier discussions utilitarian concepts and categories were rarely central. These concepts generally played no role at all, and, when they did come into question, they were often found wanting. Like other effective altruists, longtermists adopt substantial utilitarian commitments in arguing for maximizing the well-being of all. They insist that not-yet-existing beings are within the sphere of moral considerability—and that the interests of future people are on par with the interests of those who currently exist.

In the chapters of this book, we have again and again heard that EA's characteristic fixation on the greatest return in the form of quantitatively measurable indices of well-being distracts attention from unjust social structures that regularly reproduce grievous injustices. We have also heard that Effective Altruists often oppose investments of time or money in thoughtful efforts to dismantle these structures, and so actively impede work against injustice. Longtermism doesn't address these problems. It rehearses EA's familiar "utilitarianesque" moves, now with regard to future generations, in ways that replicate EAs current threats to crucial social justice work, bringing the threats into the future.

Longtermists' commitment to interventions that result in the greatest number of people whose lives go well leads them to project indefinitely into time to come. Their texts are scattered with references to enormous human populations not only millions but billions and even trillions of years in the future. The question of how best to act in reference to the potentially vast numbers of future humans is, for them, at base a mathematical one. If 100 trillion future people will exist whose lives can go better and there are only 8 billion people currently alive, then, when we crunch the numbers, the well-being of those of us living here and now is too small to really worry much about when we can improve the lives of so many more. As two prominent longtermists once put the point: "[F]or the purposes of evaluating actions, we can in the first instance often simply ignore all the effects contained in the first 100 (or even 1,000) years, focusing primarily on the further-future effects. Short-run effects act as little more than tie-breakers" (Greave and MacAskill, quoted in Samuel 2022).

The intensity of current anthropogenic human devastation of the earth has allowed this extreme movement to position itself as part of the answer to our current problems. This is ironic, because longtermists urge us to turn our attention away from the crises and injustices currently bearing down on us. The quantitative calculations they rely on indicate that these crises and injustices won't extinguish human life on the planet. So, if we have to spend billions of dollars now to ensure that smart and unprincipled (or "unaligned") machines won't someday destroy human society, or if we have to spend similar sums to construct a device that could blast a meteor out of the atmosphere before it crashes into earth, then this is what we ought to do for future people. They think we should not be swayed from these endeavors by the fact that currently existing poor people, other people who are disadvantaged, and animals who currently exist may be suffering and dying from targeted violence and the consequences of social neglect. Nor should we be swayed by the fact that immediately devoting funds and other social resources will help enormously with the desperate circumstances of these human and nonhuman groups.

There is good reason to doubt that longtermists' probabilistic calculations are reliable guides to the prospects for such urgent interventions. There is equally good reason to doubt that these calculations are reliable guides to the prospects for longtermists' own futuristic interventions. Despite lacking any plausible case for doing so, longtermists urge us to set aside the plight of existing people who are, they stress, small in number compared to future generations. And in this concern with an abstract future, longtermists largely ignore how that future will come to exist. They explore reproduction not as it is experienced by those who are pregnant, but in terms of increases or decreases in birth rates. Longtermists join other Effective Altruists in ignoring the experiences and work of those on the front lines of social justice movements.

Longtermists advocate an outlook on which protecting democracy and building solidarity for social justice here and now may not be as ethically important as taking actions that promote the most good in the very long term. They speak the language of enfranchising future people, while adopting a fundamentally apolitical stance that promises to disenfranchise not only marginalized existing humans, many of whom are actively agitating for a better future, but all existing nonhuman animals. Like other EAs, longtermists are doing the opposite of what we've tried to do in this volume, lift up and listen to the voices of those working for justice and equality for humans and other animals.

Longtermism is perhaps at its most objectionable with regard to nonhuman animals. Although, as many of the contributors to this volume explain, the welfare-oriented pro-animal interventions enjoined by non-longtermist Effective Altruists serve to strengthen social structures that cause massive animal suffering, these Effective Altruists are at least seriously concerned with animal suffering. The same cannot be said of longtermists.

Despite paying lip service to EA's characteristic commitment to animal well-being, longtermists take nonhuman animals' well-being to be dependent upon and secondary to human flourishing. They tell us that we should prioritize endeavors that give humanity a chance to achieve its potential in the long run, and—counter to current fact—suggest that doing so will give nonhuman animals their best chance at future well-being. Readers of longtermist texts can be forgiven for wondering whether this is a bad joke. The record of human treatment of animals is horrific. Human beings have developed a global enterprise of the industrial production and slaughter of animals, subjecting trillions of land and sea creatures annually to unfathomable suffering, then relentlessly killing them on assembly lines. Human activities have brought the earth into a sixth mass extinction, with species dying off at 100 to 1,000 the background rate. So, what are longtermists thinking? Alongside improbable welfare calculations that seem to show wild or nondomestic animals have such low well-being that their dying off is not to be lamented, longtermists offer us cherry-picked facts in support of a naive understanding of modernity that shows steady moral improvement, including with regard to attitudes toward animals. This magical thinking is what seems to support the idea that preserving humanity's long-term potential is nonhuman animals' best bet.

Longtermism will not save EA from the criticisms leveled at it in this book. On the contrary, by developing core themes of EA in reference to the future, it brings out yet more luridly the moral bankruptcy of a tradition that, with its deceptive talk of doing the "most good," silences marginalized voices that should be starting points in any conversation about how to move toward a livable, more just, and more compassionate future.

References

MacAskill, William. (2022). *What We Owe the Future*. New York: Basic Books.

Ord, Toby. (2021). *The Precipice: Existential Risk and the Future of Humanity*. New York: Hachette Books.

Samuel, Sigal. (2022). "Effective Altruism's Most Controversial Idea." *Vox*, September 6. https://www.vox.com/future-perfect/23298870/effective-altruism-longtermism-will-macaskill-future.

Index

For the benefit of digital users, indexed terms that span two pages (e.g., 52–53) may, on occasion, appear on only one of those pages.

Tables, figures, and boxes are indicated by *t*, *f*, and *b* following the page number